LETHAL FORCE

LETHAL FORCE

MY LIFE AS THE MET'S
MOST CONTROVERSIAL MARKSMAN

TONY LONG

EBURY
PRESS

1 3 5 7 9 10 8 6 4 2

Ebury Press, an imprint of Ebury Publishing
20 Vauxhall Bridge Road
London SW1V 2SA

Ebury Press is part of the Penguin Random House group of companies
whose addresses can be found at global.penguinrandomhouse.com

Penguin
Random House
UK

First published by Ebury Press in 2016

www.eburypublishing.co.uk

A CIP catalogue record for this book is available from the British Library

ISBN 9781785034749 (hardback)
ISBN 9781785033940 (trade paperback)

Printed and bound in Great Britain by Clays Ltd, St Ives PLC

People sleep peacfully in their beds at night only because rough men stand ready to do violence on their behalf.

Richard Grenier, derived from George Orwell

CONTENTS

FOREWORD BY CHRIS RYAN

I first met Tony on a counter-terrorist exercise in the eighties. Some of my B Squadron colleagues already knew him from previous exercises and attachments to SO19 or PT17 (as it then was), but as we shared a brew while swopping gossip in our holding area – a draughty old hanger on a disused RAF base – I learnt of just a few of his remarkable experiences, experiences he shares with great honesty in this book.

Having travelled all over the world, visiting and training with specialist police units, both as a soldier and a civilian, I still struggle to understand how the UK police have managed to maintain their unarmed status for so long when our crime rate is no lower than many other countries whose officers are routinely armed. In light of the terrorist attacks in Paris, Brussels and elsewhere, officers from Tony's old unit are trained and equipped to deal with the most serious of attacks, yet because their colleagues are unarmed they must also deal with less serious armed incidents, which, were they to happen anywhere else in the world, would be dealt with by regular cops. This anomaly makes their operators some of the most experienced in the world.

Typically, the job of an armed police officer is very different to that of a soldier, but when it comes to confronting today's terrorism the lines have definitely become blurred. In this world of sudden suicide attacks and 'active shooters', in all likelihood, it will be armed police and not the military who intervene. Although the theatre of operations for the police is the familiar streets of our major cities, their enemy is as dedicated to the same warped cause as those myself and my colleagues have confronted in Iraq, Afghanistan and elsewhere.

The PT17 teams I trained alongside in the eighties have moved on from 'blue berets' and pump-action shotguns to weaponry, tactics and expertise comparable in many ways with our Special Forces. The sheer volume of regular day-to-day work specialist armed officers now face gives them ample opportunity to put their skills into operational practice. But what is clear from reading Tony's fascinating account of life at the forefront of armed policing is that he was a pivotal part of the unit, and its evolution, for some 25 years.

Yet with only months until retirement, Tony found himself in a situation where his years of honed skills and experience were put on trial, literally, ten years after the event, and simply for doing his job. Having only ever given evidence for training purposes (in a mock coroner's court), I can't imagine what it must have been like to face an Old Bailey murder charge and the prospect of spending the rest of my life in jail.

I know that Tony, like me, was initially reluctant to come out of the shadows and tell his story. Both of us treasure our privacy. But the loss of his anonymity and the untruths that have been spread by those with an agenda forced his hand. With his name and his face now public property, *Lethal Force* tells his story, in his own riveting words, and gives him the right to reply he so rightly deserves.

Chris Ryan, 2016

PROLOGUE

'All units: state red, state red!'

Under the huge shadow of the M1 above us, our convoy of unmarked vehicles turned right at the mini roundabout. I threw down the map book and picked up my 36 and my Kevlar lid. I could see the silver VW Golf ahead, the rear-seat passenger was looking back , and I was getting a bad feeling. Graham, commander of our lead vehicle, Alpha, was now running the show and would need to pick the spot, soon. We were running out of time!

'If suitable we're looking to do it at the roundabout if he stops,' came Graham's voice over the radio, then almost immediately: 'Attack, attack!'

The G36 was already on my lap. My fingers tightened on the pistol grip and my thumb felt the resistance of the safety catch. I watched as Alpha commenced its overtake. My driver, Smudge, throttled it to close the gap on the accelerating lead vehicle and our target, the Golf, and its three edgy occupants. My eyes locked on to the rear passenger; he was in the nearside seat and unusually animated. I now had no doubt we were burnt. I sensed the atmosphere in the VW and imagined a heated discussion between the three men. I could taste the iron tang of blood. Adrenalin surged through my body.

Our car closed in rapidly. I wound down my window and felt the fresh breeze hit my face as I flipped on my Kevlar helmet. No time to worry with straps. I shouldered my weapon, instinctively brushing the safety to fire, my finger hovering beside the trigger guard. I was oblivious to anything other than that rear-seat passenger.

We were close now, just yards away. His hands were on the front seats and he was leaning forward as if he was bracing himself. Suddenly he pushed himself backwards and twisted to look over his left shoulder, then spun to look over his right. He seemed to look straight through me, oblivious to my presence.

Abruptly he threw himself down across the back seat. I was really close now, so close that if his window wasn't up I felt I could have reached out and touched the top of his head. Was he trying to hide or was he reaching for a gun? Just as quickly, he was up again, his shoulders hunched, his hands out of sight below the window of the rear passenger door.

He was armed, I was certain of it! He'd picked up the heavy, box-like, MAC 10 and was readying himself to fire. I held my breath as I aligned my iron sights on his centre mass, my finger curled around the trigger. No more time. I was going to have to shoot him and I was going to have to do it now. At any second my colleagues would be on foot and vulnerable, not only to the murderous rate of fire of the MAC 10 but also to my shots. Our car was alongside. No time to shout a warning! The rear half of the back passenger window shattered as the 65-grain soft points exploded from the stubby barrel of my Heckler & Koch.

And then he was gone.

ONE

HI-DE-HI!

There's no such thing as a typical copper. They come from all sorts of backgrounds and join for many varied reasons. I was no different. Pulled screaming into the world one cold, wet, Lowestoft morning in February 1957, my parents, Eddie and Joy, named me after the recently resigned prime minister, Anthony Eden. We lived on Pakefield Holiday Camp where Mum was the secretary to Leslie Dean, co-owner and business partner to the great Fred Pontin, the man who revolutionised British holidaymaking. Within months of my birth, Dean sold his share to Pontin, and we all moved to a smaller camp called Southdean that he'd bought on the south coast near Bognor Regis. Dad, who had worked in Lowestoft's fish market, became its bar manager. Southdean was uncannily like the camp portrayed in the eighties sitcom *Hi-de-Hi!* Mum even played a xylophone to summon campers to meals, bingo and other activities just like Gladys Pugh did in the show, her voice and the 'bing-bong' of the xylophone reverberating around the camp's tinny PA system.

I had a happy childhood. Summers were spent making new friends with the kids that arrived every week, playing in the swimming pool and enjoying everything from fancy-dress competitions to the cartoon shows that were screened daily; during winter I was content with my own company, the deserted camp my private adventure-playground

3

by the sea. Mum and Dad weren't wealthy. I always thought that our new bungalow, built for us by Leslie Dean, was part of a loyalty deal for helping him start up the new camp and I remember Mum telling me that Mr Dean had insisted they put my name down for a private boarding school when I was born.

Dorset House was a small, postcard-pretty prep school nestled by the River Arun at the base of the South Downs. As an only child, I took to boarding school straight away and, unlike some of the other lads, never suffered from homesickness. I enjoyed being part of what seemed like a large family of brothers and, like many brothers, we played and fought with each other daily. As a small, freckly and very fiery redhead, I was constantly scrapping with anyone that gave me a hard time until eventually I was left alone but my early experiences made me despise bullies. I was good at sports and got on with nearly all of the other kids who, together with the teachers, called me Eddie. I hated my given name and adopted my father's instead, thinking it sounded American and cool.

I seemed to thrive in most parts of the disciplined environment but struggled with pointless petty rules. This meant that I was constantly in trouble with the Headmaster, Mr Hutchinson. On many occasions, either because I had incurred too many demerit points or because I had broken a specific rule, I would find myself in his office where he'd give me a dressing down in his stern South African accent, occasionally followed by six of the best from his infamous cane. It was the way things were then, simple and fair, and I never resented him for it.

Hutchie had been brought up around guns, had fought in the war and owned his own shotgun that he would take out with his Labrador in the surrounding countryside. Toy guns were banned. His logic was that if you pointed them at each other as kids you'd likely do the same with a real, loaded one when you were older. However, almost all of our games involved soldiers and there was a flourishing trade in black-market toy guns. I was found with a homemade Sten gun manufactured from scraps of wood and copper tube, so WHACK!

On one rainswept day, confined to playing indoors, I ended up in a scrap with another lad with the whole school egging us on and I accidently knocked him out. Knowing I was up for the cane, I legged it into the grey, miserable afternoon. I was on the run across the Downs for about four hours before I was eventually caught and brought back to school. I don't recall any real repercussions from my 'Great Escape' although, as the first proper 'runner' in the school's history, I seemed to go up a couple of notches on the peer scale and I think I saw myself as the Steve McQueen character, locked in the 'cooler' lobbing a baseball at the cell wall.

At 13, I'd scraped through the Common Entrance exam and was accepted into Lancing College, its huge gothic silhouette dominating the South Downs landscape. It catered for about 500 pupils, which was huge after the intimacy of Dorset House. We were given free time every other afternoon and, when spending money allowed, we'd escape to Brighton or Worthing to go to the pictures or simply hang around and get ourselves into trouble. At Lancing I shed the pseudonym of Eddie and became Arnie after the Surrey and England cricketer Arnold Long. Like lots of kids, I was lazy at school but not stupid; I excelled at the subjects I enjoyed but these were heavily outnumbered by the ones I detested. I enjoyed writing and was a talented artist but I'd always had a hang up with arithmetic. Any subject that involved even the slightest amount of maths presented me with problems and I simply didn't try.

My small band of mates and I were always in trouble with teachers and prefects alike. Airguns, catapults and any other types of weapons were naturally banned but we would bring them to school anyway and cache them in the hiding places we'd find while exploring every inch of the old college.

Outside toilets or 'groves', as they were quaintly referred to, were located opposite our house and were used by the prefects and older boys for illicit smoking. If you needed to use them you, had to run the gauntlet and suffer cigarette burns and toilets being flushed on you. Tired of being the underdogs, a couple of us concealed ourselves opposite and sniped at the bullies with our air rifles before escaping into the night. My dislike of bullies hadn't diminished and I think I had already developed a deep satisfaction from bullying them.

The science labs were easily burgled and we would liberate the ingredients for homemade gunpowder and other incendiary mixtures. Influenced by a spy film we'd watched, my best mate Mark and I mixed what we thought were the right amounts of magnesium and red lead oxide, contained it in a tightly rolled cardboard tube and inserted it into the keyhole of a large iron lock set in an impressive oak door that hung in an arched stone doorway under our school house. Checking that no one was around, we lit our homemade fuse and retreated to observe the results. We were immediately disappointed by the lack of any spectacular effect and, after a cursory examination of the lock, wrote it off as another failure and walked down the hill to catch a train into Brighton.

We returned several hours later to discover that our smouldering thermite bomb had eventually ignited, not only destroying the massive lock but also burning a foot-wide hole in oak door. The fire brigade had been called to extinguish it and the housemaster had instigated an investigation but our cunning delayed action bomb gave us the perfect alibi and our train and cinema tickets were proof of our innocence. The culprits were never found and the bricked-up door still remains as testament to the brilliance of our bomb-making.

TWO

A JOB OR 'THE JOB'?

By the end of 1974, it was obvious that continuing my education would be an expensive waste of time. Two of my best friends had joined the army as officers. Like them, I wanted a job that promised excitement and was considering joining as a private soldier, but I also fancied the idea of the police.

My aunt Betty lived in Colindale, a stone's throw from the Metropolitan Police's training college in Hendon, and I would often stay with her during the school holidays. I loved exploring London on my own and whenever I took the Northern Line train, I would strain my neck to watch the cadets on the assault course and the cars spinning round the skidpan. If I caught an early enough train, I could see the columns of recruits standing to attention as their drill sergeants inspected them under the statue of the Met's founder, Sir Robert Peel.

It was American cop films like *Serpico* and *Dirty Harry* that really caught my interest, featuring renegade, plain-clothes street cops who wore their hair long and carried guns. As a teenager in the seventies, British TV police – with the exception of *The Sweeney* – seemed the opposite of cool and the image of the traditional copper seemed from an earlier time. If joining was an option, it was going to have to be as a detective in a big city and not a uniform bobby in a county constabulary.

I needed a job and sent for literature for the army, the police and the Royal Marines and while I waited for a response, I started work at the holiday camp, preparing it for the summer season. I'd forgotten about my applications until an official-looking letter arrived addressed to me. I was to attend Paddington Green police station and take part in an assessment day. Convinced I was going to be a copper, when the military's literature fell through the letterbox, I threw it straight in the bin. I was on my way.

By 1975, the Met was in the middle of a manpower crisis. Despite a background of strikes and record unemployment, they were 5,000 under strength and crime was soaring. Officers were underpaid and over-worked and it was no surprise that they were still struggling to recruit.

I duly attended my selection day where I was put through a series of underwhelming tests. Despite my expensive education I'd left without the minimum required O-levels and had to sit the standard Home Office exam. While I breezed through the basic spelling section, I floundered on the equally basic maths but did enough to scrape through. The standard eyesight test posed no problem, but having struggled with the colour-blindness one, the humourless examiner wrote 'CB' in large letters on my paper work.

'Is that it then?' I asked. 'Does that mean I can't join?'

She was poker-faced. 'You'll have to ask the doctors. Next!'

We were ushered to the next phase by a grouchy police sergeant.

'Right you lot! Get out of your clothes and into one of these splendid dressing gowns.'

I stripped off my clothes and hopped around on one leg to remove my socks while the sergeant continued his barrage of instructions.

'When I've finished talking, odd numbers will go through the double doors. Even numbers remain seated here. When your name is called you will proceed through this door where the doctors will see you. They're busy people so listen in because you will follow my instructions exactly!'

He paused for dramatic effect eyeing us like a frustrated sergeant major on the parade square.

'On entering the room you will see two footprints painted on the floor. Stand on them, drop your dressing gown, bend over and spread you arse cheeks as wide as you can! Are there any questions?' Clearly there were, but no one spoke up.

As an odd number I made my way through the double doors where I was weighed, my height was taken and the assistant loudly announced my statistics.

'Six foot and nine and a half stone!' she shouted to her colleague who dutifully recorded the details on to a form.

'Nine and a half stone, fuck me!' roared the sergeant who had followed me in to the room. 'You must have to put fucking rocks in your pockets when the wind gets up! Fuck me, the last time I was nine and a half fucking stone the old king was on the fucking throne!'

Now the centre of attention, I felt my face glowing. The sergeant had sworn! I'd heard lots of swearing before but it had never occurred to me that a British policeman would do so, let alone fit five fucks into one comment! I slinked away awaiting my next humiliation.

The sergeant inspected his clipboard. 'Long!'

I snapped to, jumped up and, with trepidation, turned the door handle and entered the room. It was empty apart from three men in white coats seated behind a large desk. In a touch of Monty Python, there was a neat row of toy cars on the leading edge of their desk. I looked around, saw the footprints painted on the floor and as instructed, turned my back, stood on them, dropped the worn dressing gown, bent over and spread my arse cheeks.

'Mr Long, not yet, thank you. Can you come over here please?'

I held my ground, maintained my bent posture and continued to pull my cheeks apart.

'I'm sorry?' I said, trying to look over my shoulder.

'Mr Long, we don't want to see that yet. Can you come over to the desk please?'

Clutching my privates I shuffled over.

'Mr Long, can you have a look at these Dinky toys and tell us what colours they all are?'

I looked at the row of toy cars, most of which were easily identifiable as primary colours, but one or two were more ambiguous. With one hand still on my privates, I pointed at the cars one at a time.

'Er, red, navy blue, green … a sort of khaki, salmony pink, yellow … er, darkish brown, er, green?'

The three white coats looked at each other and nodded.

'Thank you, Mr Long, that's fine. You may go now.'

I took their body language as a positive sign and scooping up my dressing gown left as quickly as possible, before they asked for another look at my bum.

'Medical' over, I got dressed for a short interview in front of a three-man panel of uniformed senior officers. Candidates who passed were despatched to a local hospital for a chest X-ray; and that, unbelievably, was it.

Weeks later, a letter informed me that not only had I passed my assessment, but a change in policy meant I could join once I reached 18 and a half rather than 19; although I wouldn't be allowed to perform operational street duty until my nineteenth birthday. My joining date would be Monday 11 August 1975. Detailed joining instructions would follow in due course. I was going to be a cop!

*

I knuckled down to the humdrum of holiday-camp maintenance while waiting for my joining date, and as the holiday season
approached, Mum took on more staff. Soon, the camp would open
for several weeks of OAP guests before the schools broke up and the
season proper started.

When Leslie Dean had passed away several years before, the camp
was sold to a large leisure company. Trying to compete with cheap
foreign package holidays, its friendly family atmosphere had started to
deteriorate and a series of temporary managers had failed to improve
the situation. My parents continued in their old roles for a couple of
seasons before Mum's potential was spotted and she was promoted to
general manager.

She had been diagnosed with breast cancer several years before
but after undergoing surgery had fought her way back to full health.
While she took to her new job with enthusiasm, Dad didn't fare so
well. Physically small (by 12 I was already taller than him), he'd been
a competitive cyclist as a young man but was a heavy smoker and
had a constant cough, which he suppressed with addictive linctus.
As the bar manager, he was rarely without a drink in his hand. I
put his descent into alcoholism down to his inability to cope with
my mum's illness and his behaviour, in contrast with her stoicism,
angered me.

I'd always been at school during the build-up to the season, so my
interest in the opposite sex had mainly been fulfilled by the girls who
arrived weekly during the summer season. Two years earlier, I'd lost
my virginity to a 27-year-old typist from Coventry on a fortnight's
stay with her parents. Bobby Goldsboro's hit, 'Summer (The First
Time)' – a lilting little number about a 17-year-old losing his cherry
to a 31-year-old woman – had been in the charts and as I'd clambered
drunkenly through my bedroom window, I'd sung its lyrics, which I

interspersed with Michael Crawford's catchphrase from the TV show, *Some Mothers Do 'Ave 'Em*: 'I'm a man, Betty!'

My oldest mate, Pete, and I had an unwritten rule: no dating the staff. Staff didn't just stay for a week; they were there for the summer. Nevertheless, with the OAP season underway, I was in a camp where all the guests were old and crinkly so, overflowing with testosterone, I started dating several waitresses. One of them, Kim, had earned the nickname 'Cilla' because of her uncanny resemblance to a young Cilla Black. She even came from Liverpool but had moved to the Midlands when she was little and now boasted a strong Black Country accent. One evening, I offered to buy her a drink.

'Ar, I'll have a stout and Vimto, please.'

She might as well have been talking Swahili. I could barely understand her.

'Sorry, a what?' I said.

'A stout and Vimto! Am yow deaf?'

Stout and Vimto? I should've picked up on the warning signals but we ended up an item anyway. Consequently, I was now getting regular sex, which meant, of course, I was officially in love. I put it down now to a naivety born out of ten years at an all-boys boarding school, but after a whirlwind romance, I asked her to marry me. My future seemed to be unravelling in front of me and I vividly remember a confusion of emotions ranging from apprehension to outright panic as my parents attempted to convince me not to go through with it.

No sooner had we started planning our engagement party than Kim admitted that her father was serving time for receiving an entire lorry's worth of stolen tyres, and the prospect of a copper in the family didn't sit well. Nevertheless, our engagement party was held at the camp the week before my police training started. Kim's mother and one of her older brothers came and welcomed me into their family. Mum, ever the hostess, made sure they felt welcome while my dad watched from the edge of the dance floor as we danced to 10cc's 'I'm Not in Love'.

THREE

HENDON

After the rigours of boarding school, Hendon was a breeze. I took to the discipline and routine straight away but quickly discovered that the Met was an organisation that hated change. Everything from the blue serge uniform and Victorian helmet to what were referred to as our 'appointments' (wooden truncheon, notebook, whistle on a chain and a key to now redundant police boxes) seemed from another era. Noticeable by their absence were a pair of handcuffs. Even a kid's toy policeman set had handcuffs!

To emphasise this obsession with the past, we were sent off to a tiered lecture hall to watch *The Blue Lamp*, a 1950's black and white film, flickeringly projected on to a large cinema screen. In the final scene, Constable George Dixon is shot dead while trying to persuade a young tearaway to give up his revolver, only of course to be miraculously reincarnated and later promoted to sergeant for the TV show *Dixon of Dock Green*, which, after 20 years, was still running. We were supposed to come away from the experience with a tear in our eye, sold on the subliminal message that 'it's better to die a hero's death as a quietly spoken London bobby than walk away alive with your revolver smoking like a brash Hollywood cop'. I didn't buy it.

On another occasion, we were shown an American public information film about the evils of racism, presented by the actor Robert

Culp. Culp was perfect for the part. He had played Bill Cosby's white sidekick in the sixties TV show *I Spy*, where they played the agents as friends and equals, neatly ignoring the racial issues of real-life America in a decade of civil unrest.

When the film was finished we went back to the classroom for a general discussion about the issues raised. At no point in my sheltered upbringing had I ever given a thought to racism. I'd met a handful of black kids at school, mainly from fairly wealthy backgrounds, but I hadn't really known any of them.

A Welsh sergeant started the ball rolling. 'Who in this room thinks they're going to be able to go out on to London's streets wearing a police uniform and be able to speak to a group of young black lads without experiencing problems?'

Sat at the front of the class, I raised my hand, sensing those next to me turning their heads in disbelief. I looked around to find that mine was the only hand raised. The ex-cadets, specials and those born and bred in London looked at me, grinning.

'Where are you posted to, Long?' the sergeant asked, knowing the answer.

'Er, Lewisham, Sergeant,' I mumbled. A ripple of laughter filled the room.

'Ever been there, Long?'

'Er, once, Sergeant.'

I'd briefly visited its local market with my aunt, when she'd lived in Eltham.

'Was it dark?'

'Er, no. I don't think so, Sergeant.'

'Well, I think it fucking must have been, son, for you not to have noticed all those black faces. It's like they say in *Zulu* son, "there's fucking thousands of 'em!"'

The class erupted in laughter. I took it from everyone's response that I was out of step with the consensus and made a note to keep my head down. The sergeant tried to regain the moral high ground and preached from the manual about treating everyone equally but the cat was out of the bag. I listened to those in the class who had experienced the hostility of young West Indian kids on the streets and it left me curious to know how I would be received as a young white copper by the black youth of Lewisham. The optimism born of my sheltered Sussex upbringing left me determined to at least try to communicate with them and win them round, but once out on the street I would soon realise that there was a gaping chasm between the younger West Indian community and the police that was almost impossible to cross.

Despite the method of instruction being from a bygone era, it seemed to suit me. Together with the help of down-to-earth sergeants it managed to accomplish in a matter of weeks what a decade of academic teaching had failed to achieve. I suddenly found that learning boring legislation by rote was easily achievable.

My instructors were real characters with colourful stories and language to match. Joe, a Geordie recruit was, in the words of one Scottish instructor, 'Like all fucking Geordies … just Jocks with their brains kicked in!'

The Welsh sergeant informed us that at least 50 per cent of the Met and a larger percentage of the capital's vagrants were all Scots. According to him Jocks were like piles. If they came down but then returned they were okay, but when they came down and stayed down, they were a pain in the arse! In retort the Scottish instructor would miss no opportunity to point out his fellow sergeant's sexual predilection for sheep. Initially I was shocked by the amount of swearing but as a natural chameleon, I soon found myself joining in and my language became equally colourful, my neutral Sussex accent rapidly morphing into a London one. Their comments were dished out without malice, like pellets from a sawn-off shotgun: everyone got some. My boyish looks and private education made me particularly prone to abuse. It never bothered me though; I saw it for what it was, a sign of acceptance.

'Thanks, Sarge!' I replied to one particular piece of abuse from our Scottish sergeant.

'Sarge? Is that short for sergeant, Constable Long?'

'Er, yes, Sarge,' I stuttered.

'Och, I thought so and what would be short for constable, do you think?'

'I don't know, Sarge.' I eyed him nervously as his face moved closer to mine.

'Well, I'll tell you, Constable Long! IT'S CUNT! YOU, LONG, ARE A CUNT!'

I recoiled as his spittle splattered my face.

'WHAT ... ARE ... YOU ... CONSTABLE ... LONG?' he shrieked.

'A cunt, Sarge ... er ... Sergeant.'

'Good man,' he replied calmly. 'Don't let me hear you say sarge again, laddie, okay?'

Around the campus, we would be marched under the supervision of our reluctant class captain, a former Royal Marine called Bill Dennis, and daily he'd march us to the gym or to the swimming pool for PT, self-defence or lifesaving. Despite my skinny frame I was one of the fittest in the class and threw myself into all of the physical activities, one of the more curious of which was our PT instructor's obsession with disarming techniques; presumably introduced as a direct result of George Dixon's untimely death. Partnered up and equipped with battered old Colt revolvers we would take it in turns to disarm each other. Done correctly, the PTI told us, you would take the weapon from your adversary before he could fire a shot and, if aggressive enough, rip off his trigger finger in the process. Most of us were pretty sceptical and I for one thought a better technique would be to have a gun of your own and shoot him first.

My interest in firearms had developed from cap guns and home-made Stens and, before leaving for Hendon, I'd joined a shooting club in nearby Chichester where I discovered a talent for pistol shooting; winning competitions using the club's simple, single shot Webleys and on my eighteenth birthday I'd acquired a firearms certificate and bought my first pistol, a semi-automatic Colt .22. Even then I had aspirations that one day I would carry a gun as a police officer.

One day, the PTIs decided to test our aggression with a bout of 'milling' – a crude form of no-rules boxing carried out, not in a ring but in a square arena formed of gym benches and our baying colleagues. The police cadet corps had their own boxing team and I was matched on size and weight with a former cadet champion. Needless to say, my frantic 'windmilling' was no match for his skilled gloves and after ending up on my arse twice, I was jeered out of the ring with a fat lip and a rapidly swelling eye.

Most weekends I'd spend most of my meagre wages to catch the train up to Wolverhampton to visit Kim and it wasn't long before she told me she'd missed her period and was being sick, but not as sick as I felt. She was getting bigger and wanted, understandably, to get married before her growing lump became too obvious. Kim and her mum would arrange the wedding and I would have to bite the bullet and tell my parents and, as per regulations, ask the Job's permission to marry and arrange married quarters. With the weight of the world on my shoulders, I made my way back to London.

The following day, I approached one of my intake's more thoughtful sergeants and asked for a quiet word, thinking he'd understand my plight.

'If you want sympathy,' he said, 'it's in the dictionary between shit and syphilis! Are you some sort of wanker?' Clearly, I wasn't. *If I had stuck to wanking*, I thought, *I wouldn't be in this mess.*

There followed an interrogation. Had I thought this through? Did I realise this would have an adverse effect on my chances of passing out of Hendon? Had I discussed it with my family? He seemed genuinely concerned for my future though and promised to see what could be done. Later that day, he marched me to the office of the college's commandant. Superintendent Howlett, or 'Zoom' as he was known, was a famously eccentric senior officer and I was called in to 'stand at attention' in front of his desk. I was expecting an almighty bollocking but, after being allowed to 'stand easy', received a surprisingly gentle lecture on the sanctity of marriage and the importance of doing the right thing by a young lady. I was now officially a welfare case and he would speak to the necessary people in order to get me allocated quarters. I was to go away and he would speak to me in the near future. I thanked him, returned to class, apologised to the sergeant for my absence and received a wry smile.

The following day, Howlett summoned me. Handing me a list of married quarters in south-east London, he told me that recruits were not normally told of their postings until the final stages of training. However, as I was a 'welfare case' and had to be found accommodation as a matter of urgency, his enquiries had identified a lack of probationers on P division, and although it wasn't a certainty, there was a good likelihood that I would be posted there. I was to view the properties and get back to him with my selection as soon as possible. Outside his office was a large map of the Metropolitan Police District or MPD and, checking, I discovered that P was a large chunk of south-east London stretching from Deptford and the River Thames in the north to the borders with rural Kent in the south.

Terry, one of my classmates, volunteered to drive Kim and me around to look at the various flats and the following weekend, as we waited in a café on the concourse of Euston station for her train to arrive, we were approached by a young lad who tried to sell us the proceeds of a burglary that he had in a plastic carrier bag clutched to his chest. Seeing our short hair he'd assumed we were squaddies.

'Go on then, let's have a look. I need a present for my girlfriend as it goes,' I said conspiratorially as he passed the bag under the table. I peered inside and true to his word it was full of gold and silver chains, rings and bracelets. I routed through it and asked him how much he wanted for the lot and passed it under the table for Terry to examine. After a bit of bartering I gave Terry a knowing wink. 'Tel, I'm going to check Kim's train. There's a couple of bits in there I'm interested in, mate. I'll be back in a minute.'

Five minutes later I was back with the British Transport Police and Terry and I had made our first crime arrest. Kim arrived shortly afterwards and after a busy day looking at properties we had forgotten all about it. A week later we were mid-lesson and the sergeant was in full swing when suddenly he threw back his shoulders.

'Class!' he ordered, and there was a scraping of chairs as we all leapt up and stood to attention, forcing our eyeballs to the left to see whom it was that had just entered. As our VIP walked slowly past my desk I saw that it was 'Zoom'. Tucking his flat cap and his swagger stick under his arm, he told us all to sit. My arse had just hit plastic when he said.

'Where are constables Long and O'Brien?

Terry and I immediately sprang back up to attention. The sergeant ordered us to stand easy but I expected the worst.

'Take a look at these two fine officers!' Zoom ordered the class. 'These men made an off-duty arrest of a prolific burglar, recovering many hundreds of pounds of recently stolen property. Their actions have assisted the CID to solve several previously unsolved burglaries. One of you kindly explain the circumstances.'

I felt myself going red with embarrassment but as I opened my mouth to speak, Terry thankfully beat me to it, detailing the incident at Euston as if he was giving evidence in court. Howlett congratulated us on our good work, encouraging us to keep it up, and I was only half-listening when I heard him order me to attend his office in ten minutes' time. I looked up as he put his cap back on and we all jumped to attention again as he left the room.

'You heard the superintendent, Long!' shouted the sergeant. 'Fuck off and get yourself to his office!'

Twenty minutes later I found myself again standing to attention in front of Howlett's desk. Was it to do with my married quarters or the arrest? I asked myself.

'PC Long, is there anything you would like to tell about your future in-laws?' he murmured. I knew where this was going and felt beads of sweat forming on my hairline.

'Eh, not really sir, eh, not that I can think of,' I lied, nervously. He slid a letter across the table.

'Well, perhaps this may enlighten you then,' he snorted. I unfolded the handwritten note. It read:

'Prisoner 29768 Smith respectfully requests that he be given day release to attend the wedding of his daughter Kim to Police Constable Anthony Long of the Metropolitan Police.'

It was signed Albert Smith and stamped Stafford Prison. I looked up at Howlett's stern face. He lectured me on the value of integrity and I assured him that I hadn't known of my future father-in-law's circumstances; lying that my fiancée had never spoken of him. I'm not sure whether he believed me or whether my recent arrest had swung the scales but I was dismissed and heard no more about it.

The night before my class prepared to pass off the parade square in front of our families and friends, we treated our instructors to an end of course celebration. It was a good evening, until one of the sergeants pulled me to one side for some pearls of wisdom.

'Lonnnngggg,' he said with a drunken slur. 'You've done well to get this far but at your age, with all your domestic problems, I don't think you've got a fucking chance of getting through your probationary period but good luck anyway!'

FOUR
THE BEAT

Lewisham nick was a typical old red-brick affair referred to by its coppers as 'Papa Lima' or simply 'PL', and known locally as Ladywell. Its décor, procedures and equipment seemed to have remained unchanged since the 1930s with personal radios the only significant improvement. The division had a reputation for being a good place to learn your trade. At the ripe old age of 19, as a teenage probationer, I could finally hit the streets.

Learning beats was a brief and unstructured arrangement where, dependent on your parent constable and your ability, you were cut loose relatively quickly to patrol on your own and learn your trade, often at the public's expense. One of my first unassisted arrests or 'bodies' was for the dubious offence of failing to say 'good morning to a copper under section 32 of the Lewisham Breathing Act'. I had seen a known local criminal standing at a bus stop and, as we had previously acknowledged each other in the street, had nodded at him. However, on this occasion, rather than give me a reciprocal nod of the head, he sucked his teeth and called me a *bloodclaat* so loudly that the rest of the bus queue eyeballed me for a reaction. Having learnt enough Jamaican patois to know I'd just been called a sanitary towel and not wanting to back down, I tried to search him on some spurious grounds, but he took a swing, knocked my helmet flying and took off like a rabbit. I gave chase, shouting breathlessly into my Bat phone for assistance and the cavalry arrived to find me sitting on the unfortunate guy, who had obviously just got out the wrong side of bed that morning. At magistrates' court the next day, he pleaded guilty to assaulting me, paid his fine and from that point on always said good morning.

Constantly under assessment for two years, probationers were required to 'do process' which involved reporting motorists for traffic offences. Most were decent, hard-working people who were simply late for work. I hated it but, under pressure for figures, I'd use it instead to persecute local scrotes or anyone who failed the attitude test.

Like the Lewisham Breathing Act, the 'attitude test' was not in any law book but applied to anyone who was not respectful to Her Majesty's uniform. It was simple: if I stopped you in your car, called you 'sir' or 'madam', asked you politely to turn your engine off and you complied answering my questions in a reasonably civil manner, you would be on your way in seconds. If, on the other hand, you were obnoxious, it could be a long drawn-out affair.

Calling me a liar by denying that you had gone through a red light when I'd just watched you do so 30 seconds earlier, or using phrases like 'Do you know who I am?', 'I pay your wages!' or 'I'm a personal friend of your chief constable!' were guaranteed to delay you further and get you in the book but with my sights set on joining the CID, my preference was for crime arrests.

Chief Superintendent Ted Stowe was a terrifying man to young probationers. Even by seventies standards he was considered old school and a man not to be crossed. First thing every morning he would visit the front office to check the books, taking over the station officer's desk as sergeants and constables hovered behind him like courtiers, placing the different books and logs in front of him as he checked and signed each one, pausing only to sip his tea, delivered by the PC manning the front desk. Anybody foolhardy enough to walk in on this ritual would be grilled.

'What the fuck are you doing in my front office? Why aren't you out on my fucking streets?'

He required a confident, credible answer and if he got one you'd receive a grudging permission to 'carry on', or if you were very lucky perhaps a barely perceptible wink. In an attempt to test my own nerve, I would find a reason to enter while he was carrying out this daily ceremony. Unfortunately, more often than not, the tone of his voice was so petrifying that my speedily rehearsed excuse would turn to gibberish on my lips and I would simply be told to 'fuck off!'

One day I found a scribbled note on one of my charge sheets that read 'Interesting arrest. See me.' I knew that I would have to grab my balls and knock on Stowe's door so I went back to the locker room to tidy myself up. I was growing my hair as long as I could get away with and it would need a comb and my tunic and trousers would need a quick press and my Doc Martens a shine. Twenty minutes later, I took the long walk to the top of the building and knocked on the door to his lair.

'Come!'

I took a deep breath, opened the door and stepped into the room.

'What the fuck do you want, Long?' he demanded.

'You wanted to see me, sir? You squibbed my charge sheet yesterday.'

I waited for the inevitable explosion but instead, he gave me a surprisingly warm smile.

'Ah yes, take a seat, tell me all about it.'

He seemed genuinely interested as I explained a simple arrest I'd made the day before of a conman wearing sunglasses and equipped with a white stick, a bowl of loose change and a sign that read: 'Blind and destitute. Please give generously.'

'Good work, Long. There's not enough young officers making use of their powers under the Vagrancy Act. Well done.'

He asked me how I was getting on and about my young family. Kim and I had married on a weekend part-way through Hendon and I told him proudly of my new daughter Josey who'd arrived five months later. Seemingly bored, he ushered me from the room with the back of his hand, his attention already drawn to a mountain of paperwork on his desk.

'And Long!' he barked without looking up. 'Clean your boots and get your haircut! You look like a fucking poof!'

'Sir!'

I smiled to myself as I stepped out of the office. No one ever got a complete compliment from Ted Stowe but I was already thinking ahead about how to keep him happy with other offences under the Vagrancy Act of 1824, particularly its controversial section 4, more commonly known as 'sus'. This allowed police to arrest suspects loitering with intent to commit an arrestable offence and its use was seen as a right of passage by busy coppers and particularly those with aspirations to join the CID. Its controversy sprang from its use to supress the wave of muggings and dippings (pickpocketing) that were being committed almost exclusively by young black males and was blamed for much of the tension between us and London's black youth.

There were many occasions where my colleagues and I managed to build up a fragile and temporary rapport with individuals or small groups of black youths but collectively they saw us the *Babylon*, and as an army of occupation, while we often saw them as an enemy that didn't abide by the well-established rules of our low intensity conflict.

Much of 1970s police work was still based on tradition and among the oldest practices was to have a 24-hour foot patrol presence in the capital's high streets, and as a non-driver I became a regular face among Lewisham's community of shopkeepers, traders and shoppers.

Early turn, between seven in the morning and three in the afternoon, started with a quiet stroll and a natter with the window cleaners and market traders as they set up their stalls and perhaps a brew in a favourite 'tea-hole' like the snooker hall above Burtons before a leisurely stroll back to the nick for breakfast.

As my service progressed I cultivated cafés where I could sit in a quiet corner, enjoy a free full English and stay on the ground. While I was technically accepting a gratuity – which was strictly forbidden – the café owners were happy to have a friendly police presence and the locals seemed to like the idea of chatting to a bobby over breakfast.

Once the shops opened, a lull would follow until the toe-rags had risen, after which the shopping centre, car parks and surrounding streets would become magnets for every thief for miles around. There were shoplifters, both individuals and organised teams, and kiters (those passing stolen cheques or credit-card fraudsters) and others who focused on the theft of, or from, motor vehicles and then, of course, there was the era's biggest problem, dippers and muggers. These would operate until the shops shut and then a delicate truce would ensue until pub closing time when you might end up dealing with a stroppy drunk or two or the occasional assault or criminal damage.

Occasionally, if something decent was showing, I'd take advantage of the evening ceasefire and take in a film at the old Odeon cinema that dominated the northern end of the town centre. The huge art deco building was past its heyday but the old sweats on my relief still harped back to the fifties when, following the screening of Bill Haley and His Comets's film *Rock Around the Clock*, they'd fought with the gangs of Teddy boys rioting outside.

Most large cinemas were being converted to multi-screens but the size of Lewisham's Odeon meant that it was still kept as one large venue for gigs by the likes of the Clash, Black Sabbath and Hawkwind. The movie industry was in the doldrums and its huge auditorium swallowed up the average cinema audience; it must have been losing money hand over fist.

The manageress loved her local bobbies though and enjoyed having a regular police presence to keep away the yobs, so when all was quiet on the high street and the foyer was empty, I'd slip in and after she had filled my helmet up with popcorn and given me a large Coke, I'd step over the red silk rope, walk up the once grand staircase to the empty circle and, with my radio turned down and my feet on the back of the row in front, settle in to the movie. This often meant that I saw the end of the film or the middle before I'd seen the start and, responding to the occasional radio call, it sometimes took several visits before I'd get to see the whole film, but it beat walking up and down a wet, empty street.

One evening I'd become too engrossed in the film when I suddenly realised that it was just minutes away from my booking off-time and, ditching the dregs of popcorn from my lid, I made quickly for the fire exit. Ignoring the smell of stale urine, I leapt down the steps two at a time, pushed the fire-exit door bar and stepped out into the relatively fresh air of Molesworth Street.

I closed the door behind me, making sure it was properly locked and turned round to see Ted Stowe staring at me. He was just feet away in the front passenger seat of an unmarked car driven by an APS (acting police sergeant) from the night-duty relief who shut his eyes and shook his head in despair.

'All correct, sir!' I mouthed, throwing up a smart salute, just as the Hillman Hunter pulled away.

The next day, the APS pulled me to one side as I walked towards the station gates. 'Old Ted Stowe loves you, mate!'

I'd been expecting a bollocking but now I was puzzled.

'When he saw you by the Odeon last night he said, "That young Long's a proper old-style copper. You don't see young lads checking door handles like that anymore. We need more like him!"'

I smiled.

'Good film, was it?'

'I don't know what you mean!' I said, feigning indignation, before leaving the station, grinning to myself.

Like all probationers, I longed for a driving course and the freedom of my own patrol car but I knew that I'd benefitted from my two years walking the beat. I'd learnt how to talk to people, and it had allowed me to get to know the ground better, able as I had been to explore the alleyways and cut-throughs that many of my colleagues only discovered at three in the morning when they bailed out of their warm panda to chase a burglar or a car thief.

As a non-driver, I had also spent a lot of time as operator on the Area car. Always considered a plum posting for a young copper, it had resulted in lots of good bodies and I'd built a reputation for my knowledge of local criminals, which had helped me improve the quality of my arrests. No longer a probationer and with three years' service under my belt, I was finally given a driving course.

As a provisional licence holder I had to attend a five-week course at Hendon to drive lowly pandas, GPs (general purpose cars) and small station vans and it culminated in the equivalent of a civilian driving test. I wasn't a natural, but on the Friday of the last week, much to my surprise and that of my instructors, I passed my final drive. My provisional licence was filled in and sent to Swansea, and the following morning I was driving a marked police car and two nervous colleagues around the streets of New Cross.

'Whoa! What the fuck are you doing?' shouted my front-seat passenger, gripping the dashboard. 'You just drove straight through a no entry! This is one way!'

'I'm only going one way!' I shouted back. Distracted, I'd completely missed a set of no-entry signs and was headed towards an oncoming vehicle. 'Make like we're on a call!' I cried and, screeching to a halt, I pulled the handbrake and abandoned the vehicle followed by my startled colleagues. With a wave of my hand, I acknowledged the stunned driver of the other vehicle and we scrambled over a nearby fence in search of a fictitious suspect. After several minutes hiding in someone's back garden, giggling like school kids, we straightened our faces, climbed back over the fence, waved our thanks to the patient driver and clambered back into our Austin Allegro. I pulled over to let him pass and smiled as he waved politely, proud that he'd done his bit to support his local bobbies.

My luck wouldn't hold out though and within a fairly short period of time I'd had three relatively minor police vehicle accidents or 'POLACCS' resulting in a short period of suspension. I'd not long been reinstated when, out of the blue, I was called to see the detective chief inspector. I still associated any visit to a governor's office with a bollocking but as I prepared to knock on his door I heard a conversation between him and a DI on the other side and my name was mentioned. I froze, my knuckle an inch from the worn nameplate and listened.

'He's a good little thief taker. Lots of local knowledge and some good snouts, he'll be an asset. The RCS are well chuffed at getting their hands on Tony Ali. They've been after him for months.'

My local knowledge had helped me arrest Ali two days earlier. The Regional Crime Squad (RCS) had wanted him for burgling several wealthy country homes but, being a shrewd thief, he'd avoided shitting on his own doorstep and was almost unknown in his own manor. I could almost feel my head swelling as I listened. The title of 'thief taker' seemed Dickensian even then, but was still seen as a badge of honour. I had no real idea of my own worth so was flattered to hear the title used about me. I knocked and was summoned in.

'There's a vacancy coming up on the crime squad,' the DCI said. 'We've been keeping an eye on you and we think you've got the makings of a good detective. Go and see DS Smith and he'll fill you in. You'll be starting in a few weeks, all right? Off you go then.'

I returned to my normal duties fired with renewed vigour. While I'd enjoyed uniform work and would miss the camaraderie of my old relief, I was on a new adventure, and a potential career as a detective. Even with a few salutary warnings from my older mentors to be mindful of corruption and to watch my back, my enthusiasm wasn't dampened.

FIVE

SUITS OR LIDS?

'Here, Chi-Chi, how did we let you behind the wheel anyway?' joked JJ from the backseat of the smoke-filled Hillman Hunter. I glanced up at the rear-view mirror as he spoke and caught a glimpse of my blood-shot eyes. My head was throbbing and my mouth felt like the bottom of a parrot's cage. The night before had been a major session and JJ was right: I shouldn't have been driving. Parked up in a rundown Deptford estate, we were waiting for a wanted burglar to drag his lazy arse out of bed. I wished I were back in mine.

'Why "Chi-Chi"?' asked George, who sat next to JJ, a skinny roll-up bouncing from between his lips.

'Haven't you heard? Tony's got a bit of a reputation, haven't you, Tone?' I stared at JJ and grunted. 'They call him that 'cause he's fucked so many pandas! You only did your basic driving course six months ago. How many POLACCs have you had now?'

'Just a couple,' I replied, hoping the subject would change. I closed my eyes and thought back to the night before. I'd been driving our squad's DS, an ex-Flying Squad officer, and a young DC aimlessly around the ground when I'd been told to pull up near a well-known villains' boozer in Deptford High Street. I parked so we would get an eyeball of the main door but the DS had closer surveillance in mind.

Locking the Morris Marina (a pointless gesture in Deptford), I followed the detectives into the smoky pub. Like strangers walking into a Western saloon, we were greeted by sudden silence as all conversation skidded to halt.

As the 'lid' I was expected to get the first round in, so I gave our order to the moody barman. I looked around the seedy establishment noticing at least two characters I'd nicked and several more I'd tugged before clocking three men standing at the opposite end of the mahogany bar, one of whom was a recently released armed robber.

Slowly the conversation level crept back to normal and we held our own muted discussion about a new WPC who was, by all accounts, a bit of a goer, but before we could finish our first round, the barman slid three fresh pints towards us and nodded toward the three villains opposite. One of them, an older man in his fifties with long-standing connections to the Krays and the Richardsons, raised his glass and gave us a crooked smile. A short while later, the DS returned the favour and, with the ice broken, they joined us. The DS made the introductions and hands were robustly shaken before we started to share stories. It was almost surreal, like British Tommies and German infantry playing football in no-man's-land, except that we were deep in enemy territory.

'I remember this one time,' said the villain, a huge lump with a dramatic scar on his face. 'This fucking carrot cruncher gives us a whisper about a peter full of tom that's ripe for the taking up in Norfolk somewhere, Norwich I think. Anyway, he swears it'll be a doddle so I get this peterman … You'll know who I'm talking about!'

He winked at his fellow villains.

'And we nick a motor and drive up there, meet up with this geezer who takes us round the back of this office block and points out a window on the third floor that you can get to up this metal fire escape and he agrees to keep look out for us. So me and so-n-so lug this bag up the stairs with all his tools in and the jelly and that and we manage to get through this office window and sure enough there's the fucking safe and me mate's checking it out when I hear voices in the corridor outside. So I put me ear up to the door and I can hear some geezer saying "We'll charge him in a minute, Sarge!" So I sneak a peek through the door and the place is swarming with fucking gavvers! It's only a fucking cop shop, innit? We're in the super's office, ain't we?'

We all laughed at his tall story.

'So, what did you do?' the DS probed.

'Well, we fucked off sharpish didn't we? But not before I nicked the petty cash box from off your guvnor's desk though!'

He gave us a glint of gold teeth and raised his pint. After an hour of sharing cops and robbers stories and trying to 'black cat' each other, the rest of the punters left, the doors were bolted and we enjoyed a lock in till three in the morning, at which point, we staggered out on to the pavement, shook hands and went our separate ways. I was expected to drive my equally drunken detectives back to the nick and they were asleep before I'd put the car in gear. I drove back at 20 miles an hour all the way giving a loud commentary like the instructors made you give at Hendon's driving school.

I opened my eyes. JJ was still yapping on and Pete, my operator, was still pretending to read page three of the *Sun* as he focused on the crumbling tower block's communal doors. When I'd arrived at Lewisham, the local slags had nicknamed me 'Schoolboy'. I'd filled out a bit but still looked like a teenager and, while the label had stuck, I'd developed a reputation for having a small stable of informants and some locals were now calling me 'Long Grass' instead. Grasses were something criminals feared and loathed more than anything else but while I had established loads of local contacts that fed me valuable information, none were paid snouts and my reputation was mainly an illusion that I'd been happy to perpetuate. I'd joined to be a detective and being on the Divisional Crime Squad should have been a good stepping-stone but I was starting to have my doubts about whether I was really cut out to be a 'suit'.

Pete, on the other hand, was definitely a rising star. He was a similar age to me and looked equally baby-faced but unlike me was born and bred in south London and had a much more intimate knowledge of the up-and-coming criminals and had gone to school with many of them. Add to that a passionate hatred for criminals and an analytical mind, and you had a formidable officer with aspirations to be a detective. Like me, one of his passions was linking local criminal family ties and connections and his brain was like a living genealogy chart. The Norris family in particular were high on his target list but his sights were particularly set on twenty-year-old Clifford, who was starting to dabble in serious crime and who, even at our age, was already rumoured to have bent coppers in his pocket.

'This is bollocks, Pete!' JJ grumbled. 'This little fucker isn't going to stir until the bookies are open! Let's come back later. I'm Hank Marvin!'

Pete raised his eyebrows, confirming he too had endured enough. I put the Hillman into drive and we took off, the banter continuing to flow as we cruised into Abinger Grove, a residential street bordered by low-level flats. It was still early morning and the traffic was light when we saw the two white males walking down the steps of Guillemot Court. One was carrying a heavy holdall and their attempt to look natural and relaxed wasn't working. They glanced about furtively and their body language rang all of our alarm bells.

'They're worth a tug!' George chimed, and as I steered the unmarked car to the curb my colleagues started cracking the doors ready to bail.

'That's Clifford Norris!' barked Pete, indicating the man without the bag. I took his word for it: I knew of Norris but had never had any dealings with him. The two suspects split at the bottom of the stairwell and immediately ran. Bag Man ran back into Guillemot Court while Norris ran behind our car, crossed the street and disappeared into the flats opposite with JJ and I in hot pursuit, Pete and George taking off after the bag. Like guileful urban foxes, our two runners went to ground as soon as we lost sight of them. With some surveillance training or perhaps just more experience we may have tracked them down but, out of breath, we soon congregated back at the car, cursing our luck.

'There was a shooter in the bag!' panted Pete.

'Fuck off!' said JJ. 'You're imagining it!'

Pete insisted that he'd seen the butt of a shotgun protruding from the bag. Realising that we weren't going to catch them by hanging around in the street, I encouraged everyone back into the car and made off towards Evelyn Street. At the end of the road I turned the car around and pulled up but before I could even put it in park, Bag Man was leaving the flats and making towards a parked Morris 1100. As soon as he was in the car I kicked down and steered us back down the street.

I'd only just returned to driving duties following suspension for my last minor POLACC, so wanting to avoid yet another collision, I pulled up alongside the battered Morris giving the suspect too much of a gap and he shot forward, his wing hitting the parked vehicle in front with a grinding crunch. A shower of broken tail light, filler and rust flew up as he gunned the Morris away from the kerb. The chase was on and I floored the accelerator of the underpowered Hillman in a bid to keep up with the desperate suspect, all thoughts of keeping my driving authority intact and mention of a shotgun hurled to the back of my racing mind. Pete snatched up the radio handset.

'Right into Childers Street, MP!' he shouted over the engine noise to the dispatcher in Scotland Yard's Information Room, call-sign MP. 'Left into Rolt Street, wrong side of the road, he's all over the place, MP! Through the bends in Trundley's Road. Just missed an oncoming vehicle! He's under the railway bridge, left into the railway arches! He's going to bail! He's out and running, MP!'

Pete threw down the radio mike as we all clambered from the vehicle. The suspect had driven into an alleyway between a pub and a row of railway arches, abandoning his car at the base of a footbridge. He was headed across the divisional boundary and into the wilds of Southwark's M division and the Silwood Estate, a rat-run of tower blocks and low-level flats notorious for its vehicle crime. But before he could reach that he'd have to navigate a wasteland of scrapyards and dodgy archway businesses. I realised I'd somehow left the automatic in drive and it was following me down the alley towards the abandoned bandit car. Reluctantly, I dived back through the open window and slammed the gearshift into park with a teeth-grinding crunch. Then I was off, determined to not let the suspect escape again.

My hangover was forgotten as I leapt up the steps of the railway bridge two at a time, overtaking JJ and George and hurling myself down the steps on the opposite side. I'd soon overtaken Pete as well and was closing on the now bag-less suspect but was starting to tire. I looked at my feet to avoid the deep, oil-streaked puddles and seeing half a house brick on the muddy track ahead of me, contemplated picking it up and throwing it at him but he suddenly slowed and raised his hands, collapsing with his back against the wheel of a rusty, engineless lorry and I slowed to a walk, my hands on my hips as I struggled to get air back into my burning lungs.

'Don't hit me, guvnor! I'm asthmatic!' he wheezed as I reached down, grabbed his collar and hoisted him to his feet. I shoved him up against the side of the lorry and handcuffed him.

'You're fucking nicked!' I informed him helpfully as Pete and my two other colleagues joined me. An M division panda had arrived and we were about to put him in it when we were called on the radio and advised to bring him back to the abandoned car; there was something we needed to see.

'What's in the bag?' I asked the suspect, but he denied all knowledge of any bag. I twisted his handcuffs and he yelped with pain. 'What's in the fucking bag?'

He looked at me with hate in his eyes but didn't answer and I pulled and pushed him up the railway bridge steps until we were looking down on a throng of uniform officers standing around the abandoned car. As I dragged him down the steep steps I knew, from the smiles on their faces, that Pete had been right. Mushy Parker, a big, bearded Area car driver, stood by the open passenger door of the bandit car. On the roof in front of him was the heavy-duty canvas holdall. Mushy held the bag's straps in his gloved hands.

'Bring him over here,' he said with a grin. 'You'll want to see this!'

Mushy was a divisional shot trained on the Smith & Wesson revolver and therefore authorised to 'make safe' any other firearms that came into police possession. He reached in and withdrew a side-by-side shotgun, crudely sawn off at the muzzle and at the butt. My pulse raced. Firearms finds were a rarity and recovering one with a body, rarer still. As our firearms 'expert' struggled to open its breach he swept the eager crowd with its stubby nostrils.

'Careful, it's loaded!' yelled Bag Man, flinching.

The faces of 15 coppers cracked into one unified grin. Realising his mistake, our suspect fell silent as Mushy eventually succeeded in removing two red plastic shotgun rounds from the weapon's twin breach. Also in the bag was a sawn-off .22 rifle. Also loaded, it was broken down into two parts and wrapped in two pairs of London Borough of Southwark overalls along with more ammunition, two black woollen balaclavas and two pairs of gloves. It was a coup for a lowly crime squad team and there was plenty of backslapping and congratulations all round as we placed our prisoner and our weapons cache into the car.

On the short journey back to Deptford nick our suspect faced some more questioning, this time on the whereabouts of Norris, but he'd learnt from his previous mistake and kept schtum. Back at the station came more congratulations as we processed our prisoner, placed him in the cells and got on with sorting out the exhibits. Any crime involving firearms, and particularly a potential conspiracy to rob, was always going to be a CID matter and it wasn't long before they were muscling in. My heart sank when the charge-room door opened and our allocated detective slithered in.

I'd first come across Des Brennan on a week's attachment from training school several years before. Despite my public schoolboy naivety, my initial assessment of him had been right on the money: throughout my time at Lewisham he was the only officer I'd ever been repeatedly warned to avoid and even his fellow detectives gave him a wide berth. Bedecked with a gold rope chain and sovereign rings, he looked more like a mafia hit man than a detective.

Pete was keen to start hitting Norris's known haunts but Brennan and his DS were advocating patience. Norris was going nowhere, they told us. We needed to ensure our case against Bag Man was water-tight and we should concentrate on our statements and helping them with the exhibits. Young Clifford can wait till early doors tomorrow, Brennan advised.

'You know he's gone, don't you?' said Pete, as the two of us sat nursing our pints several hours later.

'Who?'

'Norris, he's long gone. Brennan's in his pocket.'

'You can't know that for sure.'

'Trust me, I can. I can't say how I know but he's gone, we won't see him for a while. Anyway, Tone, what are you going to do? Go CID or back to uniform?'

It was a good question and one I wasn't quite yet ready to answer. The previous night's bender had caught up with me and I was struggling to finish my lager. I made my excuses and left. A persistent drizzle had me rush to my car. I jumped in and slammed the door, my head hitting the back of the bucket seat. I gripped the tiny rally wheel, closed my eyes and took a deep breath. I was 21, in a fragile marriage, the strongest part of which was our beautiful two-year-old daughter. My canary yellow Ford Escort Sport needed new brake pads, I didn't have a pot to piss in and I was at a crossroads in my short career. How had I ended up here? I started the engine and the crackly radio kicked in. It was Ian Dury and the Blockheads singing 'What a Waste'. As I pulled away I couldn't help but smile.

Soon after, having decided that I was not CID material, I returned to my old relief but was soon offered a place on the embryonic District Support Unit or DSU. Based at Lee Road nick, it covered the whole of P district from Deptford in the north to Orpington in the south and drew on officers from every division within the district.

In essence it was a mini version of the Special Patrol Group, the Met's mobile rapid-reaction force created in the 1960s to provide a pool of experienced officers to respond to everything from a missing child to major public disorder. Normally referred to simply as the SPG or by its own members as 'the Group', it had developed a feared reputation as the Met's 'heavy mob'. Having decided not to go CID, its reputation, combined with its mixture of plain clothes and uniform work, now seemed attractive and I was giving serious consideration to applying for it when it next came out in 'orders', the daily bulletin that among other things advertises job opportunities within the Met.

Small DSUs were looked down on by most on the SPG but the type of policing was similar and it attracted the same types of personalities, many of whom later went on to join the Group itself. It was full of characters, every one hand-picked from their respective divisions for demonstrating an ability to make good arrests. Each one of us knew our own respective patch and wherever we were in the boroughs of Lewisham or Bromley one of us was able get us quickly to calls and to point out local faces that were wanted or worth a tug.

We were split into pairs and I was partnered with Clive, a PC from a different relief to me at Lewisham. We knew each other from the shooting club that we had both helped form and soon found that we worked well together, developing a reputation for ourselves with the quantity, if not the quality, of our arrests.

It was a different type of policing to that which I was used to and when we ventured south away from my usual hunting grounds, I found that I had to rely on instinct rather than local knowledge. Luckily, my instincts were strong and unlike us our villains weren't restricted to arbitrary borders so we'd often spot Lewisham's oxygen thieves up to no good as we patrolled Catford and Bromley's grounds.

The Support Unit worked primarily in uniform and patrolled in an old short-wheel-based Transit carrier that was in its final days of faithful service to the Met. Its green interior paid homage to its humble beginnings as a traffic wardens' van, while its battered maroon exterior identified its more recent service with the Diplomatic Protection Group. It had very high mileage and was long overdue to be sold off. As an experimental unit, we relied on it and the civilian vehicle fleet manager at Catford traffic garage was kept sweet with bottles of scotch and regular invites to our Friday evening mess dinners and did his best to keep our old banger on the Met's books. Equally, we had to beg, borrow and literally steal our equipment, including our two-tone horns, which we liberated from a carelessly unattended ambulance. These were mounted under the bonnet on a plywood shelf, which could be quickly released in the event of the Transit having to go into the workshops.

Our blue light, originally intended for warning motorists at the scenes of accidents, was 'borrowed' from the back of an unattended traffic division Land Rover and consisted of a circular flashing light, about the size of a small dinner plate, mounted on a three-foot-high black-and-white striped pole which in turn protruded from a heavy black battery box.

Traffic had a reputation for prosecuting fellow officers and targeting the CID in particular and was generally unpopular with the rest of the force. Derided as 'black rats' or 'cheese eaters' we considered it fair game to steal their equipment.

The blue light was positioned between the legs of the radio operator in the front seat and concealed underneath an old carrier bag. When we got a call, the operator, in addition to answering the radio, was responsible for whipping off the carrier bag and switching on the light and the siren.

Friday evenings were always set aside for a 'rowdyism' patrol designed to finish after the pubs and clubs had turned out and it had all gone quiet and it always provided plenty of arrests. The governor, who had served on the SPG, decided that it would always start with a morale-boosting meal and everyone would be expected to take it in turns to buy the food and cook it for the rest of the team.

A sensible amount of alcohol was allowed, although of course the driver was restricted to soft drinks, and guests who could benefit the fledgling unit were often invited to keep the wheels oiled. Eventually the governor had to rescind the alcohol ruling after one of the crew had one too many and we were forced to handcuff him to the back seat of the van when we later went on patrol.

One evening, along with the SPG, we were to execute search warrants on several addresses in the Lewisham area. As I sat in Ladywell's yard a convoy of dark blue carriers pulled in; I felt embarrassed as the real 'Group' spilled out into the summer evening air.

Our governor introduced those of us that had shown an interest in applying for the SPG to their chief superintendent, Alex Marnock, and he made encouraging noises about our potential future, promising to look out for our faces at future interview boards. He had obviously been on the piss and I was pretty sure that he wouldn't be able to find his way home without help, let alone recognise my youthful face again, but the DSU had given me a taste of working as a team and even my introduction to its slightly inebriated commander couldn't dissuade me. When applications come out again, I was ready.

Throughout my short career, tension between ourselves and the black youth had been building to a crescendo. An attempt to deal more sensitively with the upward trend in street crime, and in particular mugging and dipping, without utilising the controversial sus laws had backfired when a ground-breaking operation, that made extensive use of video evidence, resulted in the arrests of 21 young black men.

Despite the overwhelming evidence against them, the 'Lewisham 21' became a rallying point for left-wing activists and right-wing extremists who clashed during a National Front rally through New Cross and Lewisham in the summer of 1977 resulting in us having to deploy riot shields in Britain for the first time. The Notting Hill

Carnival had also become an annual seat of trouble and as I prepared to leave the division to join the SPG, the tragic deaths of 13 black teenagers, in a fire at a party in New Cross in early 1981, stoked the boiler. As spring and the warm weather approached the pressure gauge hit red.

SIX
THE GROUP

'Try having a riot with only one shoe!' spat one of my new colleagues putting his boot into the youth's back and shoving him away. The small posse of angry youths had crossed the road and swaggered through our midst as we stood in a side street by our carriers discussing the previous night's events. It had been a brave but foolhardy gesture. Given the level of violence that Four Unit had faced in the past 24 hours, we weren't in a tolerant mood; so when one of the youths sucked his teeth loudly and another muttered 'Raasclaats', we threw them against a graffiti-covered fence where they were searched. Each had a trainer removed and thrown away before being sent in opposite directions, each one running the gauntlet of the unit before breaking free and hobbling away. There was no gloating; nothing was said. It never happened.

I'd barely arrived at Four Unit when it all kicked off. Operation Swamp 81, set up to quell another peak in street crime, was in full swing in Brixton but the SPG had been barred from getting involved and local divisional officers were handling the operation.

Under pressure from Kim, I'd taken the Saturday off for a drunken bash in our married quarters. Several guys planned to turn up after their shifts finished but it soon became apparent that some weren't going to make it. A few stragglers eventually arrived with tales of massive public disorder. The TV was turned on and the jollities stopped as we watched the nine o'clock news in shock at the severity of the rioting. I was shaken to recognise some of my new colleagues, their faces bloodied, hunkered behind their riot shields as bricks and petrol bombs rained down on them.

Based less than two miles from the riot's epicentre, Four Unit had been the first SPG on scene and were right in the thick of it. Several of us tried ringing in but with no one answering we had to sit and watch in total frustration. The following day, I arrived at work to find our ranks heavily depleted by injuries, some serious. After a hasty briefing from one of the sergeants 'acting up' in the absence of our injured inspector, we boarded up and headed for Lima Delta.

Brixton had burnt for most of the night, and while some calm had returned, damaged buildings and burnt-out cars still smouldered as nervous divisional bobbies manned cordons. The atmosphere was buzzing and we could all sense this was just the calm before another inevitable storm; 280 officers had been injured, 56 police vehicles burnt and 150 buildings damaged, while the rioters had escaped with only 45 injuries. The SPG had played no part in starting the riot – we hadn't worked Brixton for several years – but we were here now and we weren't leaving until the rule of law was re-established.

I'd always craved action; and it seemed by joining the SPG my wish had been granted. My few weeks with Four Unit had been non-stop and since that first knock on my new governor's door, strangely surreal.

'Come in!' bellowed a Geordie voice from the other side. I'd entered and behind a large desk sat a bull of a man with a broken nose and cauliflower ears, dripping sweat and chewing an unlit pipe. The scent of stale sweat and pipe smoke was overpowering. He wore a ripped sweatshirt with the sleeves cut off under a black plastic bin bag with holes cut for his large arms and, as he leapt up to greet me, I saw that he was sporting grubby shorts, rugby socks and trainers. He bounded round his desk and shook my hand with a vicelike grip.

'You must be Tony. I'm Dinger, the unit inspector. Welcome to Four Unit, son. I've heard a lot about you! I understand you're a bit of a tearaway? Good. Just what we need!'

I'd met some fairly eccentric officers of all ranks in my short service, and Dinger Bell was way up there. He seemed indestructible but leading from the front on the first day of the riots, a brick had hit him square on his helmet, splitting his scalp and leaving blood running down his face. Snapped by a press photographer he became Fleet Street's 'face of the riots' for the duration of the 'disturbances', as the Yard liked to call them.

My shoulders now displayed the characters '1162 CO'. The CO stood for Commissioner's Office and merely meant we came under central command and were not tied to a geographical division within the MPD. Legend had it that a journalist, mistaking the two silver letters as a coiled snake, wrote, with typical tabloid sensationalism, that the SPG were known as the 'Cobras of the Yard' because of their snake insignia and ability to strike at will. It was total bollocks, but the myth gave the Group an emblem and a nickname prized by its members.

Stuffed in my tunic's breast pocket, with its huge, whippy aerial secured under an epaulette, now rested an ancient Motorola radio. Unique to the SPG, it was iconic and, wearing it, I knew I'd arrived. I'd also been given a partner, known on the Group as a 'Buck'. Mine was Mac, a huge ex-Para, who immediately took me under his wing.

I wasn't much use unless I could drive and carry a gun, I was told, and as I was suspended following yet another POLLAC, my name had been immediately put down for a driving check test and a much-anticipated shots course. I would also have to attend public order training, where I would learn to work within a shield team, but with Brixton in chaos, all of that would have to wait. After a quick tour of our Cavendish Road base and an introduction to my new team, I'd boarded my allocated carrier and hit the streets running.

Back in Brixton, we set off to patrol in a three-carrier convoy, tasked with preventing disorder throughout the borough. As our carriers snaked through the tense streets we all looked on in amazement as one uniform cordon allowed a group of young black males and a few obvious white agitators to congregate on a corner.

'What's the matter with those twats?' moaned Mac, indicating the cordon officers. 'Don't they realise that they need numbers to start a riot?'

We went around the block, pulled up and waded into the growing crowd, splitting them up, confiscating their shoes and dispersing them. Our tactic was based on simple common sense: if you let a small crowd congregate it soon becomes a large one you can't control. We tried to avoid arrests as each one depleted our numbers and made us less effective. As the evening approached and the crowds grew bigger we knew we'd need all hands on deck.

Eventually, my carrier's luck ran out and we were forced to take some prisoners into one of several charging centres set up away from the rioting to process the numerous arrests. I walked up to the desk with my handcuffed prisoner. The exhausted charging sergeant scrutinised my battered charge, glanced at the Motorola in my top pocket and pushed himself out of his seat. Leaning across the desk, he checked my prisoner's single shoe, sat back and looked me in the face.

'SPG?' he smiled. 'Nice one. Keep bringing the fuckers in. I like it busy.'

Later, we deployed on foot behind our long shields as Four Unit had done the previous day when it had paid such a high price for its bravery. Each carrier had six long shields deploying ten officers behind them. We had very few small shields and anyone else was left without any protection, other than our reinforced bobbies' helmets and a pair of safety glasses designed for school children to wear in chemistry class.

Untrained, I deployed behind the shields with just a medic satchel and a fire extinguisher for protection. The rioters lobbed bricks, bottles and petrol bombs over the shields, aiming for the unprotected officers behind the 'thin blue plastic line'. With nothing to fend them off, I ducked and bobbed like an amateur boxer until half a brick hit me in the thigh, flooring me instantly.

I tasted blood in my mouth and felt a rush of adrenalin as I dragged myself up. Picking up the brick I hurled it back, watching with satisfaction as it arced over the shields striking one of the rioters who fell to the ground clutching his chest; those around him scattered.

I picked up another and another, launching them back with as much force as I could muster. Glancing to my right, I noticed a colleague following suit. Soon, several of us were nursing small stacks of ammunition to our chests with one hand while we threw them back at the rapidly thinning enemy. The shield-less rioters, happy to throw shit at us, weren't so keen at being on the receiving end.

Weeks later I was confronted by a press photograph of me in mid-fling, my shoulder numbers clearly visible. The complaints investigation officer looked disappointed when I readily admitted that it was me and defended my right to self-protection.

'The law allows me to use such force as is reasonable in the circumstances,' I argued. 'And it was the only thing I could think of to protect myself and my colleagues!'

The complaint wasn't proceeded with.

The second night was as much about looting as it was about airing any genuine grievances and with Brixton's shops and business protected, the trouble petered out, leaving the rioters to head home to count their ill-gotten gains and party the night away. With a lack of local officers, Four Unit was tasked with protecting a few looted shops, and I found myself outside an off licence waiting for its key holder. Its damaged contents were strewn across the pavement among the broken glass and I was tempted to pick up a can of lager to quench my thirst in the clammy night air.

I heard someone ranting at colleagues before I saw a small, wiry, West Indian man in his fifties shuffling towards me through the debris. I caught his eye and he pointed a bony finger at me.

'Dis am all ya fault!'

I'd had enough. I grabbed a handful of the front of his colourful shirt, spun him around and pushed him up against what was left of the plate-glass window.

'You fucking what?' I said, inches from his face.

'Ya too damned soft wid dese people!' he shot back. 'Back in Jamaica da police would na take dis shit! Dey'd take dem down an alley and break dem legs! Dis country is too damned weak!'

I lowered him gently back to his feet, released my grip and tidied his crumpled shirt. Then I picked up two cans of lager, pulled the rings and handed him one.

'You ever thought of being police commissioner?'

We put the world to rights until, content at having aired his grievances to a friendly ear, he sauntered off with a fresh can.

In April 1979 during an anti-racism demonstration in Southall, the death of Blair Peach, a teacher and left-wing activist, had brought a spotlight on to the Met's most elite uniform unit. Found dead from head injuries after a crowd dispersed, there were no witnesses to identify a culprit but the fingers of the liberal press and political agitators pointed at the SPG. In the weeks following Peach's death a media storm brewed. To the desk riders at Scotland Yard, the Group had become a liability rather than an asset.

Along with Peach, 25 demonstrators had been injured, but few remember the 97 police casualties on that day, one of whom was stabbed and another had his jaw broken in three places by a brick. I was there as part of a P district serial. I remember the crowds, the noise, the missiles and coppers covered in white paint. I remember the confusion and the long hours but I have no recollection of a death.

When I had heard about it, though, it hadn't surprised me. The level of violence could have easily resulted in deaths on either side. In fact, the whole of the seventies seemed to consist of endless violent disorder where both sides dished it out with equal vigour, but the incident would haunt the SPG and within days of my arrival on the Group, a four-year posting policy was introduced, forcing some of its most experienced members to look for pastures new.

As quickly as the riots had started, they stopped. Brixton, battered and scarred, went back to some sort of normality and, despite having restored calm, we were banished to patrol less controversial parts of south-east London. The tension remained high, however, and we all knew it would only be a matter of time before it all kicked off again and sure enough, by July, it did with the unrest spreading from Brixton to the rest of London and beyond.

Back on the frontline we were still ill-equipped to deal with this level of violence. The first deployment of riot shields in Lewisham in '77 had been a shock to those who harped back to the fictional days of Dock

Green, and the Yard had remained reluctant to relinquish the traditional image of the bobby's helmet, even though we all knew its limitations in a brawl. Finally, the level of injuries forced some action and the MOD were approached to provide us with enhanced protection.

Hundreds of green army NATO helmets that had been destined for Northern Ireland were loaded into a lorry and taken to Brixton. They were distributed on a first-come first-serve basis, and I returned from a court hearing to discover that I was one of a handful of officers not to have been issued with a helmet. I made it my mission to get one.

Chief Superintendent Bob Silence stood to attention and saluted as the Group's carriers crunched across the gravel forecourt of Dulwich College. Closed for the summer holidays and located within striking distance of the southern end of Railton Road, the seat of Brixton's riots, it made the perfect holding area for the commissioner's commandos.

Three Unit's carriers led us in a sweeping arc around the forecourt as if it was a formal inspection, playing Wagner's 'Ride of the Valkyries' over the public address system of their lead vehicle. Four Unit followed but not known for taking ourselves too seriously, our anthem of choice was Ivor Biggun's 1978 classic 'I'm a Wanker'.

Bob Silence remained in the salute with just the beginnings of a wry smile. In normal circumstances, each unit would stick to the confines of its own geographical area, coming together only for big events such as the current riots, but it hadn't always been so. When the Group was the Group, as the old sweats liked to remind us, three of its units would descend on a division for 'earlies' and the remaining three units would cover 'lates', resulting in nearly 90 extra officers policing a ground per shift.

Not only was it a massive show of force but it also meant that everyone knew each other, creating a camaraderie that was slowly disappearing as the older members started to leave or retire. For the first time in several years, we were a single entity again and while we waited for some action, old friendships were rekindled, banter filled the air and morale soared, but despite the wartime spirit, no one felt we had satisfactorily exacted revenge for Four Unit's injured.

Heavy-handed policing by local officers had allegedly triggered the 'disturbances' but they were still reluctant to employ us. I listened with dismay as divisional units were sent to deal with outbreaks of disorder while we sat in the early evening sun. Eventually, however, we were called together for a fastball operation requiring the Group's teamwork and expertise. We sat on the grass to get a better view of our command staff as they briefed us. Intelligence suggested that a derelict squat on Railton Road was a cache for a substantial number of petrol bombs. Located right in the middle of what was known as the front-line, a virtual no-go area of drug-dealing and other illegal activity, the bombs were intended for a major attack on the police that evening.

Nine of our carriers would be used, all approaching from different directions but coordinated to arrive at the squat together, and each crew was tasked with different roles. The lead carriers would immediately force entry, secure the Molotov cocktails and arrest any offenders inside. Others would act as an immediate perimeter to capture any runners and the remainder would form an outer cordon of long shields to protect us from a counter attack. The ninth carrier would contain the command element, together with a shield team to act as their protection.

Briefing over, everyone headed enthusiastically to their carriers for hasty sub-briefings and I listened as Bunrats, my carrier commander, give us our postings. I was part of the second wave, deployed to prevent squirters from escaping the target address and, as usual, was lumbered with the medic bag and a fire extinguisher. As I secured the chinstrap to my beat duty helmet and adjusted my protective glasses, I looked with envy at the others' green NATO lids. Ten minutes later, our convoy glided out of the manicured grounds and headed towards Brockwell Park. Another ten and the first two carriers peeled right to hold north of the plot. Two streets further and the next pair left the convoy to hold just south of the frontline, ready to sweep in from the east. The nearer we got, the greater the risk of compromise. The tension was bubbling over.

Finally, the two carriers in front of us, together with the command vehicle, turned right ready to seal off the squat from the west. Our carriers would be approaching from the south and all the other units would work off our call. Each confirmed they were in position and we commenced our attack run.

'Uniform four-one-one moving now,' said our operator. I eased open the rear doors, holding them ajar as we closed on our target.

'One hundred yards and all clear,' continued the operator as my heart rate climbed. 'Fifty yards … several IC3 males on the junction now … standby, standby … they're running! Go, go, go!'

Mo, our driver, kicked down, the carrier surged forward and I strained to look past my colleagues for the fleeing rioters. Other youths appeared and a volley of bricks flew towards us. One cracked our windscreen but the rest were wide of the mark. Mo stood on the wide brake pedal with both of her tiny feet and the carrier slewed to a halt at the dusty junction.

Suddenly, I was out and running towards the boarded-up squat. A stream of rioters were spewing like ants from a gap between its crumbling back wall and the wriggly tin fence adjoining it. One tried to swerve past me and I smashed my elbow into his face but my sights were set on the gap and I left him to escape or be swept up by others.

Shouts of 'Police!' and the sounds of wood splintering, glass smashing and sheet metal being flung aside filled the air. I reached the gap just as an arm, shoulder and the bearded head of a white agitator appeared in the opening. I smashed the short stubby fire extinguisher into his face, and with a cry, he recoiled back into the squat's backyard. A petrol bomb landed next to me, shattering on the pavement and covering my trousers with fuel but its smouldering rag failed to ignite it.

Pulling out the fire extinquisher's pin, I squeezed the trigger and emptied half of its noxious contents through the gap. There were screams of confusion. Peering into the yard, I could see two or three more covered in white powder clutching their faces in pain. The message had got through: that exit was closed.

Prisoners were dragged from the squat and thrown against the rusty tin fencing. Colleagues started to bring out crates loaded with petrol bombs and stack them on the pavement ready for collection as two more tended an unconscious male on the pavement, the command element looking on with concern. It had been a well-coordinated operation; we didn't need it marred by another Blair Peach.

News of our raid had spread quickly along the frontline and a large, hostile crowd was heading our way. The defensive shields started receiving bricks and bottles and yet again I found myself behind them with the half-empty fire extinguisher and the medic satchel, picking up bricks and hurling them back with as much force as I could.

An inspector from another unit, resplendent in his newly acquired NATO helmet, ordered me angrily to stop but I knew it was the only thing I could do to reduce the flow of missiles coming at us and as soon as his back was turned, I carried on with added vigour. Alan, to my right, clutched his own supply of ammunition and shouted to me above the din of the riot. 'Where's Dinger? This bloke's a right wanker!'

Several wounded officers were carted off to the rear and I looked back at our carriers, driven by the girls, following behind to pick up the casualties. I'd never felt so vulnerable and yet again found myself wishing for a NATO helmet. Suddenly my prayer was answered as a house brick struck the inspector directly on top of his gleaming new lid and he slumped, poleaxed, to the ground.

Alan and I dropped our bricks, grabbed the unconscious governor and dragged him to the shelter of a low wall. I looked back to see the last of our carriers turning right down a side street, their route blocked by a burning car. Looking back towards the shields, I was disturbed to see them now running at the retreating crowd a good 50 yards away. The situation had changed dramatically and Alan, the semi-conscious inspector and I were on our own.

Alan called up the carriers on his Motorola and Linda's reassuring voice responded immediately. She would come back around the block and collect us but we'd need to get to the far side of the obstruction. Alan and I knew what we had to do. We were on our own in enemy territory and if we were caught we were dead.

We hooked our arms under the inspector's armpits and started to drag him past the burning vehicle. The heat seared my face and I prayed that the tank wouldn't go up. Hearts pumping, we heaved our casualty into a small front garden just as a smaller group of rioters entered the street from the other end and started running noisily in our direction.

'Shit, shit, shit!' whispered Alan as we lay on top of the injured governor. 'Did they see us?'

I looked around: an elderly West Indian woman was staring directly at me from her living-room window. She looked towards the approaching gang, pulled her curtains and was gone. I started to drag some bin bags over the inspector; our only hope was to leave him hidden and try and outrun a load of teenagers in trainers but it was better than laying here and getting found, and hopefully we'd distract them from our wounded governor. I looked at his helmet and sighed, so close and yet so far!

Suddenly the front door opened behind us and the elderly woman hobbled down the short path until she was standing over us.

'Go away!' she shouted at the approaching youths. 'Don't you come down my street causing your trouble!'

The youths hurled abuse back at her, jeering and laughing.

'Don't cuss at me, ya hear? Go now, go home!'

Suddenly there was the sound of sirens, the gunning of a carrier engine and shouts of 'Babylon!'

I got up on one knee to see Linda's carrier screaming down the street and the youths running off in the opposite direction. I waved the vehicle down and Alan and I grabbed our casualty, hauled him to the carrier's sliding side door and threw him in. As Alan scrambled in ahead of me I looked back to see the old lady shutting her front door behind her. I wanted to thank her but Linda was screaming for me to get in. I clambered over the wounded governor and we were away towards police lines and safety.

I looked over my shoulder towards the old lady's house and suddenly realised how easy it had become to think that every black person hated us when all those I had come in contact with recently seemed bent on killing us, but her bravery in confronting the youths had saved us from serious injury, or worse, and her act of kindness had refocused my mind. I looked down at the moaning inspector lying on the carrier's rubber floor.

'You're going to be all right, guv. Let's have a look at your head,' I said as I undid his helmet straps.

'It's my helmet!' he whimpered.

'I know, guv, but I need to check your head.'

He closed his eyes and seemed to relax as I carefully removed his damaged lid and checked for injuries. I couldn't see any in the beam of my Maglite torch, so I left him in the recovery position and examined my prize.

The top of the helmet looked like a boiled egg bashed by a spoon but, unlike my jelly mould, it covered most of my head and more importantly had a full-face visor to protect my boyish good looks. I threw my old bobby's bucket towards the back of the carrier and pulled on my sweaty trophy, catching Alan's wry smile as I buckled it up.

'What?' I asked, innocently.

'I can't believe that you just nicked his lid!' he replied.

'Fuck him, he'll be off sick with concussion for days. He doesn't need it, I do!'

After dropping off our casualty, Linda took us to regroup with the rest of the unit. They'd continued to push the mob through the back streets all the way to Brixton Hill and were resting in the grounds of St Matthew's church. Casualties had been light and morale was high and everyone was taking the piss out of Howard, our gentle giant of a sergeant.

Six foot eight and just months from retirement, his bad back hadn't allowed him to get down behind the shields and he'd taken several hits to the head, including a Molotov cocktail that had failed to ignite but had dowsed him in petrol. He'd self-administered a huge white bandage around his head that looked like a turban with a police helmet perched on top.

'Fucking great, isn't it? Dinger gets one little scratch and he's all over the newspapers! Where's the press now?'

I took in the various characters, thought about what they had just been through and looked at their smiling faces, and realised that Four Unit's injured had finally been avenged.

*

After weeks of street fighting, we put down our battered NATO helmets, mustered as much undamaged uniform as possible, polished our battered vehicles and formed part of the huge security operation surrounding the marriage of Prince Charles to Lady Diana Spencer. Revolvers were issued to all of the unit's shots and we became the response team for the roof-bound snipers of the Met's mysterious D11 branch that watched over the processional route.

Whenever we deployed on foot we were greeted by a flag-waving public who greeted us with cheers and requests for photographs. We gladly obliged, thankful for friendly smiles after weeks of hate-filled stares. It was a brief respite. The next week we were back in the thick of it but rioting is a summer sport and, as autumn approached, the disturbances eventually subsided. Terrorism, on the other hand, was an all year round event.

The mid-seventies had been busy years for IRA Active Service Units (ASUs) operating on mainland UK but had been followed by several years of unpredictable sporadic attacks. The world had become distracted by events in the Middle East but just after the first of the Brixton riots, Irish nationalism had come back into the spotlight.

IRA hunger striker, Bobby Sands, had been elected as the Member of Parliament for Fermanagh and South Tyrone in April but by May he had starved himself to death in the Maze prison and an ASU was back on English soil, planning a full-blown offensive. In early October, a 20-pound nail-bomb detonated as a coach full of soldiers arrived at the Guard's barracks in Ebury Street. Two members of the public were killed and another 39 people injured.

With further attacks likely, we were tasked with providing security patrols in central London and two shots with their trusty .38s crewed every vehicle. Being a non-shot proved to be an advantage as it meant that I could get out on foot patrols. The West End, with its bright lights and constant activity, was the London that I had seen myself policing when I'd come up from sleepy Sussex. There was plenty to do and see, and most of the shopkeepers, business owners and public were pleased to see us. George, only months from retirement, was back on his old patch and reacquainting himself with some of his old enemies in Soho.

Back in the sixties, the seedy heart of the West End had been the dour Scotsman's beat and many of the porn merchants and gangsters that had feared him as a busy local bobby were still plying their trade. Less inclined to make arrests now, George strolled around his old patch with his young buck Frank, giving them the evil eye.

One lunchtime, as we sat in Bow Street's canteen, George and a red-faced Frank walked in. George was holding up his redundant police box key on the end of his whistle chain which, when closely examined, held a substantial sliver of curled, silver paint.

'Will ya look at that? It's disgusting!' he exclaimed to his puzzled audience. 'That's a shining example of what is wrong wi' British industry today! A Rolls-Royce and only three layers of paint!'

With that he sloped off to the counter to get himself a brew, leaving Frank to explain. They'd been patrolling Wardour Street when an irate traffic warden had approached them pointing out a silver Roller with cherished plates. It was parked on double yellow lines outside a strip-joint and the owner, a well-known gangster/semi-legitimate businessman, had refused to move it and told her to fuck off.

George wasn't a big fan of traffic wardens but detested the car's owner even more. Knowing that the cost of a parking ticket or even the minor inconvenience of sending his driver to collect it from the pound was small fry to the wealthy villain, he decided to enact his own more fitting punishment.

'Leave it to us love,' said George and after waiting for her to depart, he and Frank resumed their patrol but as they walked past the offending Rolls, Frank heard a teeth-grinding screech and realised with horror that George had keyed one whole side of the beautiful car. In George's practical mind, he figured that even his old adversary would balk at the cost of a complete re-spray. Even some of the most experienced guys at the table felt that George's daylight act of criminal damage might have been excessive even by his standards and commented that it was a noticeable shift from his normal MO of stuffing matches into villain's locks.

'Matches?' I commented. 'That's a bit old school isn't it? Hasn't he heard of superglue?'

'Superglue?' said Mac, barely looking up from his newspaper. 'He's way too tight!'

A week after the Ebury Street bomb, Sir Steuart Pringle, Commandant General of the Royal Marines, was seriously injured when a mercury tilt switch triggered a bomb underneath his car. It had exploded just seconds after I'd driven past on my way to work and nine days later I would hear and feel the blast of a second bomb as my colleagues and I attempted to evacuate London's busiest shopping street. Ken Howorth, one of the Met's most experienced EXPLO officers, was killed while attempting to defuse a booby-trapped device in the toilets of an Oxford Street Wimpy bar.

As quickly as the campaign had started, it stopped and it would be another eight months before the IRA struck again, but the Met were already preparing for an even more sinister threat and Four Unit was sent to rural Berkshire and the Atomic Weapons Establishment (AWE) at Aldermaston, made famous by CND rallies back in the sixties.

Having passed through its heavy security, we were directed to a nondescript building outside of which was parked an unusual-looking Transit van displaying a strange array of aerials on its box-like rear cab. We were ushered into a lecture theatre where an eccentric academic briefed us on the minutiae of the dirty bomb, a weapon none of us had ever heard of.

The concept was scary in the extreme but also wholly feasible. Even a warped university student, we were assured, could access highly toxic material, put it alongside crude, homemade explosives and cause havoc. We were to play a vital role in countering the threat. At first there was a degree of pride that the Group had been chosen for the task but soon cold reality hit home.

The unusual Transit van was the pride and joy of the boffins who were now our enthusiastic briefers. Equipped with powerful sensors that could detect the general location of even the smallest trace of nuclear material, they could conduct a search of an identified area and direct us to a specific grid reference where a device may be located. We would be trained to operate hand-held devices capable of narrowing the search down to a matter of feet. We looked at each other across the auditorium. Visions of sweating over whether to cut the red or the blue wire sprung to mind. We had a ton of questions.

'Why us?'

'What were we supposed to do if we found such a device?'

'Wouldn't it be better to train the Met's own EXPLO officers or better still the army?'

'Would we be given protective suits?'

We had, we were informed, been selected because of our London-wide remit and our standard police appearance. The whole concept relied on discretion and deniability and the government had approved the project on the understanding that the public would not be panicked at the sight of soldiers clad in protective clothing, scanning their doorsteps with Geiger counters.

Despite it being a thankless and potentially hazardous task, we carried out the training with as much enthusiasm as we could muster, which identified another reason for the Group's involvement. The devices were so simple that, given enough bananas, chimps could have been trained to use them.

A simple plastic box with a stubby aerial, you simply waved it around until its tone sped up to the point where it became constant and bingo, you'd found yourself a dirty bomb. After several hours of searching for small, hidden and allegedly 'safe' packages of nuclear material and plenty of larking around, like a bunch of inner-city school kids on a trip to the country, we clambered back on board our school buses and headed back to the smoke.

We would return several times to train at AWE over the coming months. Each visit was described in standard police vernacular as being an LOB or a Load of Bollocks and a distraction from our primary objective of locking up bad guys. Finally, with the riots over and the bombers gone to ground, we got back to real police work.

We'd been working Woolwich Division for several weeks, wreaking havoc among the local criminals. As always, the divisions arrest rate had gone through the ceiling but the remaining bad guys had either decided to stay at home or ply their trade elsewhere. The ground had gone dead and back driving at last, I pushed the carrier around its quiet streets. Geoff, my new buck, and the rest of my crew kept up the usual stream of banter while scanning for someone to stop; the SPG set crackled.

'Uniform Four and all Four Unit call-signs, regroup to Romeo Whiskey, Tango November, over.'

It was our HQ in Barnes. A regroup could mean just about anything but whatever it was, it was probably more interesting than punting round the ghost-like streets of SE18.

Back at Woolwich nick, Dinger and the sergeants were in a meeting. No one knew what was happening and a card school had already started as I queued for the teas. I'd recently gained a bad rep for not putting my hand in my pocket, earning myself the nickname of 'No Teas Tony', and it was now scrawled on the sweatband of my flat cap in indelible ink. It wasn't that I didn't put my hand in my pocket, it was just that there was rarely anything in it.

Kim and I were always skint and any attempt to discuss our finances just led to rows. Despite that, we'd been getting on better in recent years and had even decided to try for another child. We'd been upgraded from our pokey Job flat to a police house in the suburbs and our son Mark had been born several months previously. Although we'd been saving for our new arrival and money was tight, I'd been making every effort to get the teas in whenever I could.

Dinger and the sergeants joined us and we gathered around for an informal briefing. They hadn't been fully briefed themselves but we were to get to Lippitts Hill Camp in Epping Forest as quickly as possible to assist with a terrorist-related incident. My heart skipped a beat: Lippitts Hill was the home of D11 who, apart from being firearms instructors, were the nearest thing the Met had to a SWAT team. My mate Clive from Lewisham had joined them the previous year and had filled me with stories of the operations that they conducted. I was due to go on my shots course and was intrigued to find out what the terror-ist-related incident was all about and to get a look at D11 and their secret HQ 'reached by leafy lanes' that I had read about in the papers.

'It'll be an exercise then!' moaned Dickie, one of the old and bold. Like a morale vacuum, he could suck the enjoyment out of just about anything but a lot of the more experienced lads nodded in agreement and I felt my enthusiasm start to ebb.

We headed north on blues and twos until we reached the narrow, winding lanes of Epping Forest where we came across a mass of police vehicles parked on the narrow verges and a hive of activity out of place in the otherwise tranquil setting. A sergeant wearing a white bib emblazoned with the word 'Marshal' approached my driver's window clutching a clipboard.

'You are?'

'Four Unit SPG, Sarge. What's up?'

He checked his clipboard and watch. 'It's an exercise, you're too early, put this in your window and wait here'.

He handed me a sheet with the words 'Ex Snowdrop' on it and strode off.

'Huh, exercise! Fucking told you!' gloated our morale vacuum. We stood around in idle conversation while a few lads wandered off to see what they could find out. They never returned and an hour later the sergeant came back with his clipboard.

'Leave your vehicles here and make your way to the main gate where one of my colleagues will escort you to the canteen.' He double-checked his notes. 'Oh and you need your search kit.'

We pulled on our standard issue green mechanic's overalls and our wellies and took our missing colleagues' kit bags with us. At the main gate, huge plastic screens had been set up to prevent prying eyes and another marshal escorted us into the secret enclave and ushered us quickly towards the canteen block.

My eyes were on stalks as I took in the secret base I'd heard so much about. A Second World War prisoner-of-war camp, its wooden huts were raised off the ground by small brick pillars; presumably to stop the Italian and German prisoners from digging tunnels.

There was a mass of activity and I noticed some fit-looking young civilians with longish hair wearing dark blue coveralls who I assumed were mechanics or electricians from the Met's engineering branch.

'Oy, nobber!' shouted a familiar voice and I turned to see Clive standing with a massive grin on his moustachioed face. He was with an equally hirsute colleague and both were decked out for a small war. They wore their blue berets at a jaunty angle over grey coveralls and brown suede desert boots, their assault vests festooned with knives, grenades and magazines. Both wore Browning Hi Power pistols on their belts and had supressed Heckler & Koch sub-machine guns hanging from slings around their shoulders.

'How's it going, mate?' he said cheerfully. 'What's the SPG doing here?'

'Who knows?' I replied, admiring his kit. 'We haven't been briefed yet … situation normal!'

'I'll be around all day. I'll catch you later.'

Clive laughed as he jogged off. I looked down at my own sad rig and knew that he was part of a world more fascinating than my own. When I reached the canteen I was surprised to see our missing colleagues who informed us all that they were dead. Their nosiness had led them to sneak in to the camp where an umpire deemed that they had been shot. For dead guys they were looking good on it.

'Hello chaps, you're here then? This is all very exciting, isn't it?'

We all looked up to see our friendly boffins from Aldermaston and released a collective groan as we realised that we'd left real, albeit boring, police work to get urgently across London just to play hide and seek with fake bombs. We were taken to a quiet corner of the canteen and given a hushed briefing by one of the bibbed exercise staff.

'Terrorists have taken hostages at a stronghold near to our location and are making demands of the government,' he explained. 'In addition, they have planted a quantity of dirty bombs in the locale and you are tasked with locating them.'

He passed us over to one of our Aldermaston instructors who enthusiastically pointed at a map of the camp. 'Okay, chaps. Our specially equipped vehicle has located three strong indications here, here and here.'

We were split up into three groups to sally forth and locate them. My team were allocated a series of wooden spider blocks located opposite the canteen entrance. Equipped with our detectors and protected by our overalls and special wellies, we left the nuclear protection of the wooden canteen block to carry out our secret mission.

Our hand-held devices gave off a steady beep as we bimbled through the building casually opening doors and checking out rooms. There were several dormitories and a large communal shower block and several had signs pinned to their doors – 'D11 Forward Control', 'C13 Control', 'Negotiators' – and we could hear the murmurs of conversations and radio traffic coming from the other side. One had a sign that read 'SP Team holding area' and Geoff reached out for the door handle.

'Looks like this one's allocated to us,' he said, opening it and standing at the threshold. It was full of the young engineers in dark boiler suits that I had seen earlier. The one nearest the door seemed older than the rest though and I noticed that he was also wearing a black suede waistcoat with pockets for grenades, a pilot's escape knife and what looked like a fire axe. He had a pistol holster and magazine pouches strapped to his thighs and sported a massive moustache – their popularity seemed to extend beyond the Village People.

'Yes, gents, what can I do for you?' he said in a broad Glaswegian accent.

'We need to search this room,' Geoff stuttered, pointing at our detector.

'I don't think so mate. Fuck off!' he snapped, slamming the door in our faces.

'What the …?' growled Geoff. 'Who the hell does he think he is?'

'I think you'll find that he's the SAS,' I replied in my best public school accent. 'Which doesn't excuse bad manners!'

We returned to our task and in an alcove set aside for an ironing board, we discovered a small box, tightly wrapped in black tape that had our detector screaming. We sent a runner to get an umpire who marked something off on his clipboard and directed us back to the canteen for yet more tea.

An hour later, the marshal and our egghead returned with another exciting task. This time it only required two of us and as Geoff and I were the only ones not playing cards, we dutifully followed them to a grassy corner of the camp where, about 50 yards away, we were shown a temporary structure about the size of a garden hut. Our boffin informed us that it was the source of a strong radioactive signal. Without further ado, Geoff and I started to stride towards the grass and our radioactive objective.

'STOP!' I turned to see a Royal Engineers officer and his troops standing next to several army lorries. They began to march towards us. 'Where do you think you're going?' demanded the officer.

'I'm Constable Best and this is Constable Long from Four Unit Special Patrol Group, sir,' Geoff said. 'We've been tasked to establish whether there is radioactive material in that building.'

'Well you're not crossing that grass, I'm afraid. Minefield!' bellowed the officer.

Geoff and I looked around for our mad scientist but he'd melted away, so for the next hour we sat and watched his troops scan the grass with mine detectors and crawl on their bellies with metal probes leaving a trail of small flags to mark our safe route to the sinister shed.

'All clear, sir!' said the sergeant to the major and Geoff and I picked ourselves up and started heading wearily towards the first of the flags.

'WAIT!' shouted the major. 'It may be booby-trapped! Sergeant, get kitted up will you?'

'I don't believe this!' hissed Geoff as we watched the soldiers dressing their sergeant like serfs preparing their knight for battle. Thirty minutes later, having borrowed our scanner, the sergeant had completed his dangerous mission and returned across the grass bearing a large ammunition tin adorned with black tape, wires and an old alarm clock.

'Tickety-boo, Sergeant!' beamed the major. 'Carry on! I'm off to the ops room.' And he strode off in the direction of the spider blocks.

'Fucking Rupert!' muttered the sergeant, and the other squaddies sniggered in support. 'Sorry about him, lads,' he added as one of his troops helped him from his massive helmet. We watched fascinated as he carefully prised open the ammunition box, snipped some wires and got to his feet struggling under the weight of his protective suit.

'Done!' he announced with a grin.

'That was a bit easy, wasn't it? Wouldn't a real one take longer?' questioned Geoff, genuinely interested.

'Not if you made it yourself this morning!' said the sergeant with a wry smile. 'We put up the shed and laid the minefield too! You lads want a brew?'

The new postings policy was changing the face of the Group and we were haemorrhaging experienced members. I was already in my second year, which meant it wouldn't be long before I had to think about pastures new, and seeing Clive, dripping in 'Gucci' kit, and the SAS preparing to assault the mock stronghold had whet my appetite for D11, or 'the Wing' as it was known to its select members. I'd been allocated a date for my long-awaited shots course and I decided to watch out for applications for D11 in Police Orders. Even if I jumped through all the hoops, I theorised, I'd probably still see my time out at Four Unit.

My shots course was exclusively for SPG officers, and as I waited in the canteen on the first morning, we exchanged rumours until we were collected and taken down to Holborn's claustrophobic basement range. Sergeant Hinton, the lead instructor, welcomed us to the course and explained the format for the week's training. He stressed that we were not being taught to shoot to kill but rather to shoot to stop. We had to be able to justify our actions, and that meant a suspect had to be committing, or be about to commit, an offence so serious that it warranted lethal force. In other words, we had to believe that failing to shoot would result in ourselves or others being killed or very seriously injured.

Although the our intention was only to stop the threat, the sergeant stressed, we had to be prepared to take life. There was an awkward silence as his eyes scanned us for a reaction. Most of the class had never fired a gun before and I was sure there were some who hadn't considered the full implications.

We were taught to fire at the 'centre of mass' or, in other words, the centre of a man's chest, which provided the best chance of hitting the target when under pressure. Firing warning shots or 'winging' a suspect was out. A missed or stray round could endanger other people, and while a shot penetrating the chest but missing vital organs could prove survivable, a shot aimed at a leg could just as easily hit a major artery and prove fatal. As my instructor argued, any threat that didn't warrant a centre mass shot probably wasn't serious enough to justify discharging our firearms at all.

After a brief reminder of our legal powers to use force, we were introduced to the Smith & Wesson Model 10 revolver. We were taught to name its parts, how to carry out normal safety procedures, and how to load and unload it. Next up was aiming by using its sights, followed by how to align it quickly at close range without them employing a technique known as 'sense of direction'.

Aimed shooting involves focusing on the front sight and aligning it with both the rear sight and the target and, more importantly, keeping it aligned while controlling the trigger until you've fired. The Model 10 is a double-action revolver, meaning that when you operate the trigger it revolves the cylinder to align the next round and simultaneously draws the hammer to the rear before releasing under spring pressure, firing the weapon. This is the way it is usually fired by police officers and its longer trigger pull weighs in at about ten pounds.

'Sense of direction' was used for engaging targets at closer ranges as it uses the way the brain reacts under pressure. Keeping both eyes open to allow for maximum peripheral vision, the firer concentrates their focus on the suspect rather than the sights. Using a firm two-handed grip on the weapon, we were taught to operate the trigger twice rapidly in what was described as a double tap. This would double our chances of hitting the suspect and, if both rounds struck, double our chance of stopping the threat. The technique was taught at seven yards because that was as far back as the average shooter could go and achieve consistent success.

After the dry practice came some basic practice shoots, where we were given individual coaching, before quickly progressing to those that we would need to complete in order to pass the course. Before that though, Tom, Sergeant Hinton's attractive assistant, stood on the seven-yard line and gave a fairly lacklustre demonstration of one of the two 'sense of direction' classification shoots.

'That shouldn't be too hard to beat, should it?' whispered a PC from Five Unit, a former military policeman and experienced pistol shot. I gave a noncommittal smile. It hadn't been the best shooting I'd ever seen but they were all on the target and within the time and I wasn't going to be overconfident and make a twat of myself.

'On the point, muffs and glasses and with six rounds load!'

I loaded the revolver as smoothly as I could, conscious to carry out the drills exactly the way we'd been shown, and I smartly adopted the drawn weapons position. I was on my own and oblivious to the other shooters.

'This is a ten round, sense-of-direction shoot to be completed in 30 seconds. Your time starts when the targets turn to face you. Watch your front!'

I focused on the battered edge of the plywood target and waited. Suddenly it turned and I punched out, focusing on the target with both eyes open, aligned a rough sight picture, snapped the trigger twice and watched the two rounds strike the centre of the target within an inch of each other. I paused and lowered the weapon a fraction, just as Tom had demonstrated, before realigning my sights and firing two more that arrived within a couple of inches of the first. I followed the procedure for another pair before swinging open the cylinder and flicking the ejector rod.

Fumbling in my pocket for the last four rounds, I cursed the Met for not issuing the speed loaders that I normally used on the range, before finally thumbing them one at a time into the empty chambers. It seemed to take forever. I aligned the first round in the correct position before snapping the cylinder shut and engaged the target with my last four shots. I examined the four-inch group, dead centre, aware of a colleague continuing to fire as I ejected my spent cases and offered up the empty weapon for inspection. Fifteen seconds after my last shot the targets snapped away.

'Clear and holster, clear and holster, clear and holster!' the instructor thundered behind us as he cleared each of our weapons in turn. We waited for the last gun to be holstered before we heard, 'The line is clear, forward and check your targets!'

I struggled not to grin as the two instructors examined my group.

'Nice shooting,' the sergeant said, 'and your handling was really good … But you're aiming … this is a sense-of-direction shoot, you should be focusing on the target with both eyes open.'

'Sorry, staff, I thought I was.'

'No, you're definitely aiming if you're getting a group that size,' huffed Tom as he logged my score.

Well, you clearly weren't, I thought, as they moved on to debrief my colleagues.

The complicated lecture on sense of direction and the explanation of master eyes, binocular vision and converging images had confused even me. I resolved to stick with what I knew. If they wanted bigger groups, I would just have to spread them about a bit.

We fell into a routine that would last for the next four days. One detail would shoot and when they'd been cleared to go forward, the instructors would examine their targets, give advice, and log the scores while the next detail picked up the spent brass, threw it into a bucket and took their place on the line to await their turn. With four details of three firers this meant that more time was spent watching than shooting and struggling novices had to wait ages to put into practice the advice that they'd been given.

Minor safety infractions, failing to listen to the range orders or getting a dead-man's-click by failing to count your rounds, resulted in a small monetary fine that was deposited in a converted ammunition tin known as the 'click box'. In advance of the test later that week we would practise the same four shoots repeatedly. There were two seven-yard shoots, the one that we'd started on, and another where we'd fire a double-tap on each two-second exposure of the target, and two at 25 yards, a five-positional shoot and the single-action shoot.

The positional practice involved firing two shots double action from each of five positions. The first was standing, firing strong-handed where you could rest on a barrier to steady your aim, followed by firing weak-handed, also supported, then kneeling, sitting and prone. You had a minute and a half to complete the shoot. The single-action shoot started in the prone position with a 'make-safe' test. This involved loading the weapon with five rounds and closing the cylinder with the empty chamber under the hammer. The instructors would ask you to thumb back the hammer and complete the make-safe. This required taking control of the hammer with your support hand thumb; pulling the three-pound hair trigger and lowering the hammer under control on to a live round. It was a relatively simple task but if you got it wrong you were likely to accidentally fire the weapon and to watch some of the lads you would have thought they were defusing a homemade bomb.

The shoots weren't particularly demanding if you had some experience and I was banging all of my rounds into the centre of the target on every shoot. The instructors continued to accuse me of cheating by aiming on the sense-of-direction shoots but after completing several shoots with an instructor on either side of me watching my eyes they were satisfied that I had both eyes open and left me alone. By the final practice shoot on Thursday morning I hadn't dropped a shot and maxed the classification in the afternoon.

The following day, I found myself back at Lippitts Hill in a classroom where we received several lectures on the tactics that we would practise later in the day. The first detailed the different types of cover available to armed officers. The best was 'cover from fire', which included brick or concrete walls, substantial trees and engine blocks that would defeat bullets. The next was 'cover from view', like a wooden fence or a bush that would only provide us with concealment and not protection. To emphasise the lesson, a bullet-riddled door from an ancient Wolseley Area car was dragged into the centre of the classroom to demonstrate the futility of hiding behind one.

We were also shown the two types of body armour that were available to authorised shots. This was news to us as none of us had ever seen body armour before, let alone ever seen a shot wearing it.

There followed lectures on how to contain buildings and other structures and how to accurately report sightings of suspects and hostages using TI or target indication. This was a system that allocated each aspect of the building a colour, each door and window a number and each containment position an hour on an imaginary clock face superimposed over the building. If used correctly it was supposed to simplify and speed up communications, but with the short time allocated, it had the reverse effect when we tried to put it into practice later in the day.

The lecture on containment was followed by ones on how to conduct an armed search of a building as a team and the correct way to stop vehicles, all of which were later practised under the watchful eyes of our instructors. Each scenario seemed to be deliberately set up so that we couldn't win and while we carried drill revolvers which had their firing pins removed, the bad guys, played by more instructors in scruffy civvies, were equipped with blank-firing revolvers and shotguns so that even when we did get the drop on them and fired first, the pathetic clicks of our empty weapons were drowned by the deafening roar of their blank cartridges. If we all hadn't been so desperate to pass, it would have turned into a playground argument where we would have accused them of not 'taking their shots' and we'd have gone off to play football instead but we swallowed our pride and let them win.

At the conclusion of the war games, we were all told that we had passed. Those of us that had achieved over 90 per cent on our final shoot were given the classification of 'Marksmen' while everyone that achieved 70 per cent were categorised as 'Standard Shots'. There was no certificate or award for top shot, although I picked up the winnings as we'd all put a couple of quid in the pot and this was boosted by the contents of the 'click box'. Our instructors congratulated us and informed us that a teleprinter message would be sent to our units informing them that we were now authorised to draw firearms, and we regrouped in the 'Owl' pub opposite the camp gates to celebrate. We'd been taught just enough to make us dangerous.

Back at Four Unit, firearms operations were regular events and I soon found myself frequently deployed with a revolver. This mainly consisted of being one of a pair of shots on a carrier when we were posted to central London security but we would also be regularly deployed on raids and I found myself having to accept that in the real world no one adhered to the tactics that we'd been taught by D11. If we knew or strongly suspected that an armed suspect was in an address, we were taught to contain the building and call them out to us. This would negate us having to enter unfamiliar premises where there might be women, children or animals, and even if the location of the armed suspect wasn't known all attempts should have been made to establish that he wasn't inside first, removing any innocent parties before entering to search.

Either way, the search should have been conducted slowly and methodically using a reasonably sized, fully armed team to ensure that all areas of danger were covered and we were taught to creep silently through the building using hand signals to communicate and mirrors to clear corners and lofts.

The reality was very different though, and one of my first outings was in Clapham looking for a 19-year-old, six-foot-eight, black lad wanted for an armed robbery. Our information had him at his family home, a four-storey Victorian house that he shared with his mother, aunt, sisters, brothers and cousins. Correct practice should almost certainly have involved a surveillance operation designed to identify him when he left the house, followed by a street arrest away from the public, but eighties policing was a simpler affair and together with my fellow shots and unarmed colleagues, I found myself bailing out of a carrier, charging through the freshly shattered front door and swarming through the house in a wild game of hunt the lanky robber.

Shouts of 'Armed police!' and the screams of women and children filled the air as I came across a partially opened door on the first-floor landing. Revolver in one hand and Maglite torch in the other, I kicked the door open and scanned the room with the light's bright beam. It settled on a single bed and the head of a sleeping woman, her hair swathed in massive curlers and a hair net. She opened one tired eye.

'It's all right love, it's the police. We've got a warrant, stay where you are. I'll get a WPC.' I spoke calmly, so as not to upset her. Happy that the rest of the room was empty, I stuck my head out into the corridor and shouted for a female officer. I took my attention off the bed for a matter of seconds but when I turned around I found my eyes level with the flat chest of the gangly female who had got out of bed and morphed into our freakishly tall suspect. Why he was wearing curlers and a hair net, I never established, but fortunately he was still half asleep and totally compliant and obediently sat back down on the edge of the bed until a colleague came in to handcuff him. I holstered my revolver and patted my armour, thankful that he hadn't had a weapon to hand. It was a salutary lesson never to take anything for granted.

As a lowly PC, I knew that I wasn't going to change years of bad practice but with my application for D11 being processed, I felt that I should at least try and be professional. My mate Steve, who had transferred to the DPG several years previously, kindly liberated a set of DPG body armour for me. Despite the constant piss-taking, I always insisted on wearing it, and eventually one or two others started to don it as well. Holsters and belts were not personal issue either, so I acquired my own, which I wore together with a pouch containing a pair of privately purchased speed loaders that injected all six rounds into the gun at once rather than having to carry them loose in my pocket along with my loose change.

Years of cuffing it without any real consequences combined with a reluctance even to acknowledge the need for firearms had made the Job complacent about the way it conducted armed operations but I could see a disaster looming on the horizon. Despite my concerns, I continued to be deployed as a shot on a regular basis and by the time my interview for D11 came around I had a reasonable amount of experience under my belt.

SEVEN

BLUE BERETS

My interview for D11 was held at their Old Street base. I hadn't really studied for it and was completely unprepared. The three senior officers sitting on the other side of the desk knew my firearms course results and congratulated me on my shooting scores. Apparently, my course instructors had spoken highly of me, so I was fairly confident that an instructor's course was in the bag but then they started to ask me about my interest in private shooting and what scores I would normally achieve in specific events. I left the room realising that I hadn't been asked a single question about my policing career and uncertain that I'd done enough to win them round.

A week later I was called into Dinger's office. He handed me a letter, which I opened with trepidation, but then he offered me his hand and congratulated me: I was on the next D11 cadre course.

It was inevitable that the lack of training for 'authorised shots' and senior officers alike would result in an eventual tragedy and in mid-January 1983, while I waited to go on my instructor's course, a series of criminal offences culminated in a botched surveillance operation during which 26-year-old film editor, Stephen Waldorf, was seriously injured.

Mistaken for David Martin, an audacious, cross-dressing burglar with an obsession for firearms, he was shot five times by detective constables Peter Finch, John Jardine and a third officer. Wanted for shooting a D division PC, Martin had already been shot during his arrest for the offence but had escaped from his cell at court, bolstering his Houdini-like like reputation.

Waldorf had been a passenger in a yellow Mini with the gunman's girlfriend when he was shot and bore an uncanny resemblance to Martin, who was eventually apprehended and later convicted. The week after his conviction, in the same Old Bailey courtroom, Jardine and Finch stood trial for the attempted murder and wounding of Waldorf. Both were acquitted and Waldorf received a £150,000 pay-out from the Met. The incident sent shock waves through the Met and was the talk of my six-week course. Nearly 200 officers had applied and by the time myself and three others had passed and transferred to D11, or the Wing, the fall-out from the 'yellow Mini saga' had already started to have an effect. The basic course was extended to two weeks with far more emphasis on tactics, but typically there was to be no additional training for the senior officers who, reluctant to deploy their own shots, started to make increased use of D11's own teams. It was a very slow drift in attitude, mainly based on safeguarding their own promotion prospects rather than any real desire to deal with the job professionally. If there was going to be a fuck-up, it seemed, it was better that D11 made it rather than their own men, and we were forced to up our own game.

D11 had four operational teams, colour-coded Blue, Red, Green and Orange. Each team consisted of two sergeants and eight PCs and I was posted to Blue. Three weeks in four were spent training the Met's 4,800 authorised shots but on the fifth we'd come together as a team for our 'standby week'. Pete, my team leader, would ring us a week before and tell us what facilities he had booked and ask us to come up with some shoots or perhaps a tactical exercise. A big monster of a rugby player brought up in East Africa, he had a slightly superior, colonial way about him but he was one of the good guys. His ginger hair and ruddy, pockmarked complexion (which he tried to hide with an equally luminous beard) had earned him the nickname, 'The Cat'. He seemed to like this pseudonym, probably thinking it was a compliment directed at his agility and feline reflexes. In fact, Tony, another former SPG officer from Green team, had pointed out cruelly that Pete looked as if he'd been eating a ginger tom while being hit in the face with a shovel.

Monday morning of the stand-by week would always start with the ritual of being issued with pagers and then we would be off to the military ranges at Purfleet in Essex. Someone would always go ahead, put up the range flags and get the kettle boiling in the Portakabin. A coach would arrive with our divisional riflemen and after a natter over tea and bacon sarnies, we'd spend the rest of the day conducting joint training with them.

Pat, the team's duty action man, and I took it in turns to design the pistol shoots. I soon discovered he was obsessed with winning and practised his shoots until he could max them before we got to have a go. He had become used to always being top shot so I prided myself in beating him whenever I could. Bill, an opinionated Yorkshireman and former army sniper instructor, took the lead on rifle training, while George was our shotgun guru. He was a talented clay-pigeon shooter, who'd shot competitively and was forever breaking out the clay-pigeon trap and boxes of clays. If we'd had ever been attacked by vicious flocks of low-flying ashtrays we'd have been all over it but in terms of combat shooting, most of us felt it was pretty irrelevant and George took a load of stick from the rest of the team. Bill in particular hated skeet shooting and one morning, as we unloaded the van, he walked over feeding rounds into the magazine of a Remington shotgun.

George hadn't even had a chance to set up the trap when Bill suddenly shouted, 'Ears!'

We all rushed to put our fingers in our ears before he pumped eight rounds into three large boxes of fragile clays lying on the grass before calmly walking off with his smoking gun. George just stood there with his mouth open while we rolled around laughing.

The riflemen, our eyes and ears on security operations and sieges, came from all over the Met and while most were uniform PCs and sergeants, we also had a detective sergeant and a traffic chief inspector on our team. It was a bizarre arrangement and in my mind its part-time set-up perpetuated the impression that we were an amateur organisation, which only served to confirm the Yard's reluctance to treat firearms seriously. The rest of the week would be spent on our own using the limited facilities at Lippitts Hill or temporary venues such as old, disused hospitals where we'd practise our search skills.

As the new boy, I was conscious that I should shut up, listen and learn from my more experienced peers but I soon realised that, operations being such rare events, none of us had a great deal of experience. This resulted in heated arguments about how to tackle different tactical scenarios, and with no experience or training manual to follow, strange, theoretical tactics flourished.

Fresh from the real world, I soon realised that much of what we practised simply wasn't going to work on the street and quickly found the courage to voice my own opinions. While many shared them, some clearly didn't, but the confidence born from eight years' service, and the ruthless banter experienced during my time on the SPG, meant I wasn't shy of fighting my corner.

I also introduced 'practical pistol shoots' into our training regime. These were based on the type of competitions that some of us were taking part in and combined speed, agility, slick weapons handling and fast, accurate shooting. They were completely unlike the standard, accuracy-based shoots that the lads were used to and brought out everybody's competitive nature. Soon, standards started to soar.

More often than not our week's training schedule would be undisturbed by operations other than the occasional security gig, where we would be required to support the Special Escort Group (SEG) when they took terrorist suspects to and from prison via either Lambeth Magistrates' Court, which was always used for terrorist hearings, or the Old Bailey for the trial itself.

The SEG were only trained on revolvers, so we would ride shotgun, deploying with our heavier weaponry and our distinctive blue berets as a show of force whenever we arrived at our destination. I was always a bit embarrassed by the whole spectacle, thinking it strange that the bosses at the Yard were happy to deploy us in that role but would send a detective with a two-inch .38 to arrest the terrorists in the first place.

The only hope of a proper job rested on our pagers going off, normally in the middle of the night, for an incident that had become protracted. Wearing a pager meant that you couldn't drink and tied you to the MPD for the week but resulted in the princely sum of £10 a month, shown as 'D11 standby allowance' on your payslip. The most exciting thing about most out-of-hours call outs was the anticipation of some action and a 'fast run', where an Area or traffic car would arrive outside your house and 'blue light' you into work.

Often we'd reach Old Street or get tantalisingly close to the scene, only to find that two divisional shots had stormed in and resolved the issue. Ranger 500, a red minibus with a crew of five DPG shots, was supposed to patrol their central London patch and respond to calls to diplomatic premises but, as the only 24-hour armed asset in the Met, the chief inspector at Information Room or IR (where all 999 calls were handled) would often deploy them to the scene where they'd take great pleasure in dealing with the incident before we could arrive. A piece of graffiti scratched on to a toilet door at City Road range summed it up: 'D11 talk about it, the DPG do it!'

The IRA had been active on the UK mainland, carrying out sporadic attacks throughout my career. They had been quiet for nearly a year and then a bomb detonated at Woolwich Barracks injuring three soldiers. Eight days later at 1.21pm on Saturday 17 December 1983 at the peak of the Christmas shopping period, a huge car bomb detonated outside Harrods department store in Knightsbridge. Police had been evacuating the area and Inspector Stephen Dodd, Sergeant Noel Lane and Constable Jane Arbuthnot, together with three members of the public, were killed. Ninety others were injured, including PC Jon Gordon who lost both legs and a hand. The IRA were back in the game and, at Old Street, a second team was taken away from training duties so that 24-hour cover could be provided. Blue, the on-call team, were stood to, ready to roll at a moment's notice.

I was in the crew room when the phone rang telling us of a barricaded suspect in Croydon and within minutes we were heading south. Our destination was like any other suburban London street a week from Christmas, but the decorative lights sparkling up and down the road were overwhelmed by the police spotlights that illuminated number 27.

We were quickly briefed over the bonnet of the duty officer's car. An occupant had staggered next door with a gunshot wound to the stomach and all the victim could say before collapsing and being rushed to hospital was, 'He's killed everyone.' The inspector had two of his shots to the front, where they'd taken cover behind vehicles, and deployed another two in the rear garden. For once, a senior officer had done the right thing by not sending his men crashing in.

'We've lost enough officers today,' he lamented. 'I'm not sacrificing new lives for old. I want to explore every avenue before I authorise an entry. If everyone is dead in there but the gunman I don't want you walking into a trap just to save corpses.'

I could see his point. But we'd spent hours training for just such a situation and if innocent victims were lying wounded inside we owed it to them to make an entry. Nevertheless, protocol dictated that the local senior officer was in charge and we were obliged to follow his orders.

The first task was to relieve the divisional shots and so Tom and I made our way to the rear garden to cover the back and linked up with two wet and miserable local officers who briefed us. They'd seen no movement at all. The curtains were pulled on all of the windows, although I could see a flickering TV through a gap in the drapes that covered the large patio doors about 30 yards away. We thanked them for their efforts and they slipped quietly away, leaving us on our own. It was cold and the incessant drizzle chilled me to the bone as we maintained our vigil.

Periodically, the telephone rang unanswered inside the otherwise silent stronghold or the voice of the negotiator would echo from the public address system but there was no response. After several hours, Pat, covering the white of the building from the comfort of a nice warm house on the opposite side of the street, reported movement at the net curtains on the upper level and Tom and I cursed, realising that the duty officer was now even more likely to delay an entry.

Finally, after the Technical Support Unit (TSU) put sound probes up to the windows and adjoining walls to no avail, the local inspector finally authorised us to force entry and clear the building by hand. Pete had already formulated a plan that had us entering through the rear patio doors and Tom and I moved silently down the dark garden, staying in the shadows until we linked up with the rest of the team. We stacked up on either side of the large, double-glazed doors and with one swing of the team's sledgehammer, the safety glass shattered into a myriad of tiny cracks and then collapsed in a glittering heap on the patio floor. Cautiously, we entered.

The evening's entertainment had finished, the national anthem had played and now the TV buzzed away, the snowstorm of interference from its big screen flickering shadows across the eerily quiet room. Two young men were apparently asleep in the front half of the lounge. The first wore a dark suit, white shirt and tie and he was leant comfortably back in an armchair clasping a can of lager in his hand, his eyes closed, his legs crossed. He looked like he'd just plonked himself down in front of the telly after a hard day at the office. The second man lay in a foetal position on the floor in front of the couch. He wore a sheepskin coat as if he'd just walked in from the cold and he too clutched a tin of lager that had spilt some of its contents on to the grubby carpet by his matted hair.

My first instinct was anger. I couldn't believe we had waited outside the house for hours while these two had slept drunkenly through our attempts to contact them. There was no blood, no obvious signs of injury, but when I knelt down to shake the prone man, he was cold and as stiff as a board; he'd been dead for at least three hours. A quick glance down revealed a contact entry wound in the back of his skull and a small amount of black, congealed blood had stuck to his matted hair. Working only on hand signals we moved on. If Pat had seen the curtains move, the killer would be waiting to ambush us. Whoever he was, he probably knew the house intimately by now; we were on his territory and he had the advantage.

Guardedly, we entered the hall and found the body of an elderly man lying on the threadbare carpet. While the rest of the team moved towards the kitchen I covered the base of the stairs until I felt a hand on my shoulder guiding me backwards towards the back of the house. The team's search had led them through the grubby kitchen and into an adjoining garage where they had found an inspection pit. Someone had started tunnelling from it under the house's foundations. It would need clearing before we moved on, so rather than split the team I'd been pulled back in order to cover the bottom of the stairs from the kitchen door.

I glanced down to see the body of the elderly man who was dressed in a shabby cardigan and slippers. There was a large, dried patch of blood on the filthy hallway carpet about four feet away and I realised that the team had dragged his stiff body to prop open the self-returning kitchen door. The copper in me told me that the crime-scene investigators would be severely pissed off but, in extremis, needs must.

After what seemed like an age, the garage was finally cleared. The rest of the team re-joined me. We gingerly stepped back over the old man's corpse and made our way up the creaking staircase. The small bathroom was quickly cleared and, as open doors were always a priority, the team moved silently past a closed door to clear the front bedroom. While my fellow shotgunner covered the closed door, I covered the open one through the banisters as they made their pre-entry preparations. Suddenly my heart stopped as I saw the shadow of our suspect's head, cast by our floodlight's powerful beam, moving slowly around the far wall of the room. My gloved finger went to the shotgun's trigger and I was just about to shout out an urgent warning when I realised that the suspect had an unfeasibly thin neck. What I was actually observing was the shadow of the team's extendable search mirror as it was moved to give them vision into the room's corners. I breathed a silent sigh of relief.

The team turned their attention to the one remaining room where, unless he had escaped from the stronghold before police arrived, our killer was going to be either waiting for, us gun in hand, or dead. Both of our shotguns were now trained on the door from floor level and the doorman cautiously turned the handle and pushed. We held our breaths expecting a loud bang but it opened a quarter of the way and then stopped against an obstruction. The silence was overwhelming.

The room was in darkness and the doorman quickly put his free hand in and activated the light switch, illuminating the room and casting a ray of light across the darkened landing. Several heavy kicks and the door gave up a bit more space but, after checking with a mirror, the two entry guys were left with no choice but to force their way in.

Graham Green junior had been a survivalist. His small bedroom was not just where he went for some solitude and to sleep but was also his survival store and his post-Armageddon command post. Presumably he would have eventually moved into the man cave that he'd been constructing under the foundations of the three-bedroom semi, but until then this was his base of operations. It was crammed with canned and dried food and large plastic containers of water, military equipment, clothing and weapons. A CB radio, tuned to the local police frequency, sat on his bedside cabinet next to a pair of binoculars and he lay propped up against the wall under a brain-splattered poster depicting an atomic mushroom cloud with the ironic message: SURVIVE.

His skull had split open like the peak of a volcano. The small room was splattered in blood, brain matter and pieces of hair-covered bone. What was left of his skull was almost a hollow shell and his eyes were nearly four inches apart. Bizarrely the earphones to his Sony Walkman were still in position and a Smith & Wesson .44 Magnum, Dirty Harry's weapon of choice, lay beside him on the floor. When Clint Eastwood's most famous character had drawled the famous line, 'This is a 44 Magnum, the most powerful handgun in the world and it could blow your head clean off!' he hadn't been far off the mark.

Physically and mentally drained, and with the clearance finally complete, we left through the front door, leaving the scene for the duty officer and the detectives, and after we'd completed our notes in the bright, 24-hour canteen at nearby Croydon nick, we boarded our vehicles and headed back to Old Street.

Over the days that followed, more information about the incident filtered back to the team. I was shocked to discover that Green had once been one of us – a copper! He'd been a probationer at Tooting nick but was sacked for being substandard. Describing him as a loner, his former colleagues were amazed to discover that he possessed firearms or that he was obsessed with Armageddon.

He'd killed his father, Graham Green senior, his younger brother Gregory and Michael Skinner, a family friend, but wounded his other brother who had escaped to raise the alarm. He made a full recovery physically but was never able to tell the police exactly what had happened. So traumatised was he by the events that his mind completely shut out the horrendous memories.

In some ways I envied him. In eight years as a copper I'd seen plenty of dead bodies, mainly elderly people that had died of old age, but more than a few who had succumbed to violent deaths. Yet, in the days that followed, I thought more and more of the sudden and violent end of the Green family and their friend and it really depressed me. There was no one to discuss it with and I thought a lot about my own interest in firearms and my chosen career.

I didn't want to end up the one on the slab leaving Josey and Mark without a father, and I didn't want to be responsible for any of my colleagues ending up in the mortuary, either. I took a fair bit of flak for nearly shooting the mirror but it was small fry compared with the abuse Pat received for continuing to insist he'd seen movement at the front upstairs curtain even though we now knew that there hadn't been a living soul left in the house.

Overshadowed by the events in Knightsbridge, the tragic wiping out of a family in Croydon barely hit the news but if the IRA had wanted their bomb to benefit their cause, they had miscalculated. Its size, lack of adequate warning and the police and civilian casualty rate was frowned upon even by some of their supporters, and with one of the fatalities being an American citizen their command was worried about the effect it might have on their funding from across the Atlantic.

We couldn't have maintained our 24-hour state of readiness forever and as the IRA threat diminished, we returned to our regular monthly routine, but our operations were undoubtedly picking up.

EIGHT

YELLOW ARSEHOLE
SYNDROME

The Lippitts Hill anti-terrorist exercise I'd attended while on the SPG had been one of the first to be run since the Iranian Embassy siege in 1980. When the Wing had first been given its operational role in the mid-seventies, several of its founder members were sent to Hereford to train with the SAS and develop our capabilities. The decade had been a time of strikes, power cuts and civil unrest and shortly after this early contact, the Labour government, perhaps nervous about the military and police developing closer ties or even mounting a very un-British coup, had put a stop to joint exercises and training.

The two organisations had successfully worked together at several incidents over the years, particularly at the Balcombe Street siege in December 1975 where, after several days of impasse, the presence of the SAS was allegedly leaked to the cornered IRA trio who promptly released their hostages and surrendered.

Five years later at the embassy in Princes Gate the two units again worked together. This time the police strategy of containment and negotiation was only partially successful and the regiment was forced to carry out their famous rescue mission. Despite its success, not everything went as smoothly as the press made out and a lack of joint training and exercises had made the machine rusty.

With Maggie Thatcher in power and a new spirit of optimism in the air, the siege debrief highlighted the need for closer ties between the police and Special Forces and, shortly after I joined the Wing, we received an invite to take part in a three-day counter-terrorism exercise and Blue and Red were picked to go. While billed as an exercise, the first day was to be an under the radar training package and if questioned we were to say that it was merely exercise rehearsal and briefings. We drove to Hereford the day before, but delayed by traffic we arrived about an hour late. We were met in the Sergeants' Mess by 'Nasty Neil', a gruff, Geordie NCO who gave us our room keys, told us to be in the gym in PT rig at 0800 the following morning and left us to it.

Trips away were a rare event, so the opportunity for a team curry and a few beers couldn't be missed. Hours later I staggered back to the mess and the following morning, nursing a hangover, I joined the rest of my jaded team in the gym where we were greeted by Neil and his sidekick Mick, who had a face like Mr Punch and was the smallest, hardest man I'd ever met.

'You're late!' boomed the unhappy Geordie. 'When I say o-eight hundred, I mean o-eight hundred army time, not o-eight hundred copper's time! If you and I aren't going to fall out you'd better fookin' switch on!'

As instructors, we were used to giving out bollockings, not receiving them, and we all shuffled our feet and examined the floor like naughty school kids. The regiment's PTI's had built an assault course in the gym using benches, vaulting horses and ropes, which we were thrashed around until even Graham, one of our own PTIs, vomited into his gas mask.

We must have looked a strange bunch to our hosts. Our ages ranged from 26 to 50 plus, with a similar range of fitness abilities.

Worse for wear from our night down town we must have looked like Dad's Army on moonshine but the one thing that we could all do was shoot. Apart from George, our clay-pigeon champion, we had several county-grade rifle shooters and guys that competed at the top level of most pistol disciplines and later in the day that skill would help us save face but, in the meantime, all we could do was throw ourselves enthusiastically into the humiliation of a thorough SAS beasting.

After several hours of further abuse we drove ten miles outside of Hereford to the regiment's main training area, which was to be the next location of our continued humiliation. We started with an abseil session on their climbing tower. Being the new boy I'd never even worn a harness and one of their instructors was running me through the basics from about 20 feet up when the thump, thump of an approaching helicopter disturbed the lesson.

'That's the cab arriving, you'll be all right, you've got the basics,' he joked.

'Basics? What basics? And what's the helicopter for?'

My questions were soon answered as we took it in turns to launch ourselves, two at a time, from a tiny Scout helicopter. Soon it was my turn to sit in the small cab and be connected to the rope with my figure-of-eight descender. Tom sat next to me on the starboard side and gave me a thumbs up and a grin over the deafening roar of the rotors and the heady scent of aviation fuel. The dispatcher's mouth moved silently as he communicated with the pilot through his headset and then the aircraft began to rise vertically over the drop zone.

The dispatcher's hand signals soon indicated that we had reached 200 feet and it was time to leave the safety of the cab, get out on to the skids and shuffle into position facing back into the aircraft. Extending his hands out in a chopping motion, the dispatcher signalled for us both to lean back, straight-legged, until our heads were level with the skids and our backs were nearly parallel with the ground so that we didn't swing under the aircraft and smash our heads on the skids. It was also important that we did it together to help the pilot balance the Scout's light airframe and to insure we arrived on target together.

'Never let go of the rope with your brake hand' had been hammered home throughout my brief introduction to abseiling but no one had explained that 200 feet of rope was heavy enough to lock my descender and prevent me from moving even without my death-grip and I now found myself swinging helplessly under the helo. I looked down to see Tom disappearing gracefully down his rope while I examined the Scout's undercarriage.

I could see my colleagues far below, their hands cupped, trying pointlessly to shout advice but I was on my own. I began to tug the rope through my descender and drop in a series of jerks, several feet at a time until I realised that, by lifting it and taking pressure off the device I could pick up greater speed. The farther I descended, the lighter the rope below me became and the faster I dropped. Soon I was speeding down and had to grip the rope and lock it down violently to prevent myself hitting the ground. After several bounces I found my feet back on the red Herefordshire earth and safety. Mike, our team inspector, came up to me with a big grin and slapped my back.

'Well done, son!' he shouted over the deafening down draft. 'Not a bad effort for a first ever abseil!

Tom, who wasn't known as the brightest among us, then volunteered to experience the effects of their famous stun grenade. We looked on as Tom, dressed in flameproof coveralls, earmuffs and a respirator, reluctantly entered a derelict brick shed with broken windows.

'You can watch through the windows if you like, lads,' said Mr Punch.

We all looked at him with disbelief. Our own 'green meanie' stun grenade created enough overpressure in such a confined space to blow out the windows and damage the door, walls and roof. So even with eye and hearing protection on, we peered into the gloom of the tiny building with a degree of trepidation. Tom's eyes were like dinner plates through the lenses of his gas mask, as the black rubber grenade was posted through the door and a series of loud bangs, flashes and smoke filled the room. Tom walked out through the swirling smoke, removed his earmuffs and respirator and said calmly, 'Is that it?'

We all went back to our vehicles sharing his disappointment. The smaller multiple reports were distracting but compared with our own green meanie grenade, it was a definite anti-climax. We chatted enthusiastically about our experiences as we drove back to the camp for lunch and an afternoon in the famous 'Killing House'.

If the flash bang was an anti-climax, their equally famous Killing House was a real disappointment. After the embassy siege, I'd read a feature in the newspapers about SAS training; I should have known better than to believe it. The article described its bulletproof walls that could be moved hydraulically to reconfigure the layout, sophisticated, low-light CCTV and other computerised gadgetry. The reality was a windowless, single-storey, brick-built structure with a single briefing, loading and kit room leading to a wide corridor with two rooms on either side. One room had aircraft seats arranged in it facing a cine screen, so that their assaulters could experience firing at video images of hijackers.

The other rooms were fairly large with red, rubber Linotex sheets hanging over steel-plated walls. The 9mm rounds would pass through the rubber and smash into the steel while the Linotex would seal behind the round, capturing the bullet fragments and preventing them from ricocheting back into the room.

The control room's bulletproof windows bore the scars of several 9mm strikes and its CCTV cameras were on the blink. From here we would take it in turns to watch our colleagues burst into the room and kill the plywood terrorists while avoiding our own teammates, taking it in turns to sit as observers among the targets. Before Nasty Neil would let us do that, however, we would have to demonstrate our shooting skills.

We fired our MP5s till they glowed. Double taps to start with and then full auto, firing short bursts. We practised turning left, right and about, standing and kneeling before we progressed to our favoured weapon, the Browning Hi Power. The paper Huns Head targets were being regularly replaced now as we shot the centres out of them. As I stood waiting my turn to shoot, I thought I caught a raised eyebrow between our SAS instructors that seemed to say, 'Not bad.'

Satisfied that our accuracy and weapons handling were up to speed, we were walked and talked through basic room-combat drills. This started with two men entering the rooms at speed, the first selecting the maximum threat and engaging the targets within his arc while his number two engaged anything in the opposing arc. We walked repeatedly through it dry before progressing to live fire and then we added more men to the entry and then multiple rooms. By teatime, we had won our instructors around and our weapons skills and enthusiasm had helped compensate for our poor timekeeping and miserable gym performance.

Most of us carried minor injuries from the previous day and I staggered into the mess for breakfast nursing a strained groin and wondering what the coming one would bring. We were directed to a large briefing room where all was to be revealed and the buzz of conversation halted for a long second as their standby squadron took us in. These were the coppers they'd heard about. Exactly what they'd heard would become apparent later.

The briefing was a detailed affair covering the 330-mile move from Hereford to Beith, just south of Glasgow. We were left to find our own way.

Enthusiastic banter lasted until the outskirts of Hereford before reducing to silence and then snoring. Motorway driving was fine. With my right foot pressed to the metal we cruised along as fast as the diesel engine would take us, but when I had to use the brakes or the clutch, I found myself, like Douglas Bader, using my hands to grab a handful of denim and lift my leg to the pedals, relieving the pressure from my aching groin.

After several stops we crossed the border into Scotland and found our way to the village of Beith and the front gates of a massive MOD munitions storage area. The whole site was crisscrossed with rail tracks that provided access for munitions trucks and we were directed to a cluster of old railway carriages where Neil and Mick were waiting for us. We appeared to be the first on the scene, which made sense, as we were there to provide a police forward control and a containment group that the SAS squadron could liaise with on arrival and interact with throughout the exercise. We followed our two hosts on board the train where we were given a quick briefing by our, now slightly friendlier, Geordie.

'This carriage will be your holding area and control point. When the team turn up in a couple of hours, they'll be located in the next carriages and they'll be looking for a complete sitrep. The stronghold is a similar train located about a hundred metres from here. As soon as you've kitted up we'd like you to get your snipers out and start reporting.

'All we know so far is that an unknown number of X-rays [terrorists] have taken a number of Yankees [hostages], including the crew, and are holding them. Your own negotiators are due to arrive within the hour but so far the X-rays have made no demands. The cooks are setting up over there and you can get scoff and brews whenever you want. Any questions?'

After some brief questions, a couple of the lads got to work carrying our control equipment into the carriage while the rest of us started to get kitted up outside. We donned our coveralls, body armour and QRVs (Quick Release Vests), un-boxed our weapons and started to load our magazines with blank ammunition. As we busied ourselves, a senior police officer wearing the rank of chief constable and an army officer in standard brown brogues, cords and Barbour jacket approached us. All he was missing was a chocolate Labrador called Monty.

'All right lads?' said the local chief constable in a broad Scottish accent. 'And where might you be from?'

'Good afternoon, sir,' said Mike. 'We're from D11 – Met Police Firearms Unit.'

'Oh, I see. So you'll nae be police officers in Scotland, then?'

We all looked at each other and then to our inspector whose smile had changed to a puzzled expression.

'No, sir. We're from the Met.'

The chief constable examined our kit laid out on the floor. 'You'll nae have firearms certificates for those weapons then?'

'Er, well … no, sir.'

'Well, I shudnae have to remind you that you dinnae have the powers of constables outside of England and Wales, so I suggest that you put those away and I'll just pretend I huvnae seen them, okay?'

I caught a discreet wink from the police chief to the army officer as they turned and walked away, leaving us to stand with our mouths open in disbelief. All eyes turned to our boss. 'You heard the man, put them away!'

There followed a brief but pointless discussion about this sudden turn of events before we sorted out our postings, checked our radios and got on with the job in hand. Fifteen minutes later, we had located the train and like school kids playing cowboys and Indians, had contained it using our fingers as guns, and were starting to report back descriptions of the stronghold. Our control duly logged the information and by the time the negotiators and the SAS had arrived, we'd colour coded the train, numbered the windows and doors, identified several of the terrorists and hostages and allocated them identity codes. We had also opened a line of communication with the terrorists and established their demands.

Soon the SAS sniper coordinator was visiting our containment positions and checking out their suitability for his own two-man teams and a short while later an SAS sniper pair joined us. Each man was heavily camouflaged and equipped with a Tikka bolt-action rifle and all their ancillary equipment. The piss-taking started immediately.

'What's up fellas?'

'No guns?'

'We've got some spares if you want them!'

We grinned back, what else could we do? After a short while we were on first-name terms and the banter had started to flow. Most squaddies distrust coppers, but the reality is both professions share the same cynical sense of humour, which explains why so many ex-servicemen choose policing as a second career.

Once your average squaddie realises that we're not all church-going do-gooders, the barriers come down and they are soon fishing for tips on how to carry out the perfect robbery. After a while one of them let slip a piece of information that explained our initial reception at Hereford, the beasting in the gym and the lack of guns in our holsters. According to him, their commanding officer had attended a meeting at the Yard several weeks before the exercise, during which a senior Met officer had allegedly said, 'Of course, we don't really need the SAS in London because we have D11!'

If it was true, the naivety of the comment beggared belief. None of us thought for one minute that we were capable of doing anything more than holding the fort until the cavalry arrived. We were good instructors, we were keen and we could shoot but we only had a standby team of eight men and minimum equipment and couldn't hope to field the manpower, expertise or resources available to an SAS squadron.

When the Wing gained its operational role nearly a decade earlier, freshly funded with a large budget, its members had anticipated a blossoming future but years of not being used had dulled their passion. Now, despite the humiliation of having our guns confiscated, old hands and fresh-faced newcomers alike returned to London with renewed enthusiasm and a determination to drive our operational capability forward but Bill, our former guardsman, having no desire to relive his military past, had avoided the trip and poured cold water on our new zeal.

'You lot make me smile,' he said sarcastically, having listened in on conversations about our recent trip. 'If the SAS told you they painted their arseholes yellow, you'd be down't stores first thing the next day ordering ten gallons of yellow paint!'

NINE

MURDER IN THE PARK

By the time I'd kitted up at the base and was en route to the scene, I was already part of a second wave of D11 responders and Green, the on-call team, were already there. As our carrier forced its way through the gridlocked streets towards St James's Square, we listened intently to the radio as reserves were called up, cordons were reinforced and information was imparted. All of us held our breaths, secretly hoping not to miss the action. A quarter of a mile from the scene, the radio dispatcher announced that a WPC had died of her injuries. Later we would discover that Yvonne Fletcher had died from a single gunshot wound to her stomach sustained as she policed a demonstration outside the Libyan People's Bureau.

Uniformed officers waved us through the outer cordon and ushered back the throng of TV crews, press and onlookers and we entered a haven of calm activity. One of our armoured Land Rovers was parked at the junction of Charles the Second Street and the square with its front poking out to give its gun ports an unobstructed view of the front of the Bureau, while the rear of the vehicle remained behind the building line allowing the containment officers safe access.

A DPG officer, wearing a hastily donned set of white body armour over his dark blue tunic, directed us to a bank on the corner of the square which had been commandeered as a hasty command post. Several other DPG shared the back of the armoured vehicle with Big John Tremelling, one of Green team's snipers who waved to us as we lugged our kit into the bank, its staff already evacuated from the inner cordon.

Inside, control was up and running and several desks had been cleared of bank property while D11 and DPG officers logged radio transmissions and updated the plans and overviews that had already been hastily drawn on to sheets of large flip-chart paper and pinned to noticeboards and walls. Information was shouted across the room while a Panic, the collective term for a group of senior officers, huddled in the corner discussing strategy.

We dumped our kit bags and reported to the control to be briefed and allocated tasks. The situation was still confused. Shots had been fired from one of the front upstairs windows of the Bureau, now overlooked by our armoured Land Rover, designated as point six. From his armoured OP (observation post), JT had a poignant view over the WPC's hat, and her colleagues' helmets left in the street and the shoes abandoned by the fleeing demonstrators.

There was little information about the weapon that had been discharged, other than that it had sounded like a burst of fully automatic gunfire, but the DPG had been on scene very quickly and one of their officers had reported seeing a man try to leave the rear entrance in Babmaes Street with what he believed was an AK47. The rear containment position was designated as point one and was considered the most vulnerable.

The corner of Duke of York Street had been designated as point nine and, together with JT's position in the Land Rover, provided an L-shape arc of fire on any hostile targets leaving through the front of the premises. The corner of the square where the victims had been hit was identified as the point beyond which any police fire would have to cease for fear of causing friendly casualties. Other positions on the rooftops of adjoining buildings completed the ring of steel.

Some of the guys were sent to bolster containment positions while I was tasked to do detailed tactical sketches of the various aspects. As I left the command post with a new lad from Red team, I bumped straight into Ted Stowe. Now the commander of C division and in charge of the whole of the West End, he was his usual gruff self.

'All correct, sir!' I said, chucking up a smart salute to where my beret touched the corner of my right eye.

'Who says it's fucking correct?' Stowe snapped back.

'PC Long, sir. One of your Lewisham officers.'

'Fuck me, Long! They trust you with a gun now? The Job really is fucked!'

'I know, sir. Who would have thought?'

'How's your wife? Kim, isn't it? And your daughter?'

I was amazed. I couldn't believe he still remembered Kim's name, let alone that I had a daughter. I told him they were fine and of my young son Mark and he congratulated me.

'They've killed one of my officers, Tony,' he whispered. 'I don't want to lose anyone else. You be careful. Shoot the fuckers before they get a chance to shoot you!'

The old man winked but it barely concealed the sadness in his face. It was the one and only time he'd ever called me by my first name. He strode off to his awaiting staff car and was gone.

For the next two hours we made our way from point to point where I'd make sketches, take notes and, where necessary, give tactical advice to some of the DPG officers. With an enhanced appreciation of the stronghold and the police positions we made our way back to the control and I started to transfer my sketches on to larger A1 sheets.

The initial flurry of activity had calmed and the bosses were starting to plan for the long haul.

The Met's model for dealing with sieges was tried, tested and manpower intensive. SOPs (Standing Operating Procedures) dictated that we needed two teams to cover a 12-hour day shift and two to cover nights. Green were the standby team and were always partnered with Orange. Red and Blue would go home and be prepared to take over from the day shift at ten that evening. The Met was a huge organisation but the loss of any officer was like the loss of a family member and we all wanted to stay until the culprit was arrested or killed. Leaving our kit in the control, we boarded our transport and returned to base and then home. I set my alarm and went straight to bed.

Back at the scene that evening, things had moved on and an air of permanence had developed. To prevent press intrusion, the Job's engineers had erected large blue plastic screens supported by scaffolding frames at all of the junctions approaching the square and these were manned by an army of uniform officers who had been bussed in from all over the Met. They were only doing their job but despite us being festooned with guns and grenades, insisted on checking our IDs and even patting us down. On the other side of the screens, arc lights on hydraulic poles created an artificial daytime. Some provided general lighting for the holding area but most were directed at the imposing Georgian building that housed Yvonne Fletcher's killers.

Large generators chugged loudly, cables ran everywhere and officers queued at large urns on folding tables to fill their polystyrene cups with foul Job tea and coffee and for food from a mobile catering unit. It was like a film set but without the cameras. We made our way to the briefing room and were updated on the latest intelligence and changes to our containment plan. Elements from all of the Met's support staff were present at the scene and, aside from the screens, the generators and the lighting, the engineers had delivered sandbags to point one. One of our tasks that night would be to make a sangar to provide protection in the event of an armed break out from the rear of the stronghold.

The control had been moved to a better location and had now taken on a more serene atmosphere. A large table dominated the room and a representative from most of the departments involved had a seat and a hard-wire telephone line set up by the communications branch that connected them to the siege's own network. Thousands of yards of cable stretched out across the floors and corridors of the building, held down by black duct tape. The scene commander chaired the table and any issue coming in was discussed and dealt with quietly and efficiently.

In addition to a seat at the table of truth, each of the interested groups had a corner or an office with their own desk and the D11 control was no different. Any activity reported by the inner containment officers was logged, plotted and passed on to the scene commander where it became the knowledge of all the groups. Some other agencies present had their own rooms but weren't represented in the main control. What they knew, they would rather keep to themselves. The spooks from MI5 or 'Box', as they were better known, had an office close to the control room, as did our colleagues from Special Forces.

Nasty Neil and a few other familiar faces from Hereford had taken up residence next to the spooks but there was little for them to do. Without hostages to rescue, their role was purely advisory and the incident became an opportunity to test responses and examine tactical solutions to hypothetical scenarios. How would they force entry if they had to? What sort of charges would they use? How would they deploy their resources? In the quiet wee hours, some of us were tasked to act as guides when lads from the SAS, who'd set up in a nearby barracks, would visit the scene to carry out Close Target Reconnaissance (CTR) of the stronghold, clambering silently over rooftops and examining skylights and other potential entry points for their theoretical assault.

Despite losing a fellow officer, and the seriousness of the incident, black humour still came to the fore and I found my own outlet through my cartoons. It started one night when I was taking my turn in the control room. At three in the morning everything was quiet and the general discussion had come around to the SAS and their notional operation which was impacting, albeit slightly, on the real one that we were trying to run. This was a real murder scene with real aims and objectives, namely the peaceful surrender of the occupants of the People's Bureau, the preservation of evidence and the arrest and future conviction of Yvonne Fletcher's killers, and while we were trying to achieve that, we also had to provide the assets to assist with their conjectural operation. Copious amounts of their Special Forces magic dust had been sprinkled over the bosses at the Yard and very senior officers, who should have really known better, were insisting that the regiment be given every assistance even at times when we were actually too busy to assist.

While I listened to the conversation I doodled option one, which, as it was Easter, had an SAS assaulter disguised as the Easter bunny pushing a large Easter egg, containing another hidden assaulter, towards the front door of the Bureau. Option two followed in a similar vein with a wooden Trojan camel containing black clad assaulters.

A whole series of 'options' cartoons followed and they were to be found pinned up all over the siege site. Soon I was getting requests for cartoons from all the participating organisations and the lads were starting to complain that I was being allowed time away from the containment positions just so that I could do my drawings.

Ralph, an equally talented cartoonist, was particularly bitter and did one of me sitting at an easel drawing, while he and the rest of the lads sat on windswept containment positions. Actually, the weather was particularly mild. I spent my fair time in containment positions watching the spring sun rising over the capital's rooftops, waiting patiently for my day-shift colleagues to arrive.

The black humour didn't stop with my cartoons and it could be found everywhere as the siege dragged on. We were armed with our MP5 sub-machine guns, most of which were the suppressed SD variant, and the German weapon was fairly topical at the time. Weeks before, it had been leaked to the press that selected Met protection officers were to be trained on the stubby MP5K variant and there'd been questions in Parliament about the wisdom of giving the police machine guns. We'd had ours for nearly ten years without any dramas but it didn't stop the senior officers who were drawn to the incident like moths to a flame coming up and asking stupid questions.

'Isn't that one of those new machine guns we're getting … a Kockler or something … what do you call it?'

One visiting deputy assistant commissioner foolishly asked Tony from Green team on a daytime visit to the sandbagged sangar at point one, what was the name of his gun.

'Whispering death sir,' was the swift retort. Not picking up on the sarcasm, the DAC went on to ask why Tony needed the combat knife that he wore on the front of his assault vest.

'That, guv, is for the watches,' Tony answered in his cockney accent.

'Watches?' queried the confused DAC.

'Watches, guv. Arabs love 'em,' Rolexes, Longines, Breitlings. If it all goes to a ball of chalk and we end up in a bit of a shoot out, it's going to end up with a free for all for those watches, guv. I'm not messing around with fiddly catches and straps in the middle of a gun battle,' he said with a glint in his eye, unclipping the knife from his vest. 'I'll just cut their hands off!'

He winked as the DAC and his entourage turned and headed rapidly towards the safety of the blue plastic screens.

Most of the positions were augmented by DPG officers who were equally intrigued by our specialist weaponry and, in particular, the SD. One of the sergeants from Red team, a strange individual, was asked some technical questions about the silenced weapon on his lap. He ignored the query and started to stroke the suppressor tube of his SD lovingly.

'Don't let the nasty man upset you, my sweet,' he crooned in a Clouseau-like French accent. 'If you're a good little girl I will let you kill somebody later.'

Winding the DPG up became a bit of a pastime and Ralph and Graham, Red team's Dangerous Brothers, borrowed a spent 66mm LAWS rocket from the unit's museum and placed it next to them in the sangar for effect. They deliberately refused to answer any questions about it and the rumour that D11 were armed with anti-tank rockets spread around the Met like wildfire.

The days dragged on and after a week had passed it became clear to all that our domestic murder scene was now the epicentre of a much larger international crisis. COBRA were meeting hourly and while the Met's negotiators strived to convince the Bureau's occupants to come out quietly, the Foreign Office negotiators were conferring directly with Tripoli and their aims and objectives were entirely different from our own. The press were reporting that the government's lack of response was in fear of reprisals on British expats in Libya and some at the scene were asking unfairly why the SAS weren't planning for a hostage extraction in Libya rather than a pretend one in London. Some of us suspected that they were.

The day of Yvonne Fletcher's funeral was drawing closer and the poignant image of her abandoned cap was a daily reminder of the frustrating impasse reached at the scene. We had discussed plans to recover her hat so that it could at least accompany her coffin but senior officers refused to entertain any of them. As I arrived for the night shift the evening before her funeral, I was surprised to hear my name called and turned to see an old colleague from P district. Clive Mayberry was a good copper with an expertise in vehicle crime and was as mad as a hatter.

'All right, Clive, how's things?'

We made small talk for a few minutes then I made my excuses and went to join my team for our handover briefing.

'When's someone going to recover the poor cow's hat?' he shouted to my back and I turned, still walking and shrugged my shoulders before entering the holding area and running to catch up with my team.

At the briefing, we learnt that the negotiators had made some headway during the day and that we were likely to be deployed to prepare the corner of the square in anticipation of a negotiated surrender of the Bureau's occupants. At last it looked like we'd be doing something positive rather than just sitting, watching and reporting.

Emergency vehicles abandoned near the front of the stronghold would need to be moved before any surrender. Their radios had been left on and their batteries would probably be dead. Our mission would be to provide firearms cover while traffic officers entered the square and jump-started or towed the vehicles away. All of this was to be carefully negotiated with the besieged occupants so that there would be no misunderstandings about our intentions. The last thing we wanted to do was give them cause to open fire on more unarmed officers.

My task, together with one of our divisional riflemen, was to provide elevated cover on to the white aspect of the stronghold from scaffolding in the south-east corner of the square. Final negotiations were still taking place and it was anticipated that we would be conducting the operation at night. We were all excited at the prospect of a surrender and wanted to be the one that talked the suspect to the ground or to be the officer who, with an extra tug of the plasticuffs, cut off the circulation to the hands that had held the murder weapon, or at least to be there and to have played some part in it.

Several hours later we were given the go ahead and the two of us settled in to our sniper position and waited for the off. It was just before midnight and the two nervous traffic officers were being helped into their body armour ready to enter the square when suddenly I saw a shirt-sleeved uniformed officer complete with his bobby's helmet walking purposefully from point six, diagonally across the road towards Yvonne Fletcher's hat and I recognised his distinctive gait.

'All calls, unauthorised personnel in the square!'

It was the distorted voice of Ralph in the Land Rover at point six. The lone officer stooped and picked up the symbolic hat; it was Mayberry. He stood upright, faced the building and stood defiantly for a brief moment before turning on his heels and marching at a smart pace back to the safety of the cordon; I was sure he was smiling. The bosses weren't though; a minute later and the two traffic officers would have been about their business and who knows how the trigger-happy occupants would have reacted?

Clive's brave but foolhardy gesture was typical of him. He'd charmed his way past a perimeter WPC and completed his mission out of a passion for doing what he thought was right but blind to the danger that he might have caused. No harm was done though and, minutes later, the equally brave traffic officers went about completing their task of removing the vehicles.

Mayberry should probably have been disciplined, but he'd single-handedly achieved a small but symbolic victory that the Yard and Whitehall hadn't even thought to accomplish. The following day, the press was full of it and not one of them had a single word of criticism. It was what the great British public would have expected and the cap sat symbolically on top of Yvonne's flag-decked coffin when she was laid to rest.

Unfortunately, Clive's honourable gesture was short-lived. Behind the scenes less principled negotiations had been taking place and before we could return for another night shift, I was woken by a phone call. The situation had been resolved and we were all stood down until 0800 the following day when we were to parade at Old Street to de-service our kit. I went back to sleep until my alarm woke me and then later watched the evening news. What I saw on the screen didn't tell the whole picture. I saw, like everyone else, a steady stream of mainly suited, Middle Eastern men leave the Georgian portico and turn right to walk leisurely towards point nine. There were no hands in the air, no team on show or weapons on display, and then they were gone. They were, according to the BBC, taken to an airport and allowed to board an aircraft to Tripoli; no arrests had been made.

At least I hadn't been on duty to witness the shameful process at first hand. As I cleaned my weapon the following day, I was shocked by Green and Orange teams' accounts. They spoke of how senior officers had ordered them not to display their weapons to the suspects, speak to or search them, and how they had watched in disbelief as the killers of a fellow officer had been allowed to walk away, shielded by a non-existent diplomatic status. They had been bussed to another location where they were very briefly interviewed but the terms of their surrender didn't even allow for the taking of their fingerprints.

Then they were allowed to fly home to Tripoli and a hero's welcome on the very day that Yvonne Fletcher was buried. After ten long days, it wasn't them that had surrendered, it was us.

TEN
SIEGES AND BLAGGERS

I'd heard the final, fatal shot from my position on the floor below and had listened to the drumming of the suspect's heels on the carpeted floor as his life ebbed away. We'd run a book on where he'd shot himself: left temple, right temple and in the mouth were favourites; Tom had suggested centre chest. Who the fuck's going to shoot themselves in the chest? We all ridiculed Tom, he wasn't the brightest tool in the box, but he smiled wryly when he eventually pocketed his winnings. It was January 1985 and what had should have been a simple arrest at a house in Streatham had turned into a protracted siege.

Following the muffled shot, concerned that wanted armed robber Tony Baldessare may have set a trap, the TSU had spent several hours inserting probes into the apartment until eventually they spotted Baldessare's legs. D11's caution had proved to be the correct approach. The fugitive had barricaded the only entry point and had set up various firing positions within the flat, laying down a small arsenal of pre-positioned firearms to take us on. Before killing himself he'd burnt his ill-gotten gains in the kitchen sink. Baldessare had wanted to go out in a blaze of glory and we'd denied him his last wish. It was a classic example of why the softly-softly approach made absolute sense in the majority of firearms operations.

Earlier in the siege, concerned at the cost of the operation, Alex Marnock, now the local commander, had ordered us to assault the flat. We had politely turned down his kind invitation, pointing out that Baldessare had nothing we wanted. With no hostage to be rescued all we'd be doing was putting our lives and that of the suspect at risk. Before leaving the scene he graciously apologised for getting it wrong, but then ruined it by reminding us we were, after all, the unacceptable face of British policing.

The irony wasn't lost on us simple gunslingers. While we always advocated the calm, patient resolution that the Yard outwardly took credit for, its senior officers, who looked down on us as gun-toting cowboys, were the ones who insisted we storm in like John Wayne. At the end of March 1985, our tactics were vindicated at Southwark coroner's court: the jury heard that Baldessare had wanted to die in a police shootout but our unwillingness to play ball had frustrated him. The verdict: suicide.

The day after Baldessare's inquest, yet another armed siege tested the Met's resolve when detectives from Chelsea nick went in search of a convicted murderer and prison escapee who was working as a builder's labourer under a pseudonym and holed-up in Earl's Court, west London. Thirty-five-year-old James Baigrie had been serving life for the shotgun murder of a barman during a bungled robbery in his native Scotland. Six detectives had gone on a dawn raid to arrest him but a search of the flat had proved fruitless.

Typically, only two officers had been issued with revolvers, and as the frustrated raiding party walked down the steps to the pavement they were discussing where to go for breakfast when one of the shots, a young enthusiastic DC, saw a battered builder's Transit van parked outside. Copper's instinct took over and he bimbled over and tried to peer through the dusty windows before trying the back doors. As three of his colleagues, including his fellow shot, drove off in their Hillman Avenger, the DC was surprised when the rusty doors came open with a tug but not as surprised as he was when a balaclava-wearing Baigrie emerged from among the tools and rubbish with a sawn-off shotgun!

Despite his instinct, with his own revolver buried under three layers of clothing, all the DC could do was run for cover. What followed was a bizarre siege lasting some 36 hours that came to a bloody end when Baigrie blew his brains out after impatient senior officers ordered us to end it and we fired CS rounds into the back of his van.

The need to assault a van had never been considered before and it was decided to run a training day to debrief the incident and see what lessons could be learnt. Representatives from each of the teams met up at Lippitts Hill where a similar van was laid on for us to play with and we were split into two teams: Green and Orange, and Red and Blue. Concerns remained about the decision to assault Baigrie's van and so, to justify an intervention, we were given a scenario involving a suspect holding a hostage in the rear of the van and an hour to come up with a tactical option for dealing with it.

Orange and Green team's cunning plan involved shooting out the van's tyres and deploying a stun grenade into the rear compartment. Ours involved an armoured Land Rover nudging the van from the front to put the occupants off balance while two of us approached the rear windows. One of us, equipped with a fire axe, would then smash one of the rear windows, at which point, armed with my revolver and carrying a small ballistic shield, I would simply shoot the hostile target through the window. To register accuracy, my revolver would be loaded with plastic training ammunition. Having presented our plans, Bob Wells decided that, as our option was likely to cause the least damage, we would go first.

While the senior officers and the rival team observed with cameras and stopwatches at the ready, we initiated our plan. It nearly went like clockwork but the two plywood targets propped up in the rear compartment became dislodged when the van was nudged and as I fired my third shot into the bad guy, the hostage fell across my line of fire and my last round clipped the innocent. In reality the round would have passed through the female hostage's hair without causing injury but when the targets were removed for examination there was a fair bit of piss-taking from the rival team.

'You shot a good guy, Harry!' said one wag, misquoting a line from a Dirty Harry movie.

Aside from good-natured abuse, there was constructive criticism and Oz from Orange team took me to one side. One of only two officers in the Met entitled to wear a Vietnam medal on his uniform, Oz was one of the Wing's most experienced team members and had a reputation for being an unflappable sage. I'd worked with him on the ranges and while we were two very different personalities, I respected his opinion.

'You had two good hits on the bad guy, you should have stopped then,' he advised.

Of course, the one-dimensional plywood targets didn't react like real people but I took his point. As expected, Green and Orange team's plan caused substantially more damage than ours and their green meanie blew out the windscreen and all of the remaining glass, bulging the sides of the van and its roof. While they claimed victory based on the speed of their intervention, the rest of us were pretty sure that neither the hostage nor the bad guy would have survived the blast and the expression on Bob Wells's face told me that their plan wouldn't be going into our tool box of available tactics.

*

A few weeks later Blue team were on standby again and, in the absence of any jobs, we benefitted from some transatlantic hospitality. Instructors from the FBI's recently formed Hostage Rescue Team were doing a world tour of US embassies, providing Marine Corps embassy guards with some training in building clearance and what had become known as the modern pistol technique. We received an invitation to take part.

At the little piece of America that was the Marines's west London barracks, we were treated to a huge breakfast of pancakes and maple syrup, eggs and bacon and as much coffee and orange juice as we could consume, followed by several lectures, one of which struck a real chord. It detailed their SOPs following an agent-involved shooting, a subject none of us had ever really considered. Never having had a shooting, fatal or otherwise, the rumour was that if any of us had to fire a shot in anger, they'd be banished to division. I suspected that the dreaded policy was simply a unit myth, but the subject was never discussed in front of senior officers for fear that they might actually confirm it.

Rick gave me a knowing nod. He had joined the team the year before from P district and we had soon become firm friends. Living a few miles from each other we had taken to sharing lifts into work. A short, eccentric former soldier of Anglo-Indian extraction, he knew his subject and, despite his service in the Wing, wasn't afraid to confront the bosses if he thought they were in the wrong. We didn't agree on everything but we were both passionate about enhancing our training and, with the obvious increase in our own operational deployments, had discussed the inevitability of a shooting.

Part of the FBI lecture touched on the psychological aspects of being involved in a gunfight, and I took copious notes. One of their SOPs stuck in my mind. Their policy was that having shot someone, an agent should be whisked away so that his recollection of the dead, dying or seriously injured person would be as vague as possible. Tragedies happen, they emphasised, and the casualty might be an innocent caught up in the situation. The vaguer the shooter's recollection, the less the chance there was of them having recurring nightmares.

Lectures over, we jumped on a bus with the young Marines and drove to Bisley ranges for the pistol training. Modern pistol technique was a subject we were all very familiar with and it had divided the Wing into opposing camps for some time. Those of us that were into practical pistol shooting could see its merit while the older instructors wouldn't budge from teaching the style of shooting adopted, ironically from the FBI, nearly two decades before. Personally, I saw advantages in both styles; it was an enjoyable and valuable day and while I didn't learn anything new about modern pistol technique, I took away two valuable pieces of knowledge: if you've shot someone, get out of Dodge ASAP; and avoid pistol-packing jarheads – they're dangerous!

With our burgeoning operational experience, we were starting to accept that we could no longer rely on bad guys always surrendering or killing themselves. We had developed our own more aggressive drills to cope with those situations where we would have to intervene, but when it came to the type of intelligence-led, fastball operations performed by detective units like the Flying Squad, we still had much to learn. The D11 adage 'detectives and guns don't mix', born from incidents such as the yellow Mini saga, still resonated with many bosses and some older instructors, but many of us acknowledged that changing the culture from the outside was impossible and we should at least be pushing to work on the Flying Squad's more dangerous operations. So when the 'Sweeney' finally called for D11 support, we were eager to prove our worth, immediately dispatching Green team to south-east London to rendezvous with them.

Our bosses were still determined to prove a point though and insisted that the team deploy in their operational uniforms so when the team walked into the briefing wearing blue serge and flat caps with their pistols concealed under anoraks, they were received with looks of utter distain by the waiting techos. They had good information that a security van was going to be hit outside a bank by heavily armed robbers led by members of the infamous Arif family and wanted to conceal D11 and its additional firepower in a vacant shop close by. Unable to covertly infiltrate the team, a hasty plan was cobbled together allowing the Green Team to remain concealed in an unmarked van instead, but by the following week, our bosses had put their prejudices aside and the next team turned up in civvies to prove that plain clothes and guns could mix and would have to if we were to be an effective operational team.

Several weeks later, it was Blue's turn to cover the plot and with our Brownings now concealed under scruffy plain clothes and our shotguns hidden in old tool bags, we walked into the crowded briefing room. The awkward atmosphere made me feel like a new boy on his first day at school. Most of the detectives ignored us, some gave us looks of contempt, while one or two who I recognised, either from the range or from my previous career as a real copper, gave a tacit nod or an awkward smile.

I'd joined the Job aspiring to become a Flying Squad detective and still had a great deal of admiration for them. They were an elite, and in the same way that street criminals and yobs were terrified of the Group, serious, professional criminals were equally scared of the Sweeney. So what if some of their working practices were a little bit dodgy? They terrified blaggers and that was good enough for me.

A Flying Squad briefing was a unique experience and, for most of us, an introduction to a totally different language. A mix between cockney rhyming slang, general police terminology and their own jargon, it was almost impossible to keep up with and even years later, when we'd become as fluent as the suits themselves, a new word or phrase would often be thrown in to keep us 'Lids' on our toes.

'Listen up, we've just had word that chummy has got hold of a pair of nostrils, which he'll bring to the plot in a happy bag. He's all about and last time out he had us well burnt. His anti's a bit crude though so if he screws you, just cheese-roll him. We fancy him for that white box in Plumstead last week and we're pretty sure he's after a blue one today. We're not sure what wheels he'll be using but hopefully the OP will give us an early heads-up and get on the blower. Jacko here's passing round some smudges from last week so give your mince's a treat. Right, me and Bob will be in the flounder. Those of you with shooters, I shouldn't need to remind you of your responsibilities but just be careful 'cause we've got the old Ninjas with us today so screw the nut, okay? Any questions? No? On the plot by oh seven hundred latest then. Good hunting!'

Clear as mud! The job simply faded away; a key player may have been nicked for something else, or perhaps the robber's inside agent may have bottled it, who knew? It wouldn't be the last job to not come off but it was our first proper Squad job and as D11 and the Sweeney got to know each other better, bridges were built.

ELEVEN
MY BALCONY SCENE

NORTHOLT, 26 DECEMBER 1985

For those of us that embraced the operational role, 1985 had been a ground-breaking year. Despite a lack of IRA activity on the mainland, we'd been involved in dramatic sieges, deployed on operations with the Sweeney and experienced serious public disorder during the Tottenham riots. These resulted in the brutal murder of PC Keith Blakelock but had started indirectly as a result of an innocent black lady, Cherry Groce, being shot and paralysed during a bodged armed operation the week before. The raid had been conducted by local armed officers in Brixton and like the Waldorf shooting two years previously would have a huge impact on future training and our own operational deployments. The unit's veterans couldn't remember a year like it and it wasn't over yet. As my own family enjoyed my son's third Christmas, another tale of human tragedy was unfolding on a shabby estate in Northolt, west London.

The baddy in this Christmas pantomime was Errol Walker. A year older than me and born in Jamaica, he'd come to England as a young teenager and while I was enjoying my privileged education in rural Sussex, he'd become involved in London street crime, progressing to armed robbery. In 1982, while I patrolled with the SPG he'd married Marlene, the mother of his daughter Patricia, who sadly suffered from sickle cell anaemia. Later that year, he was arrested and charged with robbery, possession of a firearm and false imprisonment. A long stretch awaited but he rolled over and when he and his co-defendants eventually appeared at the Bailey he asked for 26 similar offences to be taken into consideration and, turning Queen's evidence, testified against his brethren. His cooperation earned him a paltry five years' protective custody. After two-and-a-half cushy years in a converted police cell, complete with TV, conjugal visits and all mod cons, he was out.

As the country's first black supergrass, he should have spent the rest of his life looking over his shoulder but rather than keep a low profile, he set up home with Marlene and little Patricia and returned almost immediately to a life of crime. Perhaps he thought he was now untouchable but he was soon arrested for theft and bailed pending court proceedings. In November 1985, police were called to their family home. Marlene had returned home after a night out with her stepsister Jacqueline Charles, and a jealous Walker had assaulted her and locked her in a room. She'd escaped through a window and called the police for help but this was the eighties and police policy then was to direct the victims of common assault to obtain a summons. Having advised her of her civil remedies they left the happy couple to sort out their own problems.

At the first opportunity Marlene scooped up her daughter and sort refuge at Jacqueline's fourth-floor flat at number 62 Poynter Court on the Gallery Gardens estate in nearby Northolt. One day in early December, as Patricia played happily with Jacqueline's four-year-old daughter Karlene, Walker managed to lure Marlene back to their home where he tied her up and assaulted her, only releasing her when she promised not to tell the police. She didn't; instead she went straight to a local firm of solicitors and made a statement. As Christmas approached, Walker made several trips to Poynter Court but was never allowed across the threshold and had to talk to his frightened daughter at the door.

On Christmas Eve, Jacqueline held a party. Walker turned up uninvited. He wanted Marlene to come home and open her presents and, despite Jacqueline's warnings, to avoid any more confrontation she made the brave but foolhardy decision to go with him. Back at the family home, Walker produced a knife and assaulted her, telling her that he'd kill her when he'd finished. In fear for her life, the terrified woman managed to grab the knife when his guard was down but he wrestled it off her and beat her violently.

On Christmas Day, while I watched my family open their presents to the cheerful sound of Paul McCartney and the Frog Chorus, Walker took his battered wife back to Poynter Court. He wanted Patricia back so that they could play happy families and, warning her not to try anything, sent Marlene upstairs to collect their disabled daughter. Jacqueline answered the door and a frantic Marlene blurted out what had happened before going next door to use the neighbours' phone. Despite her mistrust of the police, she was desperate and dialled 999. The operator tried her best to placate her and immediately dispatched local units to the scene. Meanwhile, Walker waited seething downstairs. Why was she taking so long? He'd warned her not to try anything stupid.

He bounded up the stairs to the fourth-floor balcony and, enraged, stormed into the flat through its open door and barged past Jacqueline, calling out his daughter's name. Whether it was Jacqueline or him that grabbed the large kitchen knife first we'll never know but it ended up in his hands and in a manic attack he stabbed her 14 times. Her hands were lacerated to the bone as she desperately tried to protect herself and the two girls but one of the blows resulted in the knife entering one side of her neck and exiting the other and she fell to her knees fighting for breath. The fatal strike entered by her collarbone and sliced down through her lungs and into her heart. She died on the floor at his feet in front of the terrified children.

Police arrived in time to see Marlene screaming hysterically outside the flat and Walker throwing Jacqueline's bloody and lifeless body through the shattered kitchen window and on to the balcony at her stepsister's feet. With only their wooden truncheons to protect themselves, the two responding officers wisely called for urgent assistance and the cavalry came running. They brought with them long riot shields, helmets and body armour but they were of no use. The delay had given Walker time to barricade the door and in the sanctuary of the flat he now carried Karlene with him at all times, the bloodied knife to her neck. The police now had a hostage situation that they were ill-equipped to deal with. Two divisional shots drew revolvers from the local factory and were deployed to the scene but neither felt confident enough to take the difficult shot. Two young probationers, an Asian PC and a young WPC, started to build a fragile rapport with Walker and succeeded in achieving the release of his crippled daughter before hostage negotiators and the Red team arrived at the scene. The child's release came at a cost though. To demonstrate his determination, he had cut Karlene's forearm to the bone and had been given a police radio with which he could satisfy himself that he wasn't going to be attacked. Later he would put a plastic bag over the traumatised child's head and beat her with the heavy radio as she gasped for breath, and later still would hang the child out of the back window so that her blood dripped on the faces of the firemen that waited below to catch her.

I knew nothing of this but I'd watched the first day of the siege on the TV news and I'd seen Red deploying to either side of the flat whenever the negotiators talked to Walker through the kitchen window. Our call-out system didn't allow for a second standby team over the

Christmas period, so I wasn't surprised to receive a phone call at home asking if I'd be available on Boxing Day as part of a scratch team. Much to Kim's annoyance (it was Mark's third birthday the following day), I said yes, telling her that it was highly unlikely to go on that long and I genuinely expected a cancellation message. None came though and early the next morning, Rick and I travelled into Old Street together. I was driving and the wet roads were clear of traffic. We discussed the situation and the conversation came around to weaponry. We both decided to go with our revolvers loaded with the newly authorised soft-point rounds rather than with our 13-shot Browning pistols in which we still had to use full metal jacket ammunition. Both of us felt that, as the suspect was armed with a knife, firepower wasn't an issue but, with a hostage present, over-penetration might be. We also discussed the use of the public order baton gun. We had both watched the footage of the suspect coming out on to the balcony of Poynter Court armed with a knife and felt that the baton gun might provide us with a less lethal option.

At the base, we met the rest of the team, a mixture of Blue and Green with Mike, our inspector, in overall charge. Also from Blue came our two sergeants Dave, an instructor from my cadre, and Ian, the team newcomer. Green were represented by my old mates Clive and Tony, as well as their giant Cornishman, 'Big' John Tremelling and their new and relatively inexperienced sergeant, Pete, a bit of an East End barrow boy. As we kitted up we discussed our Christmas presents, the in-laws and what had been on the box during the festive season. Mike gave us a short briefing that didn't tell us any more than we already knew from the TV news before turning to the question in hand. Rick and I both made a case for taking a baton gun but Mike turned it down on the grounds that it was only authorised for use in public order situations when the target was over 20 yards away.

We both argued that it would be easy to justify its use in the circumstances as it would provide us with an option other than lethal force but Mike wouldn't budge. Rick surreptitiously loaded it into the call-out van anyway.

We drove through empty streets direct to the scene, where a pair of wet and bored PCs removed the incident tape and waved us through. We pulled up at the base of Poynter Court and shifted our kit bags and weapons up the stairs to the fourth floor where we made ourselves at home in the living room of an evacuated flat that had become our control. While Mike and the sergeants were briefed by the on-scene commander, Red team's controller made us mugs of steaming tea and updated us on the events of the previous 24 hours. As the cheap plastic Christmas tree flickered in the corner, we studied detailed plans of the stronghold marked up with our TI system and an overview plan, all lovingly drawn by Ralph, my artistic rival.

Red team had been on duty for nearly 20 hours and were ready to be relieved. The suspect and his hostage had been sleeping and there'd been no activity for several hours, so Mike quickly briefed us in order to relieve our exhausted colleagues as rapidly as possible. 'Big' John Trem was posted to rifle cover at point five in a nearby block of flats with a view on to the balcony of Poynter Court. He would be about 50 yards away and was strictly briefed that he was there for observation purposes only. When we all queried the decision, Mike insisted that John would be too far away to judge the immediacy of any threat, because he wouldn't be able to hear what the suspect was saying.

'If, for example,' said Mike, 'the suspect holds a knife to the hostage and demands a car to be delivered within ten minutes, a shot from a sniper 50 yards away would be unjustified, as the threat to the hostage wasn't immediate!'

'What if he stabs her then?' challenged JT.

'Well then, your shot would be fired after the fact and also unlawful,' Mike argued.

The team was totally mystified. What was the point of training police snipers at all then? While the rest of us were posted to our close containment positions, JT picked up his rifle case and kit bag and stomped off angrily to commence his lonely vigil. Rick and I would be posted to point nine at the top of the stairs and at the green end of the balcony about 20 paces from flat 62 and would be supervised and supported by Dave. Clive and Tony were posted to point three; another requisitioned flat at the red end of the balcony and a mere five paces from the stronghold's front door. Ian would support them. Pete was posted on his own to the rear, or black, of the premises. His role would also, primarily, be one of observation. We were briefed that this was not a conventional firearms siege as the suspect only had a knife and we could therefore walk past the barricaded flat to get to and from point 3 without any problems. Normally we'd have had enough officers to double man each point and the control and allow for reliefs but this was Christmas and we were it.

Red team had held at their positions until the negotiators moved forward to the kitchen window to talk to Walker or whenever tensions were raised. They would then move to their FAPs (final assault positions) on either side of the flat where, for convenience, they had left their MOE (method of entry) kit – in this case a good old ten-pound sledgehammer.

The IA (immediate action) plan was to breach the front door and enter the hall while deploying distraction grenades through the kitchen and bathroom windows. When this happened Pete was to move forward on the black aspect and fire bird shot at an acute angle through the rear windows of the flat as a distraction. Normally this tactic would have been combined with the simultaneous deployment of CS rounds but this option had been turned down owing to the age and vulnerability of the tiny hostage. If entry through the front door failed, our secondary entry points would be through the kitchen and bathroom windows.

At no point were we told about the serious nature of the assaults carried out on the child the previous day and while we knew that Walker had killed the child's mother, we had no idea about the full extent of his frenzied attack on her. It would be some time before I fully appreciated the extent of the situation that we inherited that cold, wet, miserable morning. As soon as we were briefed, we took up positions at either end of the windswept balcony, still covered in the victim's blood, discarded ambulance dressings, broken furniture and abandoned riot shields. Red team would be back to relieve us in 12 hours' time.

Constant drizzle blew on to the balcony and while Rick had to cope with his inadequate dog handler's anorak, I hunkered down into the new Gore-Tex jacket I was evaluating. The jacket limited access to my belt rig, so I removed my revolver from its holster and stowed it in the jacket's map pocket and slipped my stun grenade into the left-hand pocket. My other pocket contained ambulance dressings and further med kit. Despite the biting cold I wore only my left glove, partially for warmth but also to provide me with a degree of protection in case we had to climb through a broken window to assault the flat. My right hand remained bare, as experience told me that a gloved finger could get caught in the revolver's trigger causing it to jam after the first shot. Cutting the fingers off of your issued Northern Ireland or NI gloves was considered way too gung-ho and, more importantly, would result in Bert, the store man, refusing to replace them. My big, three-cell Streamlight torch remained hung from a loop on my belt.

Shortly after we took up our positions, the negotiation team were relieved by their replacements and with the newcomers came a change of strategy. On day one the police tactic had been to keep Walker contained within the flat. Now, surprisingly, he was to be allowed greater freedom of movement out on to the balcony. A feeling of isolation and a reliance on the negotiators as the suspect's only contact with the outside world is a fundamental principle of negotiation. The change of strategy flew in the face of established protocols and when the new negotiators went forward to speak to Walker through the kitchen window they did so on their own and we were ordered to remain at our containment positions. Walker, we were told, was unhappy about the police with guns and we were ordered to keep out of sight. It seemed the deranged murderer was now running the show.

Clive and Tony at point three were reduced to taking it in turns to watch the balcony through their letter box while Ian, who had only visited them to check on their welfare, was now locked down with them for the duration. While they were isolated in the warmth of their flat, Rick and I could only take turns to peer around the corner of the louvred wooden partition that separated the balcony from the stairwell. The drizzle had now turned to heavy rain, driven sideways by the gusting wind so, as we'd obviously been relegated to a containment role, I slid my Gore-Tex leggings over my trousers, trapping my 'Streamlight' below two layers of Gore-Tex.

The close cooperation that Red team and the negotiators had enjoyed had completely evaporated and even our bosses were being excluded from strategy meetings between the on-scene commander and the negotiators. When we exercised together they would always notify our control when they were moving forward so that our containment positions could be warned to expect activity and they would always report back to our control any intelligence that they obtained while talking to the suspect, but, without warning, two of them had filed past our position several minutes earlier and were now talking to Walker through the kitchen window.

'All units from point five,' boomed Big John. 'You're not going to believe this; the negotiators are helping the suspect build a barrier at the kitchen window. Over!'

Complying with our new orders, Rick and I had kept out of sight behind the louvred partition and were relying on John's radio commentary to keep us informed but this was too strange to ignore and I peered around my cover to observe the balcony and strained to listen to the negotiators' conversation with Walker. In their suits and raincoats, the two senior officers were struggling with some unseen object through the kitchen window.

'Errol, we're not going to attack you. You can't do this while you're holding the child and the knife, you'll cut yourself, let us help you.'

JT identified the object as a glazed interior door which Walker had removed from its hinges and, in a misguided attempt to win him over, they were actually helping him to manhandle it into position on top of the sink. When they returned to their cell they made no attempt to pass this valuable information on to us. Several hours later, again without warning, they escorted Marlene Walker back on to the balcony to talk to her husband through the kitchen window. The day before, a similar attempt to talk him out failed spectacularly when he had leapt from the window, grabbed her around the neck and attempted to drag her inside. She had fought back courageously and managed to wriggle free. It was hard to believe that they were prepared to jeopardise her safety again but, with the negotiators watching on, she held a conversation with her deranged husband through the shattered window. Using an intermediary, particularly one who is in a close relationship with the suspect, is contentious at best but to let her get in close contact with a knifeman who has already murdered appeared to me insane. It seemed incredible that they would put her through this for a second time but to not involve the tactical team beggared belief.

On a recent foray to the balcony Walker had seen our sledge-hammer against the wall and saw it as evidence that we were planning to assault the flat and shoot him. He wanted it removed. Marlene passed on his request to the negotiators who agreed without hesitation and she promptly picked it up and dropped it over the railing. Four stories below, firemen were stood ready with a canvas tarpaulin in case Walker dropped his terrified hostage and the heavy sledge landed among them without warning. John reported the incident from his sniper position and Rick ran downstairs and retrieved it from a less than happy Trumpton. Yet again it seemed to Rick and I that the nego-tiators were doing their own thing without looking at the big picture and it was only through luck that no one had been seriously injured.

The radio crackled into life and we received a rare situation update from our boss Peter Harris who had now arrived at the scene. Despite holding the rank of superintendent, he'd not been invited to all of the strategy meetings but informed us that a DCI Herridge was being recalled from his Christmas holiday in the West Country. Herridge had apparently run Walker as a high-level informant in the past and the negotiators were convinced that once he arrived, the knifeman would give himself up. The DCI eventually appeared but Walker didn't rush to leave the safety of his fortress and shortly afterwards they came up with another cunning plan. This time they wanted us to pack up our kit and retreat from the scene in such a way that Walker could watch us leave. Fortunately, Commander Sparks, the on-scene commander, made one of the few sensible decisions of the day and turned down the absurd suggestion.

Every cloud has a silver lining though and their tactic of pandering to Walker's every request had resulted in him becoming bolder and bolder and, with the team now hiding in our containment positions, he'd started to encroach further out on to the balcony and further away from the security of his front door. Sometimes he would bring the terrified child with him and show her off like a trophy to the baying crowd that had gathered below but he'd also come out on his own and the germ of an idea was starting to form. We'd started to talk on our own radio net, discussing a potential plan where, if Walker strayed too far from the door, half of the team could get between him and his hostage. Mike spoke to Peter Harris and the bare bones of our plan was relayed to the on-scene commander. A short while later Commander Sparks arrived at point nine with Mike and Peter Harris.

'What's this plan then?' he demanded.

I explained that the idea was in its infancy but that with some polish we felt that we could get between Walker and his hostage and leave him without his only bargaining chip. Sparks appeared distracted as I described our proposal and, when I'd concluded, he dismissed it without hesitation, and turned and walked off, followed by Mike and Peter Harris who gave me a sympathetic shrug. A short while later we received a brief radio transmission from Mike emphasising that our plan was not authorised and that no action was to be taken without direct authority. Point by point we all acknowledged the order but carried on discussing the option over the radio, trying to develop it into a form the bosses would find more acceptable.

Hours later, Rick and I stood frozen as two more suited negotiators breezed past our position to the kitchen window, their raincoats flapping in the wind. Again they attempted a face-to-face with Walker and we strained to hear the conversation. It was clearly a one-sided affair, with him ranting and them trying to get a word in edgeways. Within seconds the two suits recoiled as Walker squirted water at them from the kitchen taps.

'Come on, Errol, we need to talk about this sensibly!' one of them bleated as another torrent of water came flying out of the window.

Rick and I gave the two soaking negotiators big cheesy grins as they retreated back past our position with looks like thunder.

'Not going well, gents?' sneered Rick.

Walker was now regularly on the balcony, playing to the crowd below and enjoying his moment of infamy, while sitting the terrified child on the balcony rail, his arm around her waist and her legs dangling over the void as he preached at the assembled crowd like a deranged Messiah.

There was clearly nothing on telly, except the usual Christmas repeats, as the crowd had been growing throughout the day. On the fourth-floor balcony, we were focused on our own little world, oblivious to the mood of the predominately black crowd below but a local uniform PC posted with us informed us that they were angry about the lack of police response. Walker was a supergrass that had given evidence against his black co-defendants. He'd brutally murdered a defenceless black woman and was now flaunting her brutalised daughter in front of them. The crowd saw our lack of action as yet another example of police indifference to the concerns of their community.

They wanted action but the senior police at the scene saw it very differently. They foresaw another potential PR disaster if Walker, the black suspect, was harmed by white police officers in front of the world's media and an angry black mob. Eventually, the crowd's patience broke and they tried to rush the police lines to deal with Walker themselves but our cordons held. What had happened to policing without fear or favour? Surely the most important person here should be the child, Rick and I argued.

'Why are we letting him run the show?' Rick asked. 'Every moment that lunatic is alone with that poor child her life is in danger. We should be doing something. Every time he hangs her over that balcony, it's a thinly veiled threat that he'll drop her!'

The negotiators' cell shared the requisitioned flat with our own control and periodically one of their team would come out for a cigarette or a breath of fresh air. One of their team, a small, bespectacled man with a nervous disposition, had been listening to Rick's rant.

'Well, I think that all depends on one's perspective,' he interrupted. 'You see him sitting her on the balcony rail as a threat, whereas I see it in another way entirely. If you notice, he has his arm around her waist and that is his way of creating a defensive barrier between himself, the girl and the rest of the outside world. Believe me, there is a very strong love bond between him and the child and he will not hurt her.'

He smiled a superior smile and returned to the negotiators' cell, leaving Rick and I to look at each other in utter amazement. It was proof, if we needed it, that the negotiators seemed more concerned with Walker's safety than that of the little girl.

Mike's voice suddenly crackled in my earpiece. 'All units stand by, stand by, door opening.'

Paying a welfare visit to JT's sniper position he had jumped in with a radio commentary freeing John to observe through his Schmidt & Bender riflescope. Rick and I were back behind our cover, keeping out of sight.

'He's crouching in the door, knife in hand, he's looking about tactically,' said Mike, calm and deliberate.

'He's eyes all about, he's out and running at a crouch towards red!'

Mike's voice raised an octave as Walker made his move. Rick and I shrunk further into the stairwell's entrance. From Mike's commentary he was running away from us. We held our ground but at the other end of the balcony Tony couldn't believe what he was hearing. It was his shift on the letterbox and he could clearly see that Walker was sprinting in a crouch not towards red but towards green and with the large kitchen knife in his hand! Walker was going for it, he was going to try and take us by surprise and fight his way down the stairwell and escape!

'Go, go, go!' Tony shouted, pulling the door open and breaking cover on to the balcony but Walker wasn't trying to escape at all. On his previous foray on to the balcony he'd seen a discarded riot shield propped up against the screen behind which we were hiding. He'd decided to grab it and use it to help boost his defences but in the time it had taken Tony to take his eye from the letterbox and open the door, Walker had reached his objective and as the team erupted from their flat they and Walker became two opposing forces in a race for the child. Walker won, throwing the shield into Tony's face as he dived through the opening, slamming the glazed door in the team's face. Rick and I suddenly become aware of the commotion on the balcony.

'Get the meanie!' shouted Tony.

Looking around the wall I saw Tony shouldering the flat door. Clive was running back towards the stronghold having retrieved his stun grenade from their containment position where it had fallen in their rush to deploy.

Ian was looking around desperately in response to Mike's frantic radio transmission.

'Go back, go back!' Mike's desperate voice crackled in my earpiece but I was aware of another voice saying 'Go, go, go!'

'You've done it now! She dies, she dies!' Walker screamed as he piled furniture against the frosted wire glass of the flat's front door.

Rick and I were now on the balcony, my green meanie in my left hand and my Model 19 in my right. I looped my right thumb through the grenade ring but I wasn't going to pull it until I knew what the hell was going on. Clive was facing me with his grenade in his hand and his finger through the ring. The look on his face read, 'Come on then!' Mine must have read, 'You first, I still don't know what the fuck's happening!' Suddenly Walker heaved a mattress against the glass, completely obstructing Ian's view of the killer, and he immediately smashed the bathroom window to the right of the front door with the barrel of his revolver. Rick started to attack the door with the sledge, sliding on the slick concrete. Clive posted his grenade into the bathroom and I immediately lobbed mine through what was left of the kitchen window. They detonated violently within seconds of each other, showering us all with glass. With no operational hearing protection, their reports were deafening. Rick was still sledging the front door but it was taking too long and I pulled some of the obstructions out of the way and started to clamber through the window and over the shattered doorframe.

The kitchen was full of smoke and Walker had placed broken furniture and kitchen appliances all over the room. It was an obstacle course. The grenade had blown the bulb, the room was in darkness and my torch was buried under layers of Gore-Tex. My ears were ringing from the meanie and I imagined that Walker was waiting for me in the smoke and darkness. I was on my own. Expecting a sudden knife attack from the swirling smoke, I pressed on towards the living room. My heart was pumping and the adrenalin flowed as I slid down the surface of the upturned fridge and entered the room, dimly lit by a glimmer of streetlight that fought through a gap in the curtains. Broken glass crunched under foot and in the gloom I saw Walker lying across the sofa with Karlene held across his chest like a limp, lifeless shield.

'She dies, she dies!' Walker screamed as I closed on him with my revolver at eye level. I couldn't see my sights and could barely work out where Walker's body and that of his tiny hostage met. I cursed myself for not having my torch to hand. All I could see was their combined silhouette. My eyes were starting to adjust to the light and I could now see their eyes and their teeth and a rough shape of his shoulder and the glint from the blade of the large kitchen knife poised at her neck.

'Drop it, you fucking bastard!' I yelled. I was very close and without sights I decided to use sense of direction and shoot at his shoulder, the furthest point from the hostage but as I started to fire he plunged the knife into the little girl. I fired a double tap, my muzzle blast briefly lighting the room and silhouetting my sights and I knew straight away from his reaction that I'd hit him. His eyes closed and he flinched, raising his right shoulder defensively and turning his head to expose his right temple to a faint shaft of light. I tried to find my sights in the dark again but my own muzzle blast had destroyed the little night vision that I'd acquired. He still held the child and I was forced to fire a third shot unsighted into his head, my only clear target. His eyes popped open and his pupils rolled back into his head and he slumped down. I thought, *That's it you've done it now! He's dead!* Training had completely taken over. It had been exactly like the shoots that Rick and I set up for the team on the B range. On the 'Go!' clamber over some barricades and engage the target with two shots to the body and one to the steel plate to stop the clock. I was surprised that I hadn't raised my free hand and shouted 'Time!' I had desperately wanted to carry on shooting the evil shit but the words of Oz after the van exercise came back to me and I knew I'd done enough.

While I was very familiar with its existence, it was my first personal experience of perceptual distortion. Firing a revolver in the confines of a small room without hearing protection should have made my ears ring painfully and yet I hadn't been conscious of the noise. Later, when I watched the incident on TV, all three shots had been fired in a single rapid burst with barely a pause between the first pair and the last shot and yet my decision to fire and the pause between my first pair and the last shot seemed to take for ever. My thought process seemed too lucid to have taken place in such a short period of time. I'll never know whether I fired before, after or at the same time that Walker stabbed his little hostage.

I was suddenly aware of Rick at my shoulder and moments later Tony and Clive appeared. Someone ripped open the curtains and I saw the handle of the knife sticking out of the little girl's neck. I felt an urgent need to do something. The seriousness of what I'd just had to do was beginning to hit home and I grabbed a shell dressing from my pocket and tore its paper wrapping open with my teeth. I took hold of the knife to try and stabilise it but it fell out in my hand as the tiny hostage slumped further into the settee. I threw it to the floor and applied the dressing to her neck while I scooped her up. She was limp and appeared lifeless. I thought one of my rounds may have hit her and, as I shouted for an ambulance, I looked up to see Tony's face inches from mine. The expression on his face read, 'What have you done?'

I was desperate to escape the tiny flat. Rick was pulling Walker's barricades away from the door. It seemed to take forever but finally it yielded and I felt the cold damp wind on my face as I ran outside. As I made my way to the stairs, slipping on the blood-soaked and rainswept concrete, I became aware, in my peripheral vision, of what looked like the handle of another knife sticking out of the child. I didn't want to look and pushed on to the top of the stairwell. Several negotiators had left the comfort of their warm cell to watch and I threw them a disgusted look as I carried on down the stairs aware of curious stares from the uniformed officers and emergency personnel. At ground level I headed straight for the grey-clad ambulance crew and handed them the fragile hostage. No words were passed, no casualty report given, they just took her and ran straight to their vehicle. I was convinced that she was dead.

The volatile mob surged forward to get a glimpse of the child and to voice their frustration. I helped shut the back doors of the ambulance and assisted uniform officers to clear a path for it as its blue light threw patterns on to the faces of the crowd. I was in the middle of them, my revolver held down by my leg, my Gore-Tex suit had no police markings, no one paid me any heed and I discreetly palmed the Smith & Wesson into my map pocket and forced my way back through the masses to the stairs of Poynter Court as the ambulance's two-tones fired up.

As I climbed the stairs I suddenly felt exhausted. Remembering the words of the FBI lecture, half of me wanted to heed their advice and remove myself from the scene, while the other half wanted to go back to the flat. I had just deliberately shot a man in the head at point-blank range; I'd seen his eyes roll up into his skull. I'd killed him. Reaching the fourth floor, I paused. Control room or stronghold? I chose the control.

I was surprised to see Bill manning the control and by the look on his face he was equally surprised to see me. The Yorkshireman had received the request to come in later than us and had been manning it for most of the day, listening to the electronic surveillance bugs that we later found had been inserted into the stronghold. I was unaware that he'd even been at the scene. The warm comfortable flat was in contrast to the windswept balcony and the wrecked stronghold that I'd just left and he had a fresh mug of steaming tea in his hand. I could smell bacon cooking in the kitchen.

'What the fook 'appened?' Bill asked.

'He was stabbing the little girl so I shot him,' I replied.

Bill looked shocked. He offered to make me a brew and a bacon sandwich. I was knackered and wanted to collapse on to the welcoming sofa but the need to keep busy remained the dominant emotion so I declined his offer. In the tiny galley kitchen there was one piece of bacon sizzling in the pan. *Jack fucker!* I thought. There had been seven of us out in the cold for hours and I filled the kettle, took seven polystyrene cups from the large ammunition tin that served as our team tea club and dropped another six rashers into the pan. I'd make brews and sarnies for the rest of the lads; they'd be back soon. Tony and Clive were the first into the small living room, closely followed by the others. I put down the butter knife and Tony gripped my hand like a vice and hugged me. This was the eighties; man hugs were over a decade away but somehow it seemed appropriate and comforting. His eyes glinted with suppressed tears as he apologised.

'What are you apologising for?' I asked. 'You've nothing to be sorry for.'

'Mate, we've got an unwritten agreement on Green that …'

I cut him short. I knew about their agreement and it was bollocks. Green team's secret pact meant that if one of their number shot someone, the nearest team member would consider firing as well to show solidarity. I'd heard a drunken Green team member explaining it weeks earlier at the unit's Christmas drinks, and told him then it was nonsense. Apart from being criminal, even if the first officer's decision to fire turned out to have been wrong, if he'd acted with an honestly held belief that lives were in danger, his actions would be deemed lawful and the second officer's involvement would be pointless. I couldn't imagine that anyone would follow the pact anyway. It was naive, senseless bravado brought about by a lack of operational experience and I told Tony so.

'I know, I know,' he said. 'But after what he did to that poor little cow! Is she going to make it?'

'I don't know, mate, she didn't look good.'

'No mate, I thought so too. We all did! Then after you left with the kid, his eyes popped opened and he begged us to finish him off. I thought he was brown bread, I nearly shat myself. I was so angry I was tempted to shoot him again but the threat was over. The ambulance just carted him away. I'm not sure he'll make it though, you got him right in the temple!'

I had to smile at Tony's down-to-earth honesty but my emotions were now totally confused. I had already come to terms with killing Walker; he was an evil bastard who had stabbed his defenceless hostage in front of me even after we'd called his bluff. I felt proud that I'd reacted in accordance with my training but was worried about the little girl's condition; praying that none of my rounds had hit her. Now I'd learnt Walker was still alive. I didn't know whether to feel relieved or disappointed.

Everyone was congratulating me, patting me on the back and shaking my hand. We were all buzzing but no one knew what would happen next. We'd been ordered not to assault without authority but the organisation had lost control of the incident and had been manipulated by a deranged psycho. We'd been forced into executing the IA, but D11's proud record of never having fired shots had been shattered and we were all in virgin territory. John Warner, the unit's chief inspector known affectionately as 'Coco', had been the first D11 senior officer on scene the previous day and had now returned to take over the next shift. Mike was tight-lipped, saying nothing. I was glad that Peter Harris was present. He took me one side and asked me to describe what had happened and then offered his congratulations.

'Well done, you've nothing to worry about, you did the right thing. We could hear everything Walker was saying in control from the microphones. I was shouting go, go, go at the top of my voice!'

I thanked him. His words were instantly reassuring.

'The negotiators have a psychiatrist working with them who's been advising on Walker's state of mind. He's offered to have a chat with you, if you like. I told him I'd ask.' he added, hesitantly.

'Little bloke with glasses? Looks like a geography teacher?' I asked.

'That's him. I take it you've met?'

I told him about his conversation with Rick and me.

'I'll take it that's a no then?' Peter said, with a smile on his face.

'Yes, sir. You can tell him to fuck right off.'

Perhaps I should have agreed to talk to him just so that I could have described Walker plunging the kitchen knife into the neck of his young hostage and remind him how convinced he was that Walker would never harm her! I was furious but it was time to leave so we quickly bagged up all of our kit and filed downstairs to our van, loaded up and made our way past the cordons and out of the now silent estate. The crowd had dissipated and the wet streets were quiet as we made our way to Southall nick. It was like a ghost ship and we wandered around looking for a suitable office to settle in. We finally set up camp in the abandoned CID office where there was a kettle, a TV and a tatty plastic Christmas tree in the corner with random blinking lights. We found some milk in a fridge and made ourselves a welcome brew before sitting down to write our notes. The news came on and we watched it enthusiastically. It didn't look very slick but a few cheers went up. Tony realised for the first time what it was that had caused the painful injury to his left hand. Under the effects of tunnel vision he hadn't even seen the full-size riot shield that had struck him and I realised that what I'd thought was a second knife sticking out of the little girl had thankfully been the barrel of my own revolver that I'd still been clutching in my right hand.

We soon received a call from the hospital. The little girl was in theatre. The wound to her neck wasn't life-threatening but they were seriously concerned about the deep, day-old injury to her arm. It was badly infected and there was a danger that she might lose it. Walker was also being worked on and despite my final round penetrating his brain he was likely to survive. Before we'd be allowed to leave for the base and home, we would have to stand fast; the commander wanted to speak to us. Eventually Sparks arrived with Peter Harris, Coco and Mike, their faces like stone.

The commander looked around the room. 'Who fired the shots?'

I slowly raised my hand.

'It wasn't very good shooting, was it?'

It was a statement not a question. I was seething. Hitting Walker without injuring the child had been an accomplishment in the conditions. I gave him a hostile glare but bit my lip.

'I was giving an interview to the press in front of the flats when you carried out your unauthorised entry. I was assuring them that we had everything under control and anticipated a peaceful resolution when I heard your bloody stun grenades going off and my first instinct was that you would all be out of a job by tomorrow morning!' He paused to take in his audience. 'But I've just come from the hospital and you'll be glad to hear that the little girl will be all right but more importantly, so will the suspect, so I have revised my decision and you now have my total support!'

We looked at each other in disbelief. He was supposed to have been in command of the operation. Could he really still be putting the life of a mad killer above that of an innocent hostage? His job was to take an overview and devise a strategy. What was he doing giving a press interview anyway? He had press officers to brief the media.

Having said his bit, Sparks turned and left, his bag carrier in tow. After a brief chat from Peter Harris we were free to go but I was to travel back separately from the lads with Mike and Coco. It was a long silent journey and even the normally jovial Coco kept his own counsel. I desperately wanted to sleep but I couldn't help but think of where my future lay. Our assumption that anyone who fired a shot would be out of the unit was at the forefront of my mind. I shut my eyes and pretended to sleep, straining my recently damaged ears above the noise of the Hillman Avenger's engine to hear if the subject was discussed, but the silence was never broken.

As we pulled up at the green metal gates to the base I could bear it no longer.

'I suppose this means I'll be back to division then?' I said jovially.

Ominously, there came no reply.

Some of the guys had already left by the time we got back. I didn't blame them: it was still Christmas and it had been a long day. Rick was patiently waiting for his lift home. He offered to drive but I said I was fine and an hour later, after dropping him off, I finally fell through my front door and headed for bed.

The press had a field day, dragging out the usual dubious experts. One suggested I should have forward-rolled through the kitchen window; another that we should have carried on lobbing stun grenades into the tiny flat as the assault progressed. I would have liked to have seen the pair of them forward roll into a room piled high with debris while I threw green meanies into the room after them.

The team had sent Karlene a teddy bear and a get-well card and, despite their grief at the loss of their daughter, her grandparents had taken the time to send the unit a card. It read:

A special thank you message to all at D11. We just want to thank you all very much for giving us back Karlene. This card cannot tell you how grateful we are. Thank you again. PS: Karlene is doing fine.

Returning to work, everything seemed normal, apart from a degree more interest from the others than in any other newsworthy job. Backslapping, congratulations and questions came thick and fast.

'I was in the kitchen when it came on the news,' said one of the lads, pulling me aside in the corridor. 'My missus called me to come through and watch it but before I could get to the TV I heard the bap-bap – bap and I said to her, "That's Longy, two to the body, one to the head, just like he had us doing on the range a month back!" Then I saw you coming out with the kid on to the balcony and I knew for sure!'

I hadn't fired the third shot to Walker's head simply because it was something I'd practised and taught on a training drill. I'd fired it because I didn't believe my first two rounds had been effective and because it was the only target unobstructed by the hostage, but he wasn't totally wrong. The fact that I'd practised for that contingency and encouraged others to do the same, made my transition from body shots to a head shot seamless and almost instinctive. To me it was a total validation of my theories about realistic training. Oz also took me to one side and congratulated me and I reminded him of his advice and thanked him. His counsel had helped me curb a natural desire to keep firing at Walker.

Bob Wells called a debrief. We started by watching the video for the hundredth time as we had already timed and analysed each stage of the final assault. There was no doubt that it appeared disorganised, and the media had been extremely critical, but they only knew what they had seen from the outside and had no idea of the full story. The negotiators and the operational commander had put us on the sidelines, allowing Walker to run free; the situation unravelling so suddenly that our response had looked hesitant and ragged. Ironically, Mike, who had told our sniper that he couldn't engage the suspect because he was too far away to know exactly what was happening, had been in that same sniper position telling us to 'Go back!' when he too had been too far away to hear what Walker was shouting at us through the door.

Each of us, starting with Ian, explained our actions. Despite the confusion and Mike's order to withdraw, he'd held his nerve, only initiating the assault when Walker had pushed the mattress against the frosted glass of the front door causing him to lose vision. While he could see Walker, he knew that he wasn't harming the child. Once he lost that vision all bets were off. The barrel of his revolver struck the glass exactly 22 seconds after Walker had grabbed the riot shield and 30 seconds before my last shot smashed through the killer's skull. If the IA had been authorised and had commenced with a 'Standby, standby' over the radio it would undoubtedly have been quicker and looked slicker but it hadn't and we'd made the best of a bad job. Mike didn't take criticism well though and went on the attack when we explained how he'd messed up the TI.

'Nothing you can say will alter my opinion that you conspired to shoot Errol Walker!' he spat, storming out.

None of us could believe what he'd just said or that he had left the debrief but after an embarrassed period of silence we continued without him. The consensus was that Sparks and the negotiators had been so obsessed with getting Walker to surrender that they had forgotten about the most important person, the hostage, an innocent four-year-old girl who had watched her mother brutally murdered.

Equipment, as always, came under scrutiny. We raised the issue of weapon's lights and I pushed for the rapid issue of a decent set of fire-retardant coveralls. Method of entry was also raised and it was agreed that it was time to look for something better than the borrowed sledgehammers and crowbars that we had liberated from the prisoners' property store.

Following the debrief, no one ever raised the subject again. Walker had wanted the police to shoot him and, having accepted that his actions had precipitated his injuries, never complained about our actions. Consequently I was never interviewed. I had undergone more scrutiny for punching a football hooligan in the mouth than I had for deliberately shooting a man in the head. It was as if the Job wanted the whole saga to disappear into the ether.

Almost a year later, Walker appeared at the Old Bailey and, to avoid the cameras, we arrived at court in the rear of an armoured Land Rover, peering through its gun ports as we disappeared down the ramp into the bowels of the old building. When I was finally called to give evidence, I climbed the steps into the witness box, gave the oath and was led through my evidence by the prosecution barrister. I glanced across at Walker. My final round had penetrated several inches into the right side of his brain, affecting him in much the same way as a stroke might have. His left arm and left leg were paralysed and he appeared to be in pain as he sat and listened. The defence barrister started his cross-examination by congratulating me on my shooting and emphasising that Errol Walker held me no malice and understood why I had shot him. Finally the judge commended me on my actions and I left the box. Many months later I would finally receive a belated commissioner's commendation for bravery.

TWELVE
BACK IN THE FIRING LINE

While normal folk had enjoyed their Christmas, and we had covered the Northolt siege, seven Arab terrorists had been preparing to attack two of Europe's busiest airports and at 08:15 the day after my balcony scene, they struck. Four of them, armed with Kalashnikovs and grenades, attacked the El Al and TWA check-ins at Rome's Leonardo da Vinci airport while a further three carried out an identical attack at Vienna International. In total, 19 innocent travellers were killed and 140 wounded.

All across the world, international airports went on high alert and our government sent troops to Heathrow. The military had been deployed there off and on as a deterrent since 1974 but something more permanent was now required. Heathrow's security section were armed only with handguns discreetly concealed under tunics, and were not equipped to confront the sort of attacks witnessed at Rome and Vienna, and despite the uncertainty surrounding my future, within days of the attacks, I found myself driving Mike to Heathrow to carry out a security survey. We hadn't yet held a debrief for Northolt and like the elephant in the room it wasn't discussed. Within days, the Home Office had agreed to a step change in armed policing and an order was placed for a quantity of semi-automatic MP5 carbines to be carried overtly by officers on security patrols.

As it would take time to train and equip sufficient airport officers, an emergency alternative was needed and Blue team were it. Exactly two weeks after Northolt, on Thursday 9 January 1986, I paraded in regular uniform at Heathrow police headquarters, ready to be one of the first officers in mainland UK to conduct overt, routine armed patrols, and the airport's commander arrived with a small entourage including the young army captain commanding the troops already deployed.

The commander emphasised that this was to be a massive departure from the image of George Dixon's unarmed police force; the world's press had been tipped off to the historic event and the eyes of the world were upon us. We would each be posted with a local armed officer as a guide but bizarrely we were all to keep our handguns concealed. We were handed a small, typed addition to our rules of engagement, stipulating that our MP5s were only to be used in their semi-automatic mode. We started to kit up but before putting on my body armour, I propped it up in the corner of the office and, pointing the muzzle of my MP5 at the centre of its chest plate, inserted a magazine and fed a round into the breach. Immediately there was a sharp intake of breath from the army captain.

'I say,' said the young officer. 'What do you think you're doing?'

'Making my weapon ready.'

He looked confused. 'Surely your breach should remain empty until you are given the order to make ready?'

'With respect, sir,' I answered, 'it's our standard operating procedure to carry the weapon with a round in the breach and the safety catch applied.'

He still looked confused. 'What sort of weapon is that anyway?'

The team gave each other sideways glances. Since its appearance on the balcony of the Iranian Embassy siege, the MP5, alongside the AK and the M16, was one of the world's most recognisable weapons and his inability to identify it summed up his firearms credentials.

'It's a 9mm, Heckler & Koch, MP5 sub-machine gun, sir.'

'A sub-machine gun?' he asked, turning directly to the commander. 'I don't think that is an appropriate weapon for the task, sir!'

'With respect, sir,' I interrupted. 'Your own men are patrolling a busy airport terminal with 7.62 SLRs!'

The army's self-loading rifle was an incredibly powerful weapon with an effective range of 800 yards but he shot me down with his simple army logic.

'My men's weapons are *not loaded*!' he stressed. 'Each soldier carries an empty magazine on their weapon together with a magazine of five rounds, taped over and stored in a pouch on their belt order in case of emergency!'

That'll work in a fire-fight with fanatical terrorists, I thought. Even the commander, who had assumed that his division had been in safe hands up to now, seemed astounded at the revelation.

Dave and I were to be the first two officers to deploy in the terminal and together with our guides were driven to departures where we were confronted by more press and film crews than I had ever seen. Dave was in the jump seat nearest the carrier's sliding side doors and, as we pulled up, I grabbed my local PC by the arm. As my sergeant stepped out into a rippling burst of flash guns and questions, we snuck out of the rear doors and slid off, leaving Dave to take the flak. Entering the terminal further down the building frontage, we merged with the crowds and spent the next hour trying to avoid the cameras. By mid-morning, the press had got what they were after and had left to catch the evening deadline and we got back to patrolling.

Contrary to Scotland Yard mythology, the credibility of the British police service and the respect and trust of its citizens didn't dissolve at the first sight of armed police, and the travelling public, familiar

Waiting for a run through on a military close quarter battle (CQB) range wearing our old grey coveralls and very basic kit, armed with a Heckler & Koch MP5 equipped with a trial weapons sight. Hereford, 1986.

Making do with nothing in the early days. Black team practises bus assaults... without a bus.

Black team poses for a group photograph during counter-terrorist training. Hereford, 1986.

[Below] In a hasty urban sniper position overlooking an IRA weapons cache as part of Operation Catnip in 1992. The weapon is an H&K 93 5.56mm rifle equipped with a Zeiss telescopic sight.

[Below] Armed with my MP5, I prepare to enter a room during live fire, close quarter combat (CQC) training. My number two prepares to post a 'flash-bang' grenade. Blue team, Lippitts Hill, 1997.

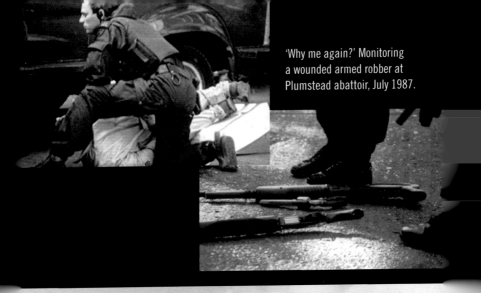

'Why me again?' Monitoring a wounded armed robber at Plumstead abattoir, July 1987.

Working with local Kittitian police in the search for the missing assistant prime minister's son and

Dressed as a cleaner in the bowels of the Millennium Dome preparing
for an operation to catch the gang trying to steal diamonds worth
£350 million on display.

A hostage rescue demonstration at the new Metropolitan Police Specialist Training Centre
at Gravesend in Kent, using purpose-built assault vehicle and pyrotechnic distractions.
A far cry from the make-do of the early days!

Members of Red team await the surrender of two failed suicide bombers at Dalgarno Gardens, West London. Operation Thesius, July 2005.

Manning a counter-sniper position overlooking Horse Guards Parade, Whitehall, during a ceremonial event in 2006. I am armed with an Accuracy International 7.62mm sniper rifle equipped with a Schmitt & Bender scope.

SFO assaulters and White team snipers during a tactical training exercise in 2008. I'm on the left with a rifle in 'India 99', the Met's helicopter.

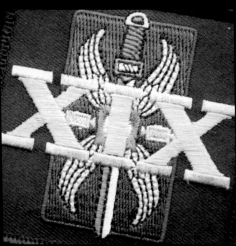

The unofficial SFO emblem of a Roman shield and sword with the the Roman numeral for nineteen.

A variant of the 9mm MAC-10 sub-machine gun that we anticipated facing when we stopped the car that Azelle Rodney was travelling in. Capable of firing 18 rounds per second, these 'lead super-soakers' had been converted from deactivated weapons by a back street armourer and had flooded the criminal market.

SFOs kit up in the backyard of a nick for a hostage rescue operation. The nearest assaulter is a Method of Entry (MOE) operator equipped with a Bennelli shotgun loaded with Hatton rounds for door breaching.

Manning a CROP (Covert Rural Observation Point), awaiting a meeting of rival drug gangs in Kent. I'm armed with a SIG 5.56mm carbine. White team, 2008.

On top of Winfield House, the US ambassador's residence, during the state visit of George W Bush, armed with a SIG 5.56mm carbine equipped with an Elcan sight.

A clash of cultures. The 'unacceptable face of British policing' meets Dixon of Dock Green at a siege involving a suspect with a bomb in central London. © Getty Images

with seeing armed officers abroad, either ignored us or took the time to tell us how reassuring our presence was. Ironically, rather than speak to my apparently unarmed guide, they seemed drawn to me for advice or directions, as if carrying a big gun somehow made me more senior or knowledgeable than my colleague. Soon Heathrow's officers were patrolling their usually benign environment with their new semi-automatic MP5s but with our fully automatic ones still restricted for use on anti-terrorist operations, we would continue to have to use our shotguns as our primary shoulder-fired weapon for the foreseeable future.

Our operational tempo had been gradually increasing to the point where we were now stretched to our limit and, to alleviate the pressure, we moved to six smaller teams, adding Black and Grey to our colour scheme. After four years on Blue, George and I crossed over to the newly formed Black. Our new inspector was Laurie, one of the old and bold. He had a weary, sarcastic way about him that conflicted with my enthusiasm and there was tension whenever we shared the same room. John, our newly promoted sergeant, was affable enough but despite his former career as a Royal Marine, never overly impressed me. We now spent four weeks on instructional duties followed by a week of second response intended as our own training week. This was followed by first response where we would take the first job that came through the door.

In 1987, D department was rebranded as personnel and training. We became PT17 and were given more manpower to create three further teams of non-instructors. Supervised by an experienced sergeant instructor, these received additional training to allow them to deal with low-end armed operations of the type previously carried out by divisional shots, releasing us to deal with situations involving hostages or suspects with exceptional firepower. The new teams went live in June and were designated as Level 2 teams. We were now Level 1.

In early July, just weeks after Level 2 went live, we were first response but had been training hard all week. On the Wednesday I was left to run the team through some pistol shooting while Laurie and John went to a briefing with 9 Regional Crime Squad (9 RCS) for a job the following day. Early the next morning we met at the base for a tactical briefing. We would be working for 9 RCS and our mission was to prevent the robbery of a security van. Tom, my old mate from Blue, was helping out and we were also supported by a single Level 2 PC and a couple of dog handlers. The previous evening John had walked his dogs through the south London plot to give himself a better appreciation and using aerial photographs, supplied by the RCS, he shared his recently acquired knowledge.

The location, a former abattoir in Garland Road, Plumstead, was now used for meat storage and distribution and was located in a small rural patch of green between the suburban sprawls of Woolwich and Bexleyheath. Woods to the north of the facility backed on to the gardens of Garland Road while those to the east and the south bordered open fields stretching away to the aptly named Shooters Hill Road.

To the north of the main building was a raised loading bay and a large concrete apron from which a narrow access road led away to the west. This led to a T-junction at the edge of the property. Turn right and it continued north into Garland Road, turn left and it soon became a grassy farm track leading south to a padlocked, five-bar gate and a farmyard that led out on to Shooters Hill. If the padlock was cropped overnight, it would be a good indication that the robbery would be going ahead and signposted a potential getaway route. The western edge of the plot was bordered by a golf course.

The intelligence was that a team of at least three robbers would conceal themselves in the woods and await the arrival of a security van delivering wages. When the guard left the safety of the van, the robbers would grab him, forcing the custodian in the rear to hand over an estimated £120,000 before escaping in a stolen vehicle driven by another member of the team. Their trademark was their willingness to open fire without provocation and the RCS fancied them for a series of violent robberies including one in nearby Woolwich where several unarmed local coppers had been shot.

Intelligence suggested they had access to an arsenal of weapons and John mentioned armoured-piercing rounds with which they could penetrate the armoured van. I made a mental note to double-check the ceramic plates in my body armour. He also suggested that they might strap improvised explosives to the guard. How much of this was actually based on intelligence and how much was supposition I couldn't tell but if his intention was to get our attention, it worked!

John started to run through his and Laurie's plan and straight away alarm bells chimed. John had a reputation for an 'it'll be all right on the night' attitude. One of his favourite expressions was 'quite simply' and he tended to use it most when he was cuffing it. Laying bets on how many times it would feature in a briefing had become a favourite sport.

'Quite simply, we'll all be in the back of a jump-off van and when the security van turns up we're going to jump out and quite simply arrest the robbers.'

John explained that we were to be driven into position by two detectives disguised as butchers. They would park us so that the rear of our vehicle faced the bay. Despite concerns there might be an employee spying for the blaggers, they had approached the assistant manager who had agreed to assist them, inventing a subterfuge to keep his workers away from the loading bay during the anticipated delivery time. The techos would remain with him in his office near the bay to maintain an appearance of normality. All the lorries were to be parked at the far end of the bay ensuring us an unobstructed view.

'What van have we got?' asked one of the lads.

'It's a Ford Luton,' John replied. 'The RCS have hired it. We took a look at it yesterday. We just need to drill some holes in the roller shutter so that we get some vision and we'll grab some gym mats for a bit of comfort.'

'How many of us are going to be in there?' I asked, suspiciously.

'Well, there's all of us, except George,' said John, indicating the Level 2 lad seconded to help us out. 'Plus the RCS DI and a couple of dog handlers.'

I did a bit of quick calculation.

'That's nine of us! Why the dog handlers? It's going to be up in the eighties today and their dogs will be panting like fuck. And why does the DI need to be with us?'

Laurie threw me an angry look.

'If the bad guys run we're going to need the dogs with us,' John explained, 'particularly if they reach the woods.'

It was a fair point.

'The DI will have an encrypted radio and I need him with me,' Laurie snapped, his lip twisted in a derisive snarl.

'You're going to be with us, Boss?' I asked. 'Surely you'd be better off taking an overview with the DI, off the plot and out of harm's way? The RCS can always lend us an encrypted radio so we can listen to the surveillance net.'

'The DI's in the van with me! End of discussion!' Laurie threw me another contemptuous look.

Overnight, an RCS covert rural surveillance observation point or 'CROP' had deployed to the junction of the farm track and the approach road. Concealed in the bushes, the lone detective would have an unobstructed view of the approach road and the loading bay and would be able to monitor the robber's movements and call the strike over the secure RCS radio net.

The rest of the RCS would be concealed in their gunships off Garland Road, deploying as an armed cut-off group, their surveillance assets controlling any suspects north of the plot and giving us an early heads-up when the security van arrived.

George had been picked because, as a former Heathrow officer, he was authorised to drive our armoured Land Rover and together with another support dog handler would hold at Shooters Hill police station until the hit was called. He would then be responsible for cutting off the robbers' southerly escape route down the farm track or across the fields; a tall order for a loan shot and contrary to the policy of only deploying shots in pairs. Strict limits of exploitation (LOEs) were laid down between the three armed groups, each of which would only deal with the suspects within their own area of responsibility, unless ordered otherwise.

For the first time on any armed operation, we had the London Ambulance Service on standby. They were moving from being casualty taxis to providing advanced first aid and had recently introduced embryonic paramedic units. Our air support unit would be airborne but holding far enough away to avoid spooking the robbers.

While Heathrow officers had been patrolling with their semi-automatic MP5s for the last 18 months, we were still using shotguns as our primary weapon and, loaded with buckshot, they were not ideal in a potential hostage situation. Our H&K 93s were longer and slightly less manoeuvrable than an MP5 but extremely accurate and their 5.56mm soft-point ammunition was less likely to over-penetrate or ricochet.

'What if the robbers get to the guard? Shouldn't at least a couple of us have 93s?' I suggested.

'It won't happen!' John opined. 'We'll get an early heads up from the CROP and quite simply catch them on the concrete. The only contingency will be if they run into the woods in which case shotguns will be ideal.'

I was convinced that the plan was flawed. Action will always beat reaction and the CROP would have to wait until he saw the gang break cover before he called it on the radio. By the time that happened the robbers would have covered a lot of ground. That's if the OP saw them break cover. What if something obscured his vision at the critical moment? What if his radio failed? What if someone else was talking on the net? What if …?

Someone raised the lack of ballistic protection in our thin alloy box and we decided to hang Kevlar blankets in the back. They wouldn't provide us protection to the rear when the shutter went up though and if we had to challenge the suspects from the back of the van while deploying, we would be like fish in a barrel.

'One of us should provide static cover while everyone else deploys,' I suggested, regretting it immediately.

'Well volunteered, Tony!' trumpeted John. 'You can stay in the van and be our cover man. Stick with your pistol and use the new shield. Oh, and take a bunch of plasticuffs: you can cuff them when we've got them on the ground.'

The heavy ballistic shield was brand new and I wasn't keen to use something that I hadn't trained with but I'd said enough already and accepted the task without further comment. Having kitted up, we headed to Eltham nick for the main briefing.

The station's snooker room was packed to capacity, the atmosphere electric. When we were told that the padlock had been cut overnight, the room buzzed with expectation and detectives and team members alike shared grins of nervous anticipation. Operation Kincraig was game on. As I walked out of the briefing there was a tap on my shoulder and I turned to see Bill Dennis, my old class captain from Hendon. We hadn't seen each other since our passing-out parade and he was now a DS.

'Watch yourself, Tone,' he said, shaking my hand. 'These aren't your usual, middle-aged, experienced blaggers. They're young hot-heads and dangerously unpredictable!'

In the yard, we prepped the Luton, drilling several spyholes into its rear shutter and sides and building a small armoured cubbyhole above the cab for the DI and his huge radio set. In the main compartment, we hung more Kevlar ballistic blankets and laid down gym mats for the rest of the team, the dog handlers and their mutts. The padlock hasp was removed from the roller shutter so that we wouldn't get locked in and John tied a length of para cord to the shutter to facilitate opening it in a hurry.

Then we rehearsed our plan, and while the rest of the team jumped from the van fanning out, I covered from behind the heavy shield until finally we were satisfied with our positions. On the last full dress rehearsal John's dodgy knot came undone and as the shutter rattled open, he flew backwards ending up in a heap on the crash mats. We all erupted in a burst of nervous laughter. Finally, we boarded the van together with the two handlers, their land sharks and the worried DI, and found ourselves a slot on the crash mats for the short journey to Shooters Hill police station to wait for the intelligence to develop. Debussing in the station yard we enjoyed the warmth of the morning sun, making small talk until eventually receiving the order to move forward to the plot. Some of us took the opportunity for a last nervous piss behind some stolen vehicles rusting in the corner of the yard and then we said our goodbyes to George and his dog handler, boarded our Trojan horse and our two detectives, now disguised in their blood-stained white coats and trilbies, drove us to the plot.

The rear compartment was light and airy with an opaque fibreglass roof and rays of sunlight pierced our observation holes lighting up the dust particles like laser beams as we rocked through the streets. The DI, perched above the driver's cab, relayed a 30-second warning and moments later the driver ground the gears as he manoeuvred us into position at the eastern end of the loading bay. John and I took the opportunity to get to our feet using the movement of the vehicle to mask our own and, as we came to a rest, I took my first tentative look through my spyhole. Shit! We couldn't see the loading bay at all! A lorry had been parked at our end of the bay no more than ten yards from the back of our van.

'That truck's in the way. Can you see the bay?' I whispered to John.

He was only a few feet to my right but I hoped that his angle might be slightly better than mine; it wasn't. He knelt slowly down to avoid rocking the truck and whispered to the nearest team member and the bad news was passed back to the DI who relayed it to the driver. I could hear the faint crackle of radio communications from the DI's earpiece as his detective responded. There was nowhere else to park but they would see if they could get the lorry moved. The driver gave us a muffled 'Good luck' before the van rocked and the doors slammed.

We were on our own and shortly afterwards the news reached us that the lorry couldn't be moved; the driver had gone home with the keys. Always the optimist, I'd realised that I could still see most of the concrete apron and the approach road through my spyhole and I'd still see the security van arrive and reverse into the loading bay. In the unlikely event that John and Laurie's plan worked and we managed to hit them between the woods and their victim, it wouldn't matter that the box was blind to us but if, as I anticipated, the blaggers got to the guard before we could react, we could deploy unseen with the element of surprise. It could all work out in our favour.

More seriously, but unbeknown to us, another lorry had parked on the approach road after the CROP had inserted and its driver was asleep in the cab. The camouflaged detective now had a badly obscured view of the approach road and the concrete apron and his role was now limited to reporting any sightings of the suspects and the approach of the money box.

As the July sun climbed higher in the sky and the temperature and the tension in the van rose with it, we started to get information that the robbers were nearby and the surveillance around Garland Road had picked up a stolen Ford Grenada driven by a known player. My earpiece crackled again as one of the team at the back of the stick relayed the DI's whispered updates. 'Subject one is on the plot in the woods and very, very close to the CROP.'

So close, in fact, that he had almost stepped on the courageous officer's hide.

'Now subject two is in sight and carrying the happy bag.'

This was the bag used to conceal their weapons and later, they hoped, their loot. Sinex (so called because he got up everyone's nose) gave me a toothy grin.

'Now all three subjects are together in the woods talking with each other ...'

But then ...

'Loss, loss, loss to OP One.'

... And silence!

The three robbers had moved deeper into the woods and out of sight of the CROP officer to conceal themselves somewhere with their own view of the loading bay but where? We had all three robbers somewhere in the woods with their robbery equipment. We had their getaway car hovering nearby. All we needed now was the star of the show but where was the security van? It was late, very late.

Several hours passed; John, Sinex and I taking it in turns to keep our vigil through the tiny spyholes while listening with concern to the dogs panting as the temperature soared. Their handlers stroked them and poured fresh water into their plastic bowls to calm them. There had been nothing from our CROP since the earlier sightings and I started to wonder whether the robbers, frustrated by the late arrival of the box, had left the scene all together. Suddenly the comms crackled into life and the DI relayed the message.

'Standby, standby, blue box approaching!'

We grinned at each other in nervous anticipation as those still seated very slowly eased themselves to their feet; grimacing as their deadened limbs came back to life. I eased my face to the metal shutter focusing on the approach road. My Browning was now drawn, my finger was off the trigger, my thumb rested on its enlarged safety catch and my weak hand gripped the fabric handle of the ballistic shield.

'The box has entered the approach road, suspect vehicle is following.'

I glimpsed back at the team; eight faces beamed back. There was no talking now, just the sound of breathing over my own raised heart-beat. I could feel the adrenalin welling up from the pit of my stomach.

'From the CROP, box turning left, left, left towards the loading bay!'

The words coincided with my first view of the blue security van moving slowly down the approach road. The sun glinted on the windscreen denying me a view of its occupants, oblivious to the awaiting danger. There was still no sight of the getaway vehicle concealed behind it.

I took a final look back towards my colleagues and winked. 'Game on!' I whispered enthusiastically, swinging back to my spyhole. The box was now carrying out a two-point turn, reversing towards the raised loading bay and revealing my first glimpse of the silver Granada as it started to carry out its own three-point turn.

The Granada had almost completed its manoeuvre as the bonnet of the security van disappeared behind the rear of the parked lorry. Suddenly there was a streak of movement from right to left, a blur of khaki jacket as someone ran from the woods within feet of our hiding place towards the loading bay. I flashed another look to my right, immediately realising that no one else had seen it.

'Go, go, go!' I whispered urgently, looking again to my right. Sinex and John looked back, their eyes wide with confusion. 'Go! Fucking go!'

I glared at John who was stooped over, his hand curled around the para cord strop, still looking at me with his mouth open. Suddenly, he seemed to register my urgency and stood up, jerking the cord and the roller shutter rattled noisily open. The concrete hard-standing was empty but for the getaway car, its exhaust fumes drifting towards the woods. No one moved, Sinex and John just looked at me in horror. What had I done? I was the only one that knew that the robbery was happening and I launched myself from the back of the van, staggering as the unfamiliar weight of the ballistic shield dragged me forward.

I stumbled headlong, fighting to regain my balance, but continued towards the loading bay. I could hear angry commands being shouted and as I rounded the corner of the parked lorry, my pistol extended ahead of me, I immediately saw three masked men and the security guard frozen like a video on pause.

The nearest robber was about four yards away. He wore dark clothing, his back was to me and he was on tiptoes looking into a small grilled window behind the driver's door. I could see the long silver barrel of a revolver over his right shoulder. The second was about seven yards away. He wore a dark green anorak, his back was to me, and he aimed a long-barrelled weapon at the legs of the security guard. He was banging his right elbow against the side of the van, shouting for the custodian in the rear to open up. The guard was facing me. He was in his fifties, his eyes wide with terror. The third robber wore the khaki jacket and was slightly behind the guard and facing me, his eyes framed by the red trim of his dark blue ski mask. Our eyes locked as he forced the stubby muzzle of a sawn-off automatic shotgun into the neck of the traumatised guard. Apart from his eyes, everything seemed to remain frozen in time.

I started to shout, 'Armed police!'

Others joined in behind me and suddenly the frozen image burst into life, as if somebody had pressed play. The two nearest robbers started to turn at once. One second I was looking at the backs of their heads, the next I was looking at their eyes through the slits of their balaclavas. Three suspects, all armed. If I waited to see if the nearest surrendered I would be vulnerable to the others.

I was in 'condition red' now, no time to analyse or think, autopilot was on and training had kicked in. Clutching the shield to my chest I fired a double tap at the nearest suspect and without pausing, a further pair at the second who had nearly completed his turn towards me. I didn't watch for effect, no time! I never saw them fall as I turreted towards my third target. He was still armed and starting to move further behind the guard. I fired a single shot, forcing myself from firing the second instinctive shot for fear of hitting the hostage.

I was back on the range; training and instinct had taken over. Just as at Northolt 18 months earlier, I had experienced the strange symptoms of perceptual distortion. My shots had been barely audible and even as I was firing I had time to think to myself, 'Come on, guys, don't let it just be me again. Someone else join in!'

Khaki jacket had moved completely behind the guard and disappeared behind the armoured van. I needed to regain vision before he used its cover to gain access to the factory. I instinctively broke right across the front of the security van, the weight of the shield forgotten. My pistol led the way as I rounded the front nearside wing and checked up the side of the vehicle.

'Armed police! Don't move!'

I glanced to my right. Laurie and Tom had given chase to the getaway car, giving up in frustration as it sped from the scene and had brought their shotguns to bear on the third suspect who now cowered behind the safety of the armoured truck.

'Show us your hands!' they commanded and I saw his gloved hands appear.

'Get on the floor *now!*' Tom shouted again and he dropped to his knees, gingerly lying face-down on the concrete. I leant the shield against the front of the van, signalled to Tom that I was moving into his arc, and walked slowly forward, covering the suspect with my pistol. Tom and Laurie closed on him as well. My mind was racing, the magnitude of my actions starting to kick in and, just as at Poynter Court, I felt an overwhelming desire to busy myself.

'Don't fucking move! Look away and put your hands behind your back. Do it *now!*'

The robber meekly complied as I holstered my pistol. I dropped my knee into the small of his back and he moaned in pain as I grabbed one of his gloved hands and applied a wristlock. Retrieving a pair of plasticuffs from the leg pocket of my coveralls I secured his wrists with a tug of each cable tie. He was trying to say something to me but between his sobs and my impatience I wasn't registering. I pulled off his balaclava immediately regretting not doing it under the watchful lens of a detective's camera.

'Shut the fuck up and stay still. You're under arrest. Detectives will speak to you in a couple of minutes. Do you understand?'

'Yes,' he replied, again trying to say something, but I was already heading for the other side of the van to secure the other two. My mind was in hyperdrive as I tried to come to terms with what had just happened. I stepped around the front of the vehicle to a scene of carnage. The police dogs were barking and straining at their leads as my colleagues worked to save the lives of the two wounded suspects but a cursory examination told me that the men were either already dead or dying.

The nearest one's feet had turned out, his face frozen like a waxwork. The other one's eyes were glazed, his head lolling as Sinex tried to control his airway. A large puddle of bright, oxygenated blood was pooling on the floor around him. I exchanged a knowing look with Sinex. I didn't need to be there. I turned and went back to search the third suspect.

Circling the vehicle, I suddenly realised I hadn't seen any guns! I knew I'd seen them when I opened fire, or had I? Self-doubt was starting to kick in. The third suspect continued to moan. I heaved him to his feet and slammed him into the side of the van.

'Aaarghh, I've been …'

'Shut the fuck up!' I hissed, searching him for further weapons.

'Brilliant shooting, Tony!' Taff, an enthusiastic transfer from Green team, appeared beaming from the front of the van.

'Never mind that,' I snapped. 'Go and see what weapons they've got!'

Taff turned and ran back to the other side of the vehicle. My suspect was still trying to tell me something but, with my eyes closed, I rested my forehead against the cool steel of the van and took a deep breath. I opened them again and there at my feet, half concealed by the bottom of the van, was the muzzle of his sawn-off Browning automatic shotgun. I breathed a massive sigh of relief just as Taff reappeared.

'We've got a Smith & Wesson Magnum and a SPAS shotgun. Well done, mate!'

A SPAS? It was the acronym for an Italian-made Special Purpose Assault Shotgun, serious kit! A wave of relief flooded over me. I'd been right all along. I knew it! The third robber had obviously thrown his gun underneath the van as he ducked behind it and I'd probably just missed the other two weapons when I was taking in the injured suspects. My mind clicked back into focus; I had a job to do.

'Aaarghh!' cried my prisoner.

'What are you moaning about?' I asked.

'I've been shot!' he rasped, gesturing towards his right side. I pulled up his jacket and spotted frothy blood bubbling from a 9mm hole in his torso. His breathing was laboured; he'd clearly been hit in the lungs. I laid him down and Tom helped me check for an exit wound and apply a seal. Then we rolled him over and used a cardboard packing box to raise his legs, allowing the blood from his lower limbs to resupply his damaged torso. I kept reassuring him, monitoring his consciousness.

'Lay still; you'll be all right. There's an ambulance on its way,' I said, surprised at my own compassion.

'How's Micky and Nick?' he asked. Lying flat out on the ground, he must have had a view under the van of his dead or dying mates on the other side.

'Not good. You're lucky to be alive. Now shut up and lay still.'

Meanwhile, the getaway car had driven through the RCS cut-offs like a knife through butter but after a short, high-speed pursuit it crashed and the driver was arrested. A woollen balaclava and a scanner locked to the local police frequency were in the smashed Granada.

Back at the scene I now knew that the other two were dead. Their arms had been secured behind their backs with plasticuffs when the team first approached them, standard procedure when dealing with any armed suspects. Perhaps the cuffs should have been cut off once it became obvious that their wounds were fatal but the lads were too busy trying to save their lives to remove them and once it became obvious that they were beyond help, they were concerned that removing them would be seen as tampering with the scene. As it was, they lay trussed up on the bloody concrete looking like the victims of a gangland execution.

The ambulance arrived and we handed the survivor over to the crew who stabilised him, placed him in the ambulance with a detective and took him away. Steve, an old friend from P District Support Unit days, approached me. Now a DC, he had the job of exhibits officer for the operation. He was apologetic but had to take my pistol. With no formal post-shooting procedure yet created, things were already getting confused. The RCS were now investigating both the robbery and a police shooting in which they were implicated, and as the only team member with an empty holster, I was now clearly marked as the shooter. Someone suggested I go inside to get out of the way. There was nothing more for me to do and I felt drained.

I stopped to have a look at the robbers' weapons laid out on the ground near the front of the security van. Within seconds of me shooting them, the lads had ordered the dog handlers to move them out of harm's way; explaining why I hadn't seen them when I'd come back to cuff them but I must have still being suffering from tunnel vision to have missed them; I'd almost stepped over them.

As I walked to the steps of the loading bay, I thought back to the words of the FBI agent and my experience at Northolt. I deliberately avoided looking at the bodies but my eyes met the guard standing on his own looking down at the aftermath of his traumatic experience. He looked beat, his hands still shaking. I asked him if he was okay.

'I'm getting used to it,' he said, his voice trembling. 'This is the fourteenth time I've been held up with shooters. Nothing like this though! Was it …?'

His voice trailed off as he nodded towards the two bodies and then me. I acknowledged with a nod.

'Thank you,' he said, shaking my hand before voicing his concerns about his young colleague in the back of the van. It was his first day on the job and his first delivery, which is why they'd been late. Now he would have to remain in the back with the money until their supervisor arrived. I left him to his thoughts, and sat down in the cool of the manager's office. I had to explain my actions to John, Laurie, the DI and other senior officers now on the scene and afterwards there was plenty of backslapping and congratulations but several of the team spoke to me quietly so as not to be overheard. They seemed to think that they had let me down because they hadn't fired but I knew that they had nothing to apologise for.

I'd been the only one to see the robbers make their move so my reactions were always going to have been quicker than theirs. In any case, as I'd predicted at the briefing, their weaponry hadn't been suitable for the task. The only appropriate target for their shotguns was the suspect furthest from the guard. I certainly wouldn't have wanted to have to engage the last two with buckshot so close to the hostage.

Taff was particularly apologetic. Seeing everyone follow me, he'd deliberately broken left to flank the suspects. He'd sprinted down the blind side of the parked lorry and leapt up on to the eastern end of the loading bay just as he heard my shots. He had immediately aligned his shotgun on the back of khaki jacket as he fled behind the security van. Taff's finger had been tightening on the trigger just as he'd thrown his hands up in response to Tom's challenge. He had nothing to be ashamed of. It had been quick thinking to break left and not just follow the pack and if the robber had still posed a threat, he'd have been perfectly positioned to neutralise it.

Arrangements were made for us to withdraw and with our Trojan horse now seized as part of the crime scene, we hitched a lift to Eltham nick in the back of a station van. As we jumped out in the station yard, a senior officer's head appeared at an office window above us.

'Have you chaps just come back from the shooting?' he asked. 'Can you tell me? Were the suspects black or white?'

Someone told him that they were white and a look of relief washed over his face. Never mind if we were all right, all he was interested in was potential political comebacks. Back in the cool of the station, we stripped off our armour and made our way to the canteen. Several of us stopped at an office to ring home and I let Kim know what had happened. She wasn't happy. I tried reassuring her, promising to get home as quickly as possible, but as I finished the call I became aware of a raised female voice and putting the phone down was confronted by a senior member of the civil staff lecturing me on making private calls on a job phone. I looked at her in disbelief.

'Why don't you fuck off?'

I snapped, leaving my colleagues to placate the woman who was now crying. I guess my pent-up adrenalin needed venting and she just happened to say the wrong thing at the wrong time. I felt bad and thought about going back to apologise but decided against it. As we completed duty statements in a quiet corner of the canteen I became increasingly self-conscious. The absence of a gun in my holster was flagging me as the shooter and I was aware of whispered comments and sideways looks in my direction. Essex police had been tasked with carrying out an independent investigation and we remained in the canteen drinking copious amounts of tea while we waited for them to arrive so that we could head home. Deputy Chief Constable James Dickinson eventually turned up in person together with a detective chief superintendent who he introduced as his senior investigating officer or SIO. He gave the usual platitudes about how he wanted his investigation to be conducted and the words 'thorough' and 'fair' received plenty of play.

He mentioned their infamous and seriously flawed investigation into the Bambi shootings, for which his force had received much criticism. Two years earlier they'd been called to a remote farm-house in a quiet Essex village. Sheila 'Bambi' Caffell, a model with a history of mental illness, had been discovered dead from an apparently self-inflicted gunshot wound to the head; next to her lay a .22 semi-automatic rifle. Also in the house were the bodies of her two children and her adopted parents. Essex CID wrapped it up as a classic case of murder-suicide but, in their hurry to clear the case, had missed some pretty basic clues, including footprints in the flowerbed, blood on a windowsill and moved ornaments. All Agatha Christie basics which, had they done the job properly, would have pointed them in the direction of the psychotic adopted brother, Jeremy Bamber. Eventually they were forced to revisit the crime and Bamber was convicted and given life.

This time, the deputy chief constable and his SIO were determined that their investigation would miss no candlesticks in the library. For some reason, there has never been any love lost between Essex and the Met and I think we all had concerns when we heard that they were involved, but true to their deputy chief constable's word they were professional, thorough and ethical throughout. After a very long day, I eventually turned the key to my front door. 'Why you again?' were Kim's immediate words of support.

The following morning I woke to sensationalist headlines, 'THE EQUALISER!' and 'AMBUSH AT THE ABATTOIR!' and was greeted at work with a mixture of congratulations and good-natured piss-taking. At Eltham nick, where the Essex team had set up shop, we were free to talk and share a coffee while we waited. Once interviewed though, the lads were shipped off so that there could be no further contact between us. We avoided any discussion about the previous day's events other than to comment on the newspaper reports, which, as usual, were full of inaccuracies and supposition.

Shortly after we arrived an RCS detective took me to a quiet corner. 'Tone, keep this to yourself, mate, but I've just been down to the mortuary and seen the bodies. Good shooting by the way!'

'Hold on,' I said. 'I thought the PM wasn't due to start till later?'

'It's not but my guvnor told me to get down there and sit in on it. I know the mortuary technician and he gave me a sneak preview. Problem was Essex turned up and got right stroppy, said it was their investigation and who the fuck was I? I told them my guvnor had sent me and to take it up with him. They belled him and I got the big fuck off so I thought I'd get back here and let you know where you hit the fuckers.' He had a good look around and carried on. 'The little one, Micky Flynn, the one with the revolver, you got him twice, right in the middle of the spine, group like that!'

He held his finger and thumb about an inch apart. It didn't surprise me that my first pair had struck Flynn in the back, I knew he'd started to turn though because I remembered seeing his eyes through the slot of his balaclava as I fired; the other two were also starting to turn and bring their weapons to bear so I'd had to start shooting or it might have been me waiting on a slab for the pathologist's knife. Flynn had been the nearest and the first to get hit. So my rounds had hit him in the back, tough: this was big boys' rules, he should've stuck to shoplifting.

'I didn't get a good look at Payne 'cause the County Mounties rocked up but I'm pretty sure he had one here and one here,' he said, indicating his right forearm and shoulder. 'Looked like he had an exit wound in his throat as well. Shame, couldn't have happened to a nicer bunch. We still fancy them for shooting the three coppers down the road and Flynn was a right little psycho! Even his mates were scared of him by all accounts! Anyway, well done. Keep that to yourself though, all right?'

'Yeah, cheers mate, that's a weight off my mind. I fired five and I knew I'd hit the one that survived and I wanted to know that I hit with all my other shots.'

'Whitelock? Apparently your bullet's lodged against his spine but they think he's going to make it. Shame, it could have been a hat-trick. You need to get back on the range and get some more practice in, geezer!'

He patted my arm, gave me a conspiratorial wink and left me to my thoughts. *Right forearm and right shoulder?* I thought to myself positioning my arms as if I was holding the SPAS. I pictured Payne spinning towards me, turning to his right and not the obvious, shortest route to his left. That made sense. I didn't know why he'd done that but it accounted for the shots striking the right side of his body.

Essex wanted to interview me last, so I spent much of Friday alone in the canteen reading the newspaper reports and waiting. The Job seemed to be rallying to support our actions. The press had been allowed access to the scene and photographs of the suspects' arsenal and the Met's head of CID was quoted as saying, 'We did it by the book.' Overall, they seemed to have sided with what they saw as an example of a strong response to an increasing armed crime problem in the capital.

By late afternoon, the rest of the team had been interviewed and the decision was made to send me home. The unit was still too small to warrant our own Federation representative and, naively, no thought had been given to consulting them or asking for legal representation. We were so convinced that we had acted according to the law and our own training that none of us saw a need. My only concession was to have Peter Harris sit in for moral support. In my 12 years' service, Peter stood high among those senior officers for whom I held the highest respect. Ted Stowe, Dinger Bell and Bob Wells would have all been worthy of the task but Peter was my current ops superintendent and had been very supportive after Northolt.

I woke up early on the Saturday and went over to the newsagent's across the street to check the papers, fully expecting any press interest to be a small piece on page five. Instead, the press had found something else to keep the story rolling and the headlines screamed 'AMBUSH COP A HERO BEFORE!'

It went on to name me personally and link me with the shooting of Errol Walker. I was furious and bought a copy of every paper that led with it and stormed home. Kim was equally angry and extremely concerned for our family's safety. I did my best to calm her and assured her that I would take it up with my bosses straight away.

Back at Eltham, I voiced my concerns to Pete Harris who immediately started making phone calls. By the time I was called in to be interviewed, my anger had barely diminished and I threw the newspapers down in front of the SIO and demanded to know how the press had discovered my name. I was pretty sure that the leak was not from them or PT17 and felt certain that someone at the Yard had probably benefitted from a drink. Still, attack is the best form of defence and for the rest of the day he and his team bent over backwards to make me feel at ease. My statement was taken under caution and recorded contemporaneously. Peter Harris sat patiently throughout, insisting that we had regular breaks, and six hours later, interview concluded, I was finally allowed home.

THIRTEEN
JAFFY

The week after the incident was a blur. This had been our first fatal shooting, let alone one where we'd shot multiple suspects. After a few days the press interest started to wane and I longed to get back to work and normality but the Job had other plans. I was summoned to see Bob Wells. I was to be the guinea pig in a new policy requiring all officers involved in shootings to visit the chief medical officer (CMO) and the welfare branch.

The force had always had a welfare fund but until recently it had consisted of a cupboard full of money at Scotland Yard with only the commissioner holding the key. The riots in Brixton and Tottenham, IRA bombings and other major incidents in recent years had changed the force's thinking and a new department had been created. Ken Rivers, a retired superintendent, had been tasked with setting it up and had been given a healthy budget, a suite of offices in the same building as the CMO and a small team of counsellors.

'Tell me they don't want me to see a shrink, sir? You know my opinion of them after my experience with that idiot at Northolt.'

I was reluctant to visit any organisation that had the word 'welfare' in its title, but being forced to see a psychiatrist was at the top of my not-to-do list.

'This will be policy from now on, Tony. If everybody goes through it, there'll be no stigma attached. I'll pass on your concerns to the CMO but ultimately it will be his decision.' As if to sweeten the idea, Bob added, 'Take Kim along. She'll be entitled to help as well. Ken's a good man. I understand his team's done a sterling job for those who've had problems coping after the King's Cross fire.'

'I'm not having problems coping, sir, and neither is Kim.'

'I'm sure that's the case, Tony, but you're going anyway.'

Conversation over.

I was due for a week's leave and, low on funds as usual, Kim and I planned to stay with my dad and stepmother. After Mum had died in 1978, Dad had fallen apart and sunken deeper into alcoholism but Yvonne, an old family friend, herself a widow, had taken him in, fed him and weaned him off the booze. Now happily remarried, they were living near the Suffolk Broads.

Kim took to the idea of a meeting with welfare with an unexpected relish and the next day an unmarked car, driven by one of the new Level 2 lads, picked us both up at home and chauffeured us uptown to the CMO's office.

We were ushered into a newly decorated room furnished with thick carpet, subdued lighting and comfortable chairs, where a lady took our order for tea or coffee. It looked like a meeting room in an expensive hotel.

'Ken will be with you in just a moment,' she said, before gliding out of the door. Kim and I took in our surroundings. A bookshelf dominated one wall and I studied the books' titles. Most were on the subject of post-traumatic stress disorder or PTSD, but one in particular captured my attention. It read, *Stress in the Police Service – Post-Shooting Experiences*. *They'd cut their teeth on the Kings' Cross fire*, I thought, *I bet they must have been gagging for a shooting to come along,* and I wondered what preconceptions they would have about my mental and emotional state.

Ken Rivers entered and introduced himself. He was clearly passionate about his new role, explaining that he had been pushing for a more humane approach to the way that officers were dealt with and wanted to help in any way he could, emphasising that no stigma would be attached to our meeting.

'Now Tony, I know that you have been involved in a shooting incident before but this is different. Two men are dead this time and another seriously injured, you must feel differently about it?' he said gently.

'Not really, sir. It's my job.'

Kim tapped my ankle with her foot and shot me a sideways glance.

'Well, Tony, you're a police officer not a soldier. It's not your job to kill people is it?' he chided.

'I'm not a soldier, sir, but I do carry a gun and if someone poses a threat that requires me to shoot them, I will. If I wasn't prepared to take that responsibility, I wouldn't carry a gun.'

I responded as politely as possible while trying to ignore the increasingly persistent kicks to my ankle. Ken Rivers seemed perplexed as if he thought my confidence camouflaged my inner demons.

'Actually, sir, from a purely professional point of view, I feel better about this incident than the last one.' I explained. 'In the previous incident, I fired three shots at almost point-blank range and only had one effective hit. This time I was shooting single-handed at three suspects and at longer distances. I fired five shots and got five good centre-mass hits. So professionally, I think I performed better.'

Whack! Kim's heel struck my ankle but this time with more vigour and Ken Rivers seemed genuinely shocked.

'You don't really mean that, surely?'

'Well …'

Another vicious kick from Kim.

'Well, what I meant was, I'm happy that I performed my job to the best of my ability. I didn't make the suspects take guns out to commit robbery. They were responsible for their own destiny ...'

And another!

'Obviously I regret the loss of life but that was their decision, not mine.'

No kick this time, I glanced at Kim to see her smiling innocently at Ken. He seemed happier after my demonstration of contrition and changed the subject to the future and what he and his team could do for us. So far, aside from being named in the papers, we had escaped any press intrusion to our home life but it wasn't for lack of trying. If they could find us, so could the villains. We lived in south-east London, their stomping ground, and the security of our young family was our main priority. We voiced our concerns as Ken made copious notes. He offered our family counselling, but we politely declined.

As the meeting came towards its conclusion Ken piped up. 'I understand that you're on leave next week, that's good. It will do you all good to get away for a while.'

'Well, I'm not very happy about it, actually!' moaned Kim. 'It's not a proper holiday; we're only staying at his dad's. He's very proud of Tony and he's just going to want to talk about it all the time!'

Ken interjected enthusiastically. This was something he could help with!

'Quite right. You need a proper holiday, somewhere like Spain or Portugal ...'

This was going well, I thought. I didn't think the job would stretch to a holiday!

Visions of lying on a beach in Spain with a cold *cerveza* were suddenly interrupted by Kim.

'Los Angeles!'

It was my turn to kick her under the coffee table and throw her a sideways glance.

Ken Rivers looked bemused. 'Oh, Los Angeles ... well I don't know if ... why Los Angeles, Kim?'

'Tony's got a friend in Los Angeles who will put us up!'

Have I? Who the f—? Suddenly, I realised who she was talking about. Several months previously I had been running Marylebone range when the local duty officer introduced me to an American visitor. John Robertson, a former Los Angeles police officer, visiting London on holiday. When he'd heard there was a firing range on the top floor he'd been intrigued; they always were. American cops are fascinated by the fact that their British counterparts don't carry guns and when they discover that we do have an armed capability are equally fascinated by what it consists of.

As a consequence they were regular visitors to the unit, to such an extent that a lot of senior officers saw looking after them a chore. More often than not, those tasked with the visit, having stripped the visitors of their gifts, would give them a lacklustre tour of our facilities before pointing them in the direction of Old Street tube station. I called it JAFFY, or Just Another Fucking Yank syndrome, and the attitude annoyed me intensely. Every worthwhile piece of material on the police use of firearms came out of the States and if they had all the experience, I wanted to learn from it. I had given John a couple of hours of my time and after saying our goodbyes, I hadn't expected to hear from him again but a week or so later I was surprised to receive a thank you letter and the kind offer of a place to stay if I ever found myself in LA. By pure chance I'd posted a reply two weeks before Kincraig.

Ken went to his desk and fumbled among the books and paper-work, pulling out one of the free magazines they gave away at tube stations, and started thumbing through its pages.

'San Francisco … here we are, Los Angeles … well, that's quite reasonable,' he said passing us the magazine, opened at a page where bucket-shop airline prices were displayed. He walked back to his desk, picked up the phone, dialled and then cupped his hand over the handset.

'I'm sure that we can stretch to four-return fares. You'll need spending money, of course. Do you think a thousand pounds should cover it? No, perhaps two.'

While Ken spoke to the Met's travel department, Kim and I chuckled to ourselves like naughty schoolchildren. Before we knew it, it was a done deal: we were going to California. Disneyland, here we come! We said our thanks to Ken as he ushered us from his office and escorted us to the lift for my next appointment with the CMO. This time I wouldn't have Kim for support.

I was ushered into his office by his secretary, leaving Kim in the waiting room with a coffee and some worn copies of *Police Review*. Dr Bott, the Met's chief medical officer, leapt from his swivel chair and shuffled around his desk to greet me. His red face held a genuine smile and his podgy fingers gripped mine in a firm handshake.

'My dear boy! How are you?'

This wasn't the reception I had expected at all! He looked like a village GP with a penchant for a lunchtime sherry and, if it hadn't been mid-morning, I would have sworn he was already pissed.

'Now, I've spoken to Mr Rivers and he tells me that you're off to America! You don't need a personal physician to come with you, I suppose?' he guffawed. 'Mr Wells has told me about your distrust of psychiatrists. Quite understandable, strange bunch, but don't worry about that for now, plenty of time for all that malarkey when you get back. I will want you to have a sit down with one eventually, of course, but the one I've got in mind is a bloody good chap, ex-RAF, knows what's what. You'll like him, I'm sure.'

We agreed I should visit him again when I returned and I was guided to his door where we parted with another hearty handshake. Back at home we broke the news to the kids. They were going to meet Mickey Mouse.

From then on, events moved at speed and before we knew it, we found ourselves sitting on board our flight to LA, drinks in hand, pinching ourselves at our good fortune. The Yard had received reliable intelligence that elements within the south London underworld had put a price on my head and it suited the job to get me out of town while they planned a response. At the time I was unaware of this, so I couldn't help thinking that they had massively overreacted to the whole affair.

It was a wonderful trip and everyone we met treated us with kindness. It proved to be the perfect place to go in the circumstances and the Americans' laid-back attitude stood in stark contrast to the uncomfortable reception I often received in the UK. It was summed up on my last day when I was given a flight in an LAPD helicopter.

The unit's commanding officer introduced me to the crew. 'Tony here dumped a couple of assholes so they told him to get out of Dodge.'

The pilot looked confused. 'They send you on vacation when you shoot someone? Do you have any vacancies in the Met?'

FOURTEEN
THE CORONER

Back at work, it was business as usual and I remained on Black team. Payne and Flynn's funerals were held while we were away and angry members of the funeral cortège had attacked the press but other than that there'd been no repercussions. Following Northolt, Bob Wells had called me into his office to discuss my 'future'.

'Tony, I want you as a sergeant in the Wing. You command everyone's respect and write better reports than any of my inspectors. Go away and give it some thought.'

Promotion would mean more money but I was into my work and didn't really want the responsibility that came with rank. Besides, passing the exam would mean returning to division. Nevertheless, I started to attend promotion classes and was given projects allowing me to devote my time to studying but I struggled to find the motivation. The sound of colleagues working outside my office attracted me like a moth to a flame and I'd leave my books to join them. At home, my young family also demanded my attention and after a long day at work, I'd invariably fall asleep on the bed surrounded by my books. I knew it wasn't going to work and months later when I sat the exam at Hendon, I failed miserably.

I decided to try again, but after Kincraig and the trip to the States, I had missed classes and put it off to the following year. To keep Kim happy, I'd agreed to come off ops and the bosses were happy to oblige but, two months later, Kim had endured enough. I was a pain in the arse to live with and I went back to the team. Our cycle of instructional and operational duties continued unabated and it seemed that Kincraig had, if anything, created more work for the Wing with squads and divisions crying out for our services. Our lack of surveillance capability was identified as a limiting factor on our ability to provide units with effective support and the bosses, still looking to keep me out of harm's way, sent me on the Met's surveillance course. It was three weeks away from regular duty and a revelation. I had plenty of plain-clothes experience but none of it had benefitted from any proper training and I winced when I discovered the basic mistakes that I'd made.

The first two weeks ran from a nondescript building in Pimlico and consisted of lectures and exercises around central London to test our burgeoning knowledge. Our instructors were passionate about passing on their craft and demanded perfection. Getting 'burnt' by the role players, or showing out to the ordinary public, along with myriad other errors, resulted in fines that went, in standard Met form, towards the end-of-course piss-up. We aimed to be 'grey' by avoiding 'trigger points' such as distinctive clothing, props or mannerisms. One fundamental technique was simply to avoid eye contact. Only three types of person, we were told, looked strangers in the eye in a lift or a train carriage: gay men, black youths and coppers. I was by no means a natural but I thoroughly enjoyed it and wished that I'd been taught these simple common-sense techniques at the very beginning of my police career. After mastering the basic principles of foot surveillance using just hand signals, we were issued with covert radios equipped with an induction loop that sent transmissions wirelessly to a tiny peanut concealed in our ear.

The final week of the course was spent working from Hendon mastering the art of mobile surveillance, something that, with my driving reputation, was fraught with danger. On one exercise, our stooge entered the Underground at the furthest point on the map. My passenger jumped out and followed the suspect into the ticket hall and, after earwigging the destination, followed our man down to the platform.

'Euston, Euston, Euston!'

He muttered into his radio and I frantically flipped open the geographia (a thick, hard back A–Z map book of London uniquely gridded for the Met) searching desperately for the correct page. I knew where Euston was but hadn't a clue how to get there from my current location. There followed a frenzied drive through heavy traffic, the map balanced on my lap as I turned the pages while speeding down the wrong side of the road, passing through red lights and breaking every traffic law imaginable before skidding to a halt outside Euston with seconds to spare.

The final exercise was equally testing and we were briefed to pick up a jewel thief when he was released from Wormwood Scrubs. Intelligence suggested that he would go straight to recover his ill-gotten gains and after a long day of twists, turns and clues worthy of a crime thriller, we followed our man to the countryside. Our team leader directed part of the team to a car park at a natural beauty spot where he'd deduced our baddy was heading.

Our subject arrived and Sharon, my partner for the exercise, and I played a couple. While pretending to nibble my ear she whispered a commentary into her hidden microphone. Suddenly she burst into laughter, spraying my ear with spittle, and I strained to see what was making her wet herself.

There behind us was Pete, another student on the course, fighting to remove an angry Jack Russell from the rear of his car. Clutching the wriggling, yapping trigger point to his chest, he took off after our suspect who was also trying to suppress a fit of the giggles. Ever resourceful, Pete had located a nearby farmhouse, flashed his warrant card and requisitioned the farmer's dog. By now, the instructors were also struggling to take their exercise seriously and calling 'endex' we all retired to a nearby pub for a well-earned pint and a debrief.

In April, the trial of the surviving abattoir robbers commenced at the Old Bailey. Whitelock and Parfett, the getaway driver, pleaded guilty, receiving 15 and 8 years respectively. Soon I'd have to explain my actions at the coroner's court.

The Met applied for us to give our evidence from behind a screen, a dispensation that SAS troopers had been granted several months previously at the inquest into the controversial shooting of three IRA suspects in Gibraltar. Our team of blaggers had hardly been terrorists but they all came from south-east London, as did half of our team, and there had been rumblings about possible reprisals. The coroner, Mr Monty Levine, listened to the Job's application and dismissed it out of hand. We would be giving our evidence in full view of the press, the public and the dead criminals' families. Security and press interest were high and I was whisked in through the back entrance to avoid photographers. Entering the panelled grandeur of the old magistrates' court I climbed into the elevated witness box, took the oath and the coroner addressed me.

With his waxed moustache and dodgy toupee shifting on his head, he reminded me of Hercule Poirot and I struggled to keep a straight face. I was handed my labelled Browning and asked to demonstrate how I'd fired. Clutching an imaginary shield to my chest, I poised with my pistol at the ready. Producing a stopwatch he asked me to mime firing it so that he could work out how long it had taken me to fire my five rounds and with his thumb poised on the button he looked at me over the rim of his glasses.

'Three, two, one, go!'

I punched out, my mind racing. I wasn't sure what noise to make to simulate firing. Not wanting to be that kid who made shit gun noises, I immediately ruled out 'percheow, percheow!' and 'bap, bap' and in an instant decided on simply saying, 'One, two, one, two, one!'

Traversing the pistol from right to left to simulate engaging Flynn, then Payne and finally Whitelock. Levine looked up from the stopwatch.

'One point three seconds,' he stated, asking me to repeat the process.

I didn't want to give the impression that I'd fired too quickly to have made a correct assessment and consciously slowed my next demonstration.

'One, two, one, two, one!' I repeated.

'One point five six.'

I was in a bizarre game of *Play Your Cards Right* with half of my brain shouting 'higher, higher!' while the other screamed 'lower, lower!' Finally, after several more goes, he settled on a mean time of one point eight seconds and we moved on to other matters.

I looked down on a sea of wigs representing the families, the Met and, as an afterthought, myself. We hadn't seen a need for me to be separately represented and it was only last-minute advice from the Federation that identified the need for me to have my own barrister. The Met's barrister was there to represent the commissioner, not the cannon fodder.

The family's barrister accused me of going rogue, calling the strike and leaving the van first. He suggested that I was a glory seeker by not sticking to my role as cover. I explained that, as no one else had seen the robbers break cover and as they had clearly reached their victim, my role had become redundant. If I hadn't left the vehicle and confronted the suspects, the guard would have been left at their mercy.

Despite my caution, I felt my confidence rising as his line of questioning led me deeper and deeper into familiar territory. I still spent most of my time teaching officers how to shoot but also about their legal responsibilities. It was like being my own expert witness and the laws covering reasonable force, our rules of engagement and Job policy all rolled confidently off my tongue. I knew, as Levine finally granted me leave to step down from the witness box, that I'd performed well.

Laurie and John's planning of the operation came under closer scrutiny than my decision to shoot. The jury might look with sympathy on my split-second decision to open fire but if poor planning had put me there when another, safer option could have prevented the confrontation, then the actions of those responsible for the plan might at least be considered negligent, if not criminal.

Finally, after days of evidence and a summing up by Levine, the jury of nine men and women were sent away to consider their verdicts. When they eventually came they were both 'lawful killing'. The verdict on 29-year-old Payne, armed with a loaded shotgun and shot in the front, was unanimous, but worryingly, that on 24-year-old Flynn, armed with an unloaded revolver and shot in the back was based on a seven to two majority. The team were elated but the second verdict concerned me.

What had those two jurors been thinking? I had explained in depth that with three armed men all turning at once, I hadn't the luxury of waiting. Had they expected me to somehow know that Flynn's revolver was empty, or did they just consider it unsporting to shoot someone in the back? I would never know, but it was finally over.

FIFTEEN
MY MATE MARMITE

'Tony, you've done a brilliant job but now that it's all over, we need to discuss where your career goes from here,' Bob Wells said awkwardly. 'I need you to take a back seat and let others take the lead.'

That seemed reasonable, although I wasn't sure how it would work out in practice.

'And the CMO wants you to have a chat with a psychiatrist,' he added. A massive whiff of dead rat hit my nostrils.

'Sir, this stinks!' I said angrily. 'By the time I got back from the States, the CMO had changed his mind about me seeing a shrink. Now I'm exonerated, he wants me to see one again? If I needed a shrink, why have I been kept on ops all this time?'

He assured me that it was just a formality but I left the office with my mind spinning. Black team were first response for the week and the day after we were called to Acton where a job was brewing. Taff and I were immediately dispatched to reconnoitre the plot, a busy high street about five minutes away from the nick. The local crime squad had no surveillance capability and our plan needed to be simple. After a quick walk through we headed back to the local nick, and as I drew a hasty map on to the white board we suggested a plan to Laurie and John. Taff and I would sit in a McDonald's opposite our target premises, providing a direct radio link with the team. When our suspect left his flat, we'd give a radio commentary until the team deployed on to him from the sliding doors of our covert van. In the event of them being held in traffic, we'd be able to deploy on foot and keep eyeball on the suspect until the team could catch up. Mindful of Bob Wells's directions and as our only surveil-lance-trained officer, it seemed the ideal role for me. John went away to a corner with Laurie to bottom out their final plan while Taff and I got kitted up.

I slipped into my covert radio harness and, with the peanut in my ear, asked for a signal check. Laurie looked up from his conversation. Happy that my comms were working, I put my armour on under my shirt, double-checked my weapon and filled my jacket pockets with my plot cap, med kit and plasticuffs before taking a seat for the briefing. The local DS ran us through the background of the operation before John called me up to brief on the ground. Pointing at my hand-drawn map, I gave a detailed description of the target premises and surrounding area before returning to my seat. John then detailed our plan but when he came to our postings my name wasn't mentioned and Sinex was now partnered with Taff in the OP.

I raised my hand. 'John, so I'm not in the OP then?'

He looked embarrassed; Laurie answered for him. 'I've got strict instructions that you're to take a back-seat shag, so you'll be sitting here monitoring it on the radio.'

He'd watched me get kitted up but had chosen to say nothing until we were in the middle of the briefing. I clenched my fists with rage but knew it would be unprofessional to respond. It would have to wait. The team were deployed for several hours while I sat alone in the canteen and by the time the job had been stood down, I had decided not to confront Laurie. We didn't like each other; there was no point. I'd take it up with the Boss.

The next day Bob Wells listened patiently to my grievances, accepting that Laurie may have taken the phrase 'taking a back seat' too far and apologising for his tactless approach. I'd thought about it overnight and told him I wanted off operations until I'd undergone the psychiatric assessment. I had real concerns that I was being fitted up and wanted everyone to know that I'd withdrawn myself and not been taken off by the CMO. He seemed relieved and I reluctantly agreed to go training on the understanding that I'd be allowed back on ops as soon as I got the CMO's all clear.

I was put on a small cadre of full-time instructors whose job was to provide the continuity in training we'd lost as our operational role expanded. Run by an inspector and two sergeants, our team was responsible for writing new content and supervising its introduction. I would be one of two experienced PCs on the new team. My new colleagues were all older, solid, reliable guys who had all volunteered for the role but were, I thought, unimaginative and resistant to change. With five years in the Wing I was full of ideas and pretty sure I was seen as a young upstart. I was, however, given the responsibility of running training packages with little or no supervision, and being posted to Lippitts Hill gave me time to get back into my promotion studies. After two sittings, the psychiatrist declared that I was sound of mind but, with a smile, denied my request for a certificate to prove it. I would like to have had it framed and put up in the office as proof but at least I could now leave training and return to the teams.

My euphoria was short-lived. Unfortunately for me, Bob Wells had retired weeks before and the new man in the chair hadn't signed up to previous promises. Bob had been a key player in the Wing's development and had always held my respect. Rick Johnson, his replacement, had a hard act to follow. Sat in his office the day after my final session with the shrink, I happily announced that I'd been given the all clear and asked to be reinstated. Johnson, who had come to us from the Special Escort Group, looked surprised and his response knocked me backwards.

'Tony, you must realise you are a political embarrassment to the Metropolitan Police. You'll never carry a gun again!'

Bob Wells had given me his word but he was gone and suddenly I was faced with what appeared to be an insurmountable wall. I left his office angry and confused but determined to fight on. The following week I was summoned to the CMO. Expecting it to be about my psychiatric assessment, I duly attended but this time there were no smiles, no handshake and no charming bedside manner.

'You know why you're here, Long.'

Gone too were first names.

'You have the worst hearing of any officer in the Met. I am recommending that you be removed from firearms duty and be returned to divisional uniform duties immediately. That will be all!'

He ushered me to the door with the back of his hand. In a state of shock I turned and meekly left the room, tears welling up in my eyes, I pushed open the toilet door and walked in. I looked in the mirror at the face of a stranger, turned on the tap, splashed water on my face and gripped the sink until my knuckles matched the porcelain. I felt anger welling up from the pit of my stomach. Picking up a bar of soap I hurled it at the wall before storming out and heading straight for the CMO's office, my fists balled in rage.

We were all required to have annual hearing tests and were acutely aware of the danger to our hearing but our issue protection was barely adequate and on ops, we had nothing. Even in training, we were often unable to wear protection against the noise from shotgun rounds, blanks and our fiercely loud stun grenades and the incidents at Northolt and Plumstead had both given my ears a battering.

My last test had been about eight months previously and the results hadn't been brilliant. Like a lot of the guys, I had hearing damage in both ears but particularly in my left, which being right-handed was always nearest the muzzle. The specialist had given me the usual lecture about taking care of my ears and told me that he'd see me in six months rather than a year. I'd been given a couple of 'six-mon-thers' before; it wasn't unusual. I was by no means the only instructor to get them and was certain my hearing couldn't be worse than every other officer in the Met! I'd had no notification of a second test and hadn't been about to volunteer myself for one.

'Excuse me! You can't go in, he's got a – '

The CMO's secretary leapt up from behind her desk but it was too late, I was already entering his office. The chief medical officer didn't look well; his usual ruddy complexion was draining rapidly as he pushed back in his swivel chair and attempted to stand.

'Now see here! You can't come barging in here! I have another patient!'

Sitting next to his desk was a pallid officer, probably pushing for early retirement and an ill-heath pension.

'You'll have to make another appointment!' the CMO added, trying to regain his composure.

'Let me get this right, sir,' I said, turning the screw. 'My last hearing test was over eight months ago and the result was bad enough to warrant a six-monthly test but, without the benefit of a second one, you're telling me that my hearing is so bad I have to go back to division immediately. Is that right?'

The penny dropped and he sat clumsily back in his seat. I glanced at his patient who had left his chair and was slowly edging towards the door.

'Knowing that, you've subjected me to a further eight months' hearing damage! Is that what you're telling me, sir?'

He knew I had a case and immediately started back-peddling but I wasn't letting him off the hook. I told him of my suspicions about the psychiatrist and he waffled a response.

'Rubbish! You were hoping that the psychiatrist's report would give you an excuse to bin me but when that didn't work you've come up with this crap about my hearing! I'm not stupid.'

He grudgingly offered me another hearing test and I left, having won a temporary reprieve. I was certain now that the bosses wanted me out of the Wing and using the CMO had been their easy option.

With an increase in manpower we had finally elected a Federation representative and Colin was my first port of call. The larger Federation were reluctant to get involved but after a lot of cajoling funded an independent hearing test. A week later, a Harley Street specialist ran me through a series of tests far beyond the basic ones performed at the CMO's. I had high-frequency hearing damage but no worse than he'd expect from someone that worked around firearms and he saw no reason why, provided I took care, I shouldn't remain in my chosen profession.

'High-frequency damage? What does that mean in real terms?' I asked.

'Don't waste a lot of money on a good stereo,' he replied.

Word finally came through from the CMO that I was cleared to return to full instructional duties. It was a victory but I was still no closer to returning to the teams.

Studying for the sergeant's exam was going well and I'd already attended several classes when Mike summoned me to his office. I was running some abseil training at Old Street and had been hanging from a rope halfway down the building when he'd stuck his head out of the window. I unhitched myself and knocked on his door.

'Come in and shut the door,' he said picking up my personnel file from his cluttered desk. 'I'm afraid I have some bad news. Your supervisors have marked you down on your sergeant's assessment. I'm afraid you don't have sufficient points to sit the exam.'

I was staggered. The job had just introduced a points system and applicants had to be assessed by an inspector and two sergeants. As an experienced instructor, it should have been a formality and, knowing that inexperienced divisional officers in my promotion class had already been given leave to sit the exam, it seemed inconceivable that I hadn't.

'How can that possibly be, Boss?' I was incredulous. 'What have they marked me down on?'

He looked up from the file, chewing forcefully on his unlit pipe, always a reliable indication of his stress level. 'I'm sorry but I can't say!'

In those days, we were still a disciplined force and not yet a service and there was no such thing as a grievance procedure. He wouldn't budge, and I stormed from his office slamming his door behind me. I looked at my watch; it was three o'clock. The bosses would be thinning out shortly and I made my way to the administration office to have a quiet word with one of the girls I always flirted with.

Rick had already taken down some of the ropes but when I told him what had happened he agreed to help and we rigged up the one remaining one to drop past the secretary's open window and waited for the bosses to leave. An hour later, satisfied they'd gone, I abseiled down, clambered into the locked office, photocopied the report and left the way I'd arrived, closing the window behind me. We packed away the ropes and Rick gave me a lift home via the pub where, over a few pints, we studied the report and discussed my options.

It was a pathetic attempt at a fit up. None of my supervisors' criticisms were evidenced and had there been any valid ones, no one had ever taken the time to point them out. I laboured over my response but satisfied that I had answered all of their points, I bypassed Mike and hand-delivered it to Johnson. Several days later I was called back to his office where he commended me on the quality of my report and, overriding their assessment, granted me permission to sit the exam. He'd gone up in my estimation and I stood up, shook his hand across the desk and thanked him, but I'd already decided that they could poke their promotion. If I passed, I'd be sent back to division as a sergeant, never to return. If they wanted rid of me I was going to make them work for it!

The Wing's museum in Old Street's basement was a shambles. The armourer doubled as its curator but it had grown beyond his control and its ramshackle design made supervising and monitoring the hoard of seized weapons problematic. Stuck on training, I had volunteered to redesign it, making it more secure and user-friendly. Everyone agreed that it was a good idea and I was left to arrange my duties to get it completed.

Shortly after I'd undertaken the thankless task and was busy in the museum, Johnson walked in sporting a face like thunder. 'Long! In my office, now!'

I knocked on his office door having no idea what I had done wrong and wasn't prepared for what was to follow. A torrent of wild accusations flew from his lips but the most serious was kept until last: I had, he insisted, been carrying my issue pistol off duty. He'd checked the armoury personally and it wasn't there. Straight away I knew the source of this particular piece of misinformation.

The previous day I had been called away from the museum to help man the range at nearby City Road. I'd drawn my issue Browning from the main armoury to practice with in my lunchbreak and was in the Level 2 crew room. I was stuffing the pistol into my day sack on top of my uniform before cycling to the range when the Level 2 baseman had walked in.

'Expecting some trouble, Tone?' he said with a cheeky smile.

Dave, one of the two sergeants who had marked me down on my promotion assessment and a former friend from Blue team, was reading the paper and sipping his tea.

'Well, you never know, do you?' I replied sarcastically, nodding towards Dave. 'I'm wearing stab-proof armour underneath all this as well!'

When I'd returned six hours later, the base was empty. All of the teams were out on jobs, the armourer and all the bosses had slid off early and the lone baseman was holding the fort. Unable to open the main armoury, and after proving it unloaded to the baseman, I'd deposited my Browning in the Level 2 pistol safe in their crew room.

'Show me!' Johnson ordered.

'If you don't believe me, sir, I suppose I'll have to!' I countered, leading him downstairs. The baseman unlocked their safe and un-prompted, supported my account while I removed my pistol for his examination.

'Put it in the armoury!' Johnson ordered, storming off.

'Sorry, sir. Was that an apology?' I retorted.

'Just get it put it away,' he snapped back as the baseman moonwalked from the room.

Twenty minutes later, pistol back on its rack, I was back in the museum. I looked around at the jumble of lethal weapons and realised that by taking responsibility for it I was leaving myself vulnerable to further wild allegations. I found myself knocking again on Johnson's door. He had calmed visibly and I asked if we could talk candidly. I made it clear that I saw the CMO's involvement, the promotion fiasco and this morning's allegation, together with his own 'political embarrassment to the Met' comment, as proof that I was seen as a liability and that concerted efforts were being made to force me to leave.

I told him I was on to them, and that I wished to relinquish my responsibility for the museum. I was surprised by his response. Rank-conscious as he was, he fell short of criticising his inspectors and sergeants but hinted that he was unhappy at being dragged into a witch-hunt. He had worked with strong characters like me on the SEG, saw their value and knew how to handle them, adding that he respected my knowledge and enthusiasm and didn't want to lose good talent. Accepting my request to step away from the museum, he warned me to watch my back before shaking my hand. I wasn't sure whether to trust him but I was certain I couldn't trust my immediate supervisors and decided to heed his advice.

When the 9mm Browning High Power first appeared in 1935, its compact design and 13-round magazine made it an instant success. Used by both sides during the Second World War, it had become Britain's main service pistol but was getting tired. With the exception of Special Forces, the military had never considered the pistol as a serious weapon and its limited operational value meant that replacing it wasn't seen as a priority; it would soldier on for a further 30 years. For police, however, pistols were still primary weapons and by the late eighties the Browning had had its day. Bob Wells had ordered a search for a modern replacement and we'd looked at several including the radically new Glock 17 but, following his retirement, the project stalled until one day the armourer gave me the new compact version to play with, with one proviso.

'All I ask is that you give it a fair go and put something on paper afterwards.'

It came with its own box, the usual two magazines, a plastic holster and a magazine pouch and I kept it for nearly a month before it eventually won me around. Although it had internal safety features, I had concerns over its lack of a manual safety catch but it was robust and reliable. Reluctantly, I handed it back with a one-page report concluding with the line: 'I would personally be happy to carry the Glock 19 as an operational weapon.'

The following day I was summoned to see Johnson. *What now?* I thought, but he was all smiles as he offered me a seat.

'Just read your report, excellent. We're going with your advice and I'm replacing all of the unit's Brownings with Glocks.'

It was just one man's opinion, I argued, and it would be wrong to commit to the purchase of a new weapons system without running a proper, comparative trial. We didn't have time, he insisted. The Wing was expanding, we had a new intake of instructors and he had to decide whether to buy more Brownings or to go for something different. The armourer was unhappy with the quality of the most recent batch of Brownings and he'd made his mind up: we were going for the Glock. I got some flak from those who hated change but soon most took to the new pistol but for one thing: the Glock was issued with only two magazines whereas, up until then, operators had carried a minimum of two spare mags for their Brownings. Johnson was adamant that as the Glock magazine took 17 rounds versus its predecessor's 13, no additional mags would be issued.

I'd been taking each of the six teams to Hereford for a week's training using the SAS's range facilities. The issue of weapon's lights still hadn't been resolved since the Northolt siege and I had acquired an attachment designed to allow the fitting of a small, Mini-Maglite torch to the base of a Glock magazine. The armourer had provided a magazine and fitted the device and while I wasn't convinced that it was the perfect solution, it seemed better than nothing. Mindful of the criticism I'd received over the Glock, I was determined for it to be tested by as many lads as possible over the six-week cycle. On the last Friday of the training we returned late to an empty base and after our kit and weapons were stowed away, we bomb-burst for the weekend. It was half-term the following week and I'd taken it off to spend time with the kids.

I returned to work to find that, on discovering some officers had ignored his third magazine edict, Johnson had instigated a bag search: anyone with a third magazine was in the shit. Four lads had already been dragged upstairs and rumour had it that they would be returned to division. I was the fifth and could expect to be hauled before Johnson later that day. I laughed it off. I had no doubt that when he heard my explanation he'd realise that the armourer had issued me with it to trial the light attachment. Rick was my most trusted teammate and if our duties merged, we still shared lifts to work, putting the world to rights as we sat in the rush-hour traffic.

'Don't trust Johnson,' he advised. 'And make sure you've got your Marmite file with you!'

The 'Marmite file' was a dossier of facts discussed on our regular journeys together. It contained useful snippets of information about our supervisors known only to us and gained its title from a TV campaign that used the annoyingly repetitive catchphrase of 'my mate Marmite'. The idea was that if you found yourself in a corner with no way out, you'd pull out the file and, before revealing what you had on them, would say, 'You don't want to sack me, sir. I'm your mate …'

Our file was bulging with misdemeanours and fuck-ups and while some might consider it blackmail, we preferred to call it insurance. Forewarned is forearmed and I took a stroll over to the armourer's workshop for a brew and chat. The armourer greeted me with a cheery smile and told me that Johnson hadn't spoken to him and, as far as he was concerned, was unaware that I'd been issued the spare mag for evaluation. Cuppa in hand, I walked over to the big corner cupboard where the armourers stored their goodies. They had first pick of any seized firearms and I always enjoyed a nose around on my regular visits. There was nothing new of interest but looking at the packed shelves sparked a recollection and I knew straight away what I would be pulling out of the Marmite file first.

Later that day, as expected, I was summoned to Johnson's office. This time I wasn't offered a seat and his speech was short and to the point.

'Right, Tony, you know why you're here. You have been found in possession of an extra magazine in direct disregard of my written instructions. I run this department and I can't have my orders ignored. I've told you before that I value your knowledge and your enthusiasm but I'm afraid I have to let you go and you will be returning to division as soon as your transfer can be arranged.'

I had expected at least some questioning first and tried to explain but he was having none of it.

'There is nothing to discuss, Tony. I have made my decision, now kindly leave!'

There was nothing for it; I was going to have to go for the big guns. I took a deep breath, looked him in the eyes and opened the Marmite file at page one.

'You don't want to sack me, sir ... I'm your mate!'

Apart from D11 courses, royalty close protection officers also attended training provided by the SAS, whose instructors poured scorn on their puny revolvers. Selected officers were also trained on the stubby Heckler & Koch Kurz sub-machine gun but they wanted to replace their revolvers with a high-capacity pistol and, having friends in the very highest of places, eventually got their own way.

Our move to the Glock had left our old Brownings available as a stopgap and senior members of my training team had run hurried conversion courses for them. Under normal circumstances the course should have taken a week but, keen to be helpful, my obsequious inspector had agreed to run abbreviated weekend courses. The rest of us watched on, convinced it was a recipe for disaster, and were soon proved right.

Within weeks of completing his abridged course, a close protection officer managed to have a negligent discharge (ND) through the floor of the Queen's armoured Rolls-Royce and, while the gunshot's echo reverberated around Buckingham Palace's Georgian quadrangle, the consequences would be heard further afield. News of the embarrassed officer's ND was soon known around the Met. The next day, Rick and I had visited the armourer's shop for a brew and a chat and were having a nose in the large store cupboard when we heard one of our senior officers walk in and I watched him hand a pistol-sized exhibits box to the armourer.

'This is the royalty Browning from yesterday's embarrassing little episode,' he said, conspiratorially. 'Give it a once over will you? Nothing on paper though, I'd like to try and keep this in-house if we can.'

As we were concealed behind the cupboard's open door, he was completely unaware of our presence. Rick and I looked at each other with raised eyebrows, remaining hidden until he had left. It hadn't surprised either of us. Royalty Protection attracted a sycophantic following from many senior officers who would do anything they could to keep in favour with them, even if it meant pulling a few strings or turning a blind eye. It was definitely one for the file.

Back in Johnson's office I played my ace card and watched with a degree of satisfaction as the colour drained from his face. Over the next 30 minutes, I threw in jar after jar of the black sticky stuff and he stuttered a few feeble responses. I still had plenty left but the fight had left him.

'Right, Tony, this is getting us nowhere. You've raised some issues that I will have to look into but my gut feeling is that I will still be sending you back to division. We'll speak next week.'

I went downstairs, changed into my cycling gear, jumped on my bike and headed home. Johnson had gone from definitely returning me to division to thinking about it. It was a substantial shift but, still concerned, I changed direction and headed for Rick's. Surprised to see me, we cracked some beers and discussed the meeting, the Marmite file and the future. Several hours later, slightly the worse for wear, I cycled home.

Kim wasn't pleased to see me. 'The Federation guy has rung; you need to ring him back as soon as possible. I'm going to bed.'

I rang Colin straight away; he had good news. Johnson had changed his mind; none of us would be sacked.

I was to ring Johnson back but Colin offered some advice. 'I think he actually likes you, Tone, I'm pretty sure he didn't want to sack you. Go easy with him; you need him on-side.'

It was late and I was still pretty drunk, but I picked up the phone and dialled. Johnson answered on the second ring.

'Ah, Tony, I've thought about our conversation and I've decided not to sack you.'

'I know,' I answered rudely.

He wanted to talk face-to-face about the issues I'd raised so we scheduled a meeting for the following week. I'd won yet another skirmish but the battle dragged on. Too drained and too drunk to celebrate I fell to sleep on the sofa.

Mike joined us for the meeting and I sensed the ice-forming as soon as we sat down together. Johnson started the ball rolling. He was genial and re-emphasised how he valued my expertise and enthusiasm but repeated that he couldn't have me ignoring his orders. Mike was almost chewing through the stem of his pipe and the vein on his temple was pulsating with anger as he waited to speak. Eventually Johnson passed him the ball.

'You, mister, have got a problem!' he spat, stabbing at me with his mangled pipe stem.

I wasn't going to let him turn my victory into defeat and there followed a heated argument about my attitude, position and credibility in the department, and my willingness to criticise senior officers. I couldn't believe the irony of it. I hadn't lost a moment's sleep following the shootings at Northolt or Plumstead, actions forced on me by circumstances beyond my control. I'd even coped with their protracted aftermaths but when they'd been satisfactorily concluded, the very senior officers that should have been supporting me had put me under ridiculous pressure and all because they weren't robust enough to handle me.

If I walked away now I would have won just another battle; it was time to win the war. Being taken off operational duties for doing what I was trained to do was unacceptable, I argued. If shots found themselves in a position where they had to open fire but thought they might be treated the same way, it was only a matter of time before someone hesitated with tragic consequences. I wanted to be reinstated to full operational duties immediately and, if that didn't happen, I wanted an interview with the commissioner.

The meeting was concluded and I left, struggling not to swagger as I walked down the corridor. It was time to move on.

SIXTEEN

BACK IN THE GAME

My ultimatum finally forced a decision and within weeks I was leaving Lippitts and heading back to the fold. Laurie refused me back but the 'Cat', now an inspector, and Russ, his larger-than-life sergeant, snapped me up and I joined Green.

Times were changing. We were still operating on our two-tier system and instructors were still dividing their time between training and ops, but multiple operations were now a daily event. Working hand in glove with the Flying Squad during my absence, twelve more team members had been forced to open fire, killing four armed robbers and wounding another five, and many of London's busiest blagging teams had packed up and moved to safer ventures. One gang had been taken out in Hoxton Street only a few hundred yards from our back gates. The well-disciplined professional team were planning to take out a security van collecting from a sub post office but when the blaggers appeared, wearing wigs and bearing sawn-offs, our team caught them bang to rights and were amazed at the speed at which they hit the deck.

We later discovered that they'd planned for three eventualities. Confronted by unarmed bobbies, they would threaten them at gun point or, if push came to shove, take them hostage. If it was detectives bearing shiny guns, shouting 'Armed police!' (Flying Squad detectives had changed to stainless steel revolvers in 1984), they would shoot their way out, but if faced with guys carrying long black guns, they would surrender immediately without waiting to be told. They even admitted practising their surrender, timing themselves as they lay their weapons down.

Word had spread among the criminal fraternity that PT17 was a newly formed squad with specific orders to kill armed criminals and we'd become known as the 'Execution Squad', earning a quite undeserved reputation for shooting without warning. It wasn't true, of course, but the Yard seemed happy for criminals to believe it and equally happy with the plummeting robbery statistics.

A DC approached me from Flying Squad's Tower Bridge office. He had an informant close to a busy south-east London firm and during the course of a meeting the mid-level criminal retold rumours he'd heard about PT17.

'That's bollocks, there's no such thing as a police execution squad,' the DC had told him.

'Oh yeah?' replied his snout. 'What's that Tony Long then if he isn't a fucking hitman?'

Robbery aside, the country was suffering an epidemic of drug-related violence. Jamaican 'Yardie' gangs had shifted from just importing their native 'ganja' to more lucrative South American cocaine, converting it to crack for sale in fortified drug dens. North London's Turkish gangs were responsible for the resurgence of heroin, and with a supply chain from its source in Afghanistan, Kalashnikovs and other military-grade weaponry started to appear. Meanwhile, home-grown, white London gangs had diversified into the drug trade. Still performing robberies to fund their bigger transactions, they too were concentrating on the large-scale importation of cannabis and cocaine, and the production and distribution of ecstasy.

Detached from normal street duty, the extent of the drugs problem wouldn't truly come home to me for several years, but the blossoming criminal activity was having an impact on the type of operations we were deployed on. The three full-time Level 2 teams were also being run ragged and the line that divided them from Level 1 was becoming increasingly blurred. We were all now armed with semi-automatic MP5s and Glocks and, aside from hostage operations and rapids, we were doing the same work. The writing was on the wall: sooner rather than later we would merge, and I for one looked forward to full-time ops.

It was the nineties, the start of a new decade, and in the preceding 12 months, three Met officers had been killed in the line of duty prompting, as always, calls to arm the police. The Yard was a long way from letting that happen though, and a ground-breaking compromise was reached. Other UK forces had used armed response vehicles (ARVs) for years but the Yard had resisted the move. Now the decision had been made to create them in the Met and they would come under our control. Overnight the unit doubled in strength.

With the increase in manpower and the new emphasis on operations, we kept our training responsibilities but left personnel and training and moved to specialist operations. We were now SO19; a new era was born and with it came the merger of the two tiered teams. The Level 2 lads underwent a testing selection course and those who passed joined instructors such as myself to become specialist firearms officers (SFOs) while those that didn't make the transition joined the ARVs. The coloured designations remained and I found myself as 2IC of the new Green team, with Russ as my team leader. Exciting times loomed.

*

The Job was ill prepared for its newborn problem child. We had insufficient weapons, only two teams' worth of ancillary kit and almost no budget but nothing could dampen our enthusiasm. With the ARVs' arrival at Old Street, we took over the basement area and, despite its peeling paint and crumbling brickwork, turned it into our base room, begging, borrowing and often stealing whatever we needed to make it habitable.

Transport was more problematic with just two armoured Land Rovers and two battered vans to be shared between six eight-man teams. It required the efforts and contacts of our senior officers but negotiations eventually acquired a brand new unmarked white van and our existing, liveried, call-out van was swapped for a white Ford Transit that looked like a laundry van. They were converted to my design so that they were capable of carrying all of our kit and could still conceal a fully equipped team. They became an immediate success. On the outside they both looked like commercial vans and we had magnetic signs made to conceal their real purpose. One, not too subtly, read, 'H&K Carriers – we aim to please', while another advertised us as 'pest control' specialists. In the back were padded seats, black-out curtains, windows with one-way film and covert radios.

The remainder of our fleet remained woefully inadequate but we discovered a quantity of almost unused Range Rovers gathering dust in a warehouse. They had been purchased at huge public expense for royalty close protection and were armoured to stop high-velocity rifle fire but their added weight made them too slow to keep up with the likes of Princess Anne, who liked to drive her own car at speed. We managed to secure three of them and straight away our credibility soared.

A spotter could tell that their fragile alloys had been replaced with Land Rover wheels and that their windscreens were thicker than a regular Chelsea tractor, but they blended in well with London traffic and were reasonably low key. Loaded with four big guys and all their kit, they weren't the most stable of vehicles but with leather seats and air-con they oozed kudos. It would be several more years before our fleet would get anywhere near matching our manpower though.

Previously, one of the team's primary functions was responding to out-of-hours' calls, but now the 24-hour ARVs were responding immediately, and swiftly resolving most situations. Our workload was changing accordingly and operations could be broken down into dig-outs, rapids, squad jobs and 'others'.

Dig-outs were where we would go to an address specifically to arrest an armed suspect. They were our bread and butter and the objective was always to get the suspect to come out to us. Entering unfamiliar premises where women, children or vulnerable persons might be present was always a last option and the humble dig-out became our safest and most reliable tactic. If dig-outs were our bread and butter, rapids were our jelly and ice cream. The term was lifted straight from the pages of the SFO manual, which described the tactic as: 'a rapid entry, followed by a rapid internal deployment'.

A rapid was planned and executed in exactly the same way as its tamer cousin up until the breach, at which point, rather than hold at the door, we would enter at speed, clearing the building room by room and securing the occupants before they could resist or destroy valuable evidence. We had always frowned on armed entries simply to secure evidence, but with local authorised firearms officers marginalised and the city's boroughs plagued with drugs we were their only option.

Our tactics and old school raids were worlds apart though. Gone were ten unarmed 'bobbies' and two shots with holstered 'equipment' crashing blindly into the unknown, to be replaced by disciplined operators carrying out well-practised drills. Those performed on rapids were almost identical to those used on a hostage rescue and so each one was a rehearsal for the main event.

Dig-out or rapid, they were always planned with the same degree of care and imagination. Any excuse to use a trained tactic or technique was rarely missed and we were always looking to push the envelope. Executing a drugs warrant on the fourteenth floor of a tower block might give us the perfect excuse to have two of the team abseil down, smash a window and dominate from the outside, or if the circuitous route to a target took us through a rough housing estate, the recce team, armed with cans of spray paint, would add their own unique tags to the graffiti-covered walls steering the team to their target.

Reconnaissance became an art form and team members with a talent for it became indispensable assets. Disguises, props and cover stories were used to infiltrate even the most hostile estates and those with artistic skills were particularly sort after as SO19 briefings became legendary for their thoroughness and for their elaborate visual aids; no other unit in the Met planned their jobs with the same attention to detail.

We were constantly learning and regardless of the hour, and often accompanied by beers in the crew room, every job finished with a thorough debrief. No one could leave until it was finished and they could be brutal affairs. Mistakes, however small, were always learnt from and SOPs adjusted to prevent them happening again.

Larger or repeat mistakes resulted in punishment. Fitness standards within the team were pretty high but, unlike some other units, rather than resort to physical punishment like press ups or pull ups, the offender had to buy cakes. Minor infractions might involve a visit to the bagel shop in nearby Brick Lane for a team's worth of cream cheese and salmon bagels; for something more serious a trip to Harrods patisserie might be in order.

Squad jobs would normally be for the Flying Squad but the term could equally refer to other CID units. Intelligence-led, they were divided into either mobile or static as dictated by the quality of the information. If they were behind a team of active armed robbers but didn't know where they were going to strike next, it would be mobile and we'd simply be passengers in the Squad's gunships, but if they had precise intelligence of a time and location then it would be a static plot. The Sweeney had been doing this for decades without us and were sometimes reluctant to have us on board. I could understand their reticence; if they'd been behind a good team for several months, it was only natural that they'd want to lay on hands, but times were changing and they were required to use us if certain criteria were met. The rivalry and banter was constant: they were always suits and we would forever be mere lids.

'There's nothing more dangerous than a techo with a gun!' one of the lads joked as we waited for a briefing.

'Except a ninja in the witness box!' a wag at the back shot back and everyone laughed.

Our lack of transportation meant relying on the Sweeney when it came to mobile ops and we'd just sit kitted in the rear while the driver and the detective on the maps did all the hard work, only deploying to do our thing when the 'attack' was given. It never sat well with me that we were reliant on officers that we hadn't trained with, expecting them to drive us, unarmed, into what might potentially be a full-blown gunfight. Even when we worked with the anti-terrorist squad (SO13) we were forced to use Flying Squad vehicles and crews and our ultimate aim was to become self-sufficient with our own fleet of gunships.

If the job was a 'static plot', the Squad were duty bound to use us but they'd often twist the intelligence to allow them to do the job themselves and we'd only learn about it after it went wrong, which it sometimes did. Their priority as detectives was to arrest the bad guys with the maximum evidence to secure a conviction and, while our job was to facilitate that, our priority was the safety of not just the public and ourselves but, if at all possible, that of the suspects. The two priorities often clashed. Mobile jobs, by their nature, were fluid and when they came off they required us to think on our feet but, above all, rely on our training to win the day. A good static plot would allow our imaginations to run wild and any technique, piece of kit or subterfuge, however wacky, would be used to achieve our objective. One typical static involved the robbing of a wages delivery in a rough industrial part of the East End. The blaggers planned to use a mechanical digger and a lorry to block the armoured security van in a stretch of potholed, cobbled street bounded on both sides by 20-foot wriggly tin fencing bordering scrap and haulage yards. There was nowhere to conceal a team and any police activity would have stood out like a bulldog's bollocks so we had the Met's engineers modify a large skip so that it appeared full of rubbish but could still conceal a small team. Laid down by a skip lorry in the early morning, our team waited patiently for hours before bursting out on to the oily cobbles to take out the startled blaggers without firing a shot.

The 'other' category of operations covered less dynamic but equally rewarding operations. It could be to provide a Counter Ambush Team (CAT) for a state visit, or it might be to provide discreet protection to an undercover officer as he made a drugs buy in a McDonald's car park or an MI5 officer placing a tracker on a terrorist's vehicle or, occasionally, if you were lucky, a protection gig in some far-flung corner of the former British empire.

I could recall almost every job I'd done as a part-timer in the first decade of my service; now I was on full-time ops, I was hard-pressed to remember ones I'd done the previous month and I was personally hitting several hundred ops a year. We would try our hand at anything and our reputation for planning, preparation and our can-do attitude started to win over even our keenest critics.

One week in six, our training team at Lippitts Hill would take us through a refresher programme and at least one day would be spent in our close quarter combat (CQC) range where we'd spend hours moving as a team through its reconfigurable rooms firing live ammunition at the hostile targets while avoiding the innocents until we could almost do it with our eyes closed.

In between our structured training programme, the team's own instructors would be expected to fill our downtime with additional training. In the absence of jobs, team 'fizz' was a daily event and would normally consist of a local run along the nearby canal path and through the fume-filled streets of Shoreditch, followed by a session in the gym. We'd spend hours applying our abseiling skills or in an activity where one of us would lead the team around the rear of the old building, free-climbing up old cast-iron drainpipes, pulling ourselves up and over railings and leaping over stairwells and voids. We were rarely roped on and, as health and safety didn't yet exist, we would constantly push the envelope attempting to scare the crap out of each other and, in particular, visitors from other teams. Soon our reputation spread and we became known as the Green team dangerous sports club.

The new system also allowed me to push our shooting to new levels. Our nearest range was at City Road police station, a five-minute drive away. In a typical session, our small team would often fire several thousand rounds in the space of a few hours. Nearly all of our shoots involved a competitive element and we were always pushing ourselves to shoot more accurately and to draw, shoot and reload with ever-greater speed. We'd fire, reload and clear stoppages single-handed with both strong and weak hands to simulate being injured, and much of our training was done firing from unusual positions or on the move, sometimes balancing on gym benches or clambering over range furniture.

On top of our crime operations, with the IRA active on the mainland and with SO13 taking the national lead, we found ourselves increasingly deployed across the whole country for weeks at a time; kipping in sleeping bags on the floor of Territorial Army halls with all of our kit while the detectives slept comfortably in nearby hotels. From our joint efforts, though, there stemmed some spectacular results breaking up Provisional IRA cells and thwarting bomb attacks but in January 1993 Harrods again became a target. This time, fortunately, no one was injured. When video of the scene was examined, a hawk-eyed Special Branch officer recognised the two bombers. By early March they'd been housed in Stoke Newington and Blue team were tasked to arrest them. As they made their final preparations to breach the door they came under fire from inside but carried on with their assault regardless. The shooter had suffered a malfunction on his pistol and his accomplice was frantically trying to load an AK47 when the team stormed in and detained them both without firing a shot. The suspects were secured and as the team cleared the rest of the property they came across explosives, some already connected to PIRA's trademark Time Power Units (TPUs). Elated at the result and relieved to have escaped casualties, Blue retired to the base for tea and medals and Green were called in on the hurry up to carry out further searches.

Our first address was a ground-floor council flat in Camden and, pre-warned of potential booby traps, we entered through the kitchen window. A short assault ladder was placed, the window was raked with a 'Hooley bar' – a method of entry tool – and I clambered in with my MP5 at the ready. When I saw a Bobby Sands poster on the kitchen wall next to a Delia Smith book I knew we had the right address. With shouts of 'Armed police!' we cleared the flat, only to find it empty. A warm coffee cup told us that our suspects had only recently left and, strangely, the smashed remains of a portable TV were littered through the flat. My first thought was that a heated argument must have taken place before our suspects had fled but then I looked down at Russ's leg holster and saw a cable and plug wrapped around it. Last through the window, he'd somehow become entangled and had dragged the TV with him. Adrenalin flowing, he'd been completely oblivious.

Within minutes, we were back in our covert van, being led by a surveillance car at break-neck speed through the dark winter streets. The flat's occupants, a man and a woman, had been located and followed to a nearby railway station where they were waiting on a platform. Head to toe in black assault kit, we were ill prepared for surveillance but with confusion on the radio net, we split and made our way to the various platforms. As Russ and I emerged on to ours, we saw the two suspects being confronted by team members on the neighbouring platform. Totally focused on supporting our team mates we jumped down on to the tracks, hopped over the live rails and clambered up on to the other platform.

Back at the base, elated but coming down from the adrenalin high, we debriefed over a cold beer and reflected on the night's activity. Blue had done everything right but had been lucky not to take casualties, but 20 seconds after Russ and I had reached the safety of the platform, a fast train had sped through the station. We all agreed it had been a foolhardy and pointless manoeuvre and logged it under 'lessons learnt'. It was Russ's second mistake of the night but as team leader he dished out the fines but *never* paid them and so I escaped a trip to the cake shop.

SEVENTEEN
TROUBLE IN PARADISE

Against all expectations, Kim and I had managed to stay together for 18 years. There'd been good times, but I was too dedicated to the Job and we'd slowly drifted apart, so despite sleeping under the same roof we were living separate lives. While I considered myself a good dad, I was a useless husband and I'd been cheating on Kim for a while, so I could hardly blame her for seeking solace elsewhere.

One day, I asked her a simple question.

'Can you see us staying together once the kids have grown up?'

Her answer sealed the deal and we immediately started divorce proceedings. While Josey struggled with our decision, blaming herself for Kim and I getting married in the first place, Mark simply shrugged and asked if he could carry on playing football. Days later, Kim drove me over to a teammate's house armed with some newly purchased bedding and a few boxes of meagre possessions. After a tearful goodbye I was a single man. Almost.

As the Met's Christmas party season approached I was determined to party as hard as possible. SO19 would normally rent an East End nightclub, and we had developed quite a reputation for attracting women from all over the Met. But the best bashes, by far, were hosted by the Flying Squad. Despite my determination to stay single, at the first piss-up I attended I met Lyn, a detective on their surveillance teams, and come Boxing Day Mark and I were eating turkey with her and her family. Within months, we'd moved in together.

Lyn couldn't have been more different to Kim, and for a while we were very happy. She was great with Mark and soon became his second mum but I knew I had jumped from one pan straight into another. Soon, I was playing the field again. Lyn knew I wanted my own place, but despite realising it would crush our relationship, she bravely helped me get a mortgage. However, with maintenance and child support commitments to meet, I was still struggling to get a deposit together. Then fate intervened in the shape of a very distant murder.

In October 1994, as part of a small team from 19, I was despatched to the tiny Caribbean island of St Kitts to provide armed protection to detectives from SO1 – the Met's International and Organised Crime branch. Earlier in the year two of them had investigated the mysterious disappearances of the former UN ambassador Dr William Herbert, along with a group of family and friends – who had vanished without trace while out sailing on his yacht. Months later they had returned to investigate the disappearance of the Deputy Prime Minister's son, Vincent Morris, and his girlfriend, Joan Walsh. As if vanishing VIPs weren't enough for a small island, on the morning of the detectives' most recent arrival, their local counterpart and lead investigator, Superintendent Jude Matthew, was gunned down in his jeep as he set off to meet them. International cocaine smuggling was at the heart of the matter; and the prime suspect in the disappearances was local 'businessman', former Jamaican 'Shower Posse' kingpin and DEA informant, Charles 'Little Nut' Miller.

Out of their depth, the two detectives called the Yard for more investigators and armed protection and I arrived in St Kitts to find myself embroiled in a James Patterson thriller, populated with a cast of Colombian drug barons, psychopathic Yardies, FBI, DEA and CIA agents and now Scotland Yard.

Our CID team was too large and their enquiries too widespread for our small team to provide them all with protection, so our first task was to give them an abbreviated firearms course. The normal two-weeks were crammed into a morning on a makeshift range and, with the detectives armed, we became responsible for minding the SIO who, just months short of retirement, sensibly decided not to carry. As we each took it in turns to be his personal protection officer (PPO), the rest of the team put our on copper's heads and bolstered the enquiry team; it was like being back on the crime squad in 1978 but with a gun, sun and palm trees. I loved it.

The island's 50-strong Special Service Unit or SSU were a paramilitary unit, clothed and equipped by the US government as part of a Caribbean-wide anti-narcotics programme. Along with Keith, an old mate from Red team, I took them on the range to build bridges and run them through some training with their Vietnam-era M16s, 40mm grenade launchers and a belt-fed M60 machine gun. Their pistols and revolvers came in a variety of calibres, colours, makes and models – all seized from criminals. Despite our cultural differences we quickly bonded. We trusted the men and women of the SSU to protect us at night while we slept, and far from complain, they took to the task with enthusiasm. Whenever we went back to our hotel rooms after a late night in the bar, amid the deafening sound of tree frogs and crickets I'd hear familiar voices coming from the shadows.

'Good evenin' Scotland Yard.'

Barely visible in the bushes, their teeth and eyes glistening in the dark, would be a pair of camouflaged SSUs armed with M16s. Normally, like vampires, they'd be gone as the first rays of sunlight crept over the horizon; but one morning, while enjoying breakfast outside, the night-duty pair appeared on the veranda. In the early hours, they said, they'd watched a 'Spanish' man apparently spying on our accommodation and signalling with a torch to a boat in the bay. They'd arrested him and he was now in custody at police HQ. Keith and I were sent to question him. The local inspector made available the station's parade room and the handcuffed man was brought in and plonked on a rickety chair. Casually dressed in designer gear, he looked like an extra from *Miami Vice*. His jet-black hair was slicked back into a ponytail revealing his pockmarked olive face. As the inspector sent for a Spanish-speaking officer Keith and I waited, doing a double-take as a chicken strutted through the parade room. Eventually, an overweight female constable arrived and we started our interrogation. Who was he? How had arrived on the island? Why was he spying on us? Whose boat had he signalled? The constable conveyed all of our questions but he just sat there, impassively, with contempt in his eyes.

'Tell him that he can rot in the cells and we'll to speak to him later!' Keith said. She relayed the message in Spanish.

He grunted a reply, looked down and spat on her shoes. Without warning, she picked up a large leather-bound ledger and whacked him on the side of his head with such force that he fell to the floor, where she continued to pummel him. Her inspector watched nonchalantly until finally she stopped and walked out without saying another word.

'Hell hath no fury like a woman scorned,' quipped the inspector before returning the battered prisoner to his cell. Some weeks later, Keith and I walked past his office.

'Scotland Yard, Scotland Yard!'

I heard the inspector's chair scrape as he rushed from behind his desk into the corridor.

'Yes, sir. How can I help you?' I asked.

'The Spanish man? You still want to speak to him?'

I'd completely forgotten about the prisoner. We hadn't arrested him nor completed any paperwork. As far as I was concerned, he wasn't our responsibility. Clearly, the inspector thought otherwise.

'No thanks, sir. I think you can let him go now,' I said, supressing the urge to laugh.

The tiny cells were meant for drunks and other miscreants held pending a visit to the magistrate and weren't equipped for long stayers. I watched as our prisoner was taken through the release procedure. His basic diet had left his now soiled clothing hanging from his gaunt frame; his once arrogant face now looked like a mask of misery as he shuffled out into the bright sunlight past the small crowd of relatives carrying baskets of food to their loved ones.

Nepotism and corruption had left much of the population with a deep mistrust of their police and information about every imaginable crime was bombarding our enquiry office; most was about cocaine. St Kitts seemed awash with the stuff, and while the disappearances of Herbert and Co were undoubtedly connected to drug trafficking, our SIO felt it was distracting the main investigation, so I was ordered to follow up all of the drug-related information and see where it took me. I was given free rein to liaise with the DEA office on the nearby US Virgin Islands and use the SSU if need be. Soon I was getting amazing results, retrieving kilos of high-grade coke.

Eventually, we discovered the bodies of Vincent Morris and Joan Walsh in the boot of a burnt out car in a cane field; both executed by a single bullet to the head. Tension on the island had heightened and as I returned from an inquiry, I saw a glow over the island's capital, Basseterre. As I drove towards the town's centre, its streets became blocked with crowds of excited locals and I shrunk back into the shadows created by my hire car's heavily tinted windows. Hostile faces stared in at me and I drew my pistol from its holster, wedging it under my thigh. Blocked at every turn I was forced to point it at one particularly intimidating mob who tried to force open my doors but, heart pounding, I finally made it back to my hotel to find its residents and the rest of my team barricaded inside. The island's prison had burnt down, all of the prisoners had escaped and the local population were having a celebration carnival.

A Canadian guest at the hotel had been mugged and badly beaten and most of the hotel's other residents seemed to hold us responsible for the state of emergency, but we kept a stiff upper lip as we sat down for supper in the hotel's restaurant, a bagged MP5 at my feet, as if it were all perfectly normal. Within days, all of the prisoners had either surrendered or been recaptured and were transferred to a temporary prison set up in old warehouse. An uneasy peace returned.

Unbelievably, it transpired that 'Little Nut' was also an informant for the RCS back in the UK and his handler, a DS, together with his DI, were dispatched to the Caribbean to see if they could make him talk. When they arrived we were all called to a meeting in the SIO's hotel suite to discuss tactics. Entering the room, I heard an audible groan from a familiar face. The newly arrived DI smiled as he walked over and offered his hand.

'All right, Tone? 'I hope you're not going to cause me as much writing as the last time we worked together!'

Just weeks before departing for the Caribbean, I'd been on a drugs rapid in Woolwich and wound up shooting the suspect's dog – a not uncommon occurrence.

A plan was thrashed out to collect Miller from prison the next day, but we needed a safe location to interview him. Our options were limited so it was decided to bring him back to our hotel. It was a risky plan but the best under the circumstances, so the following day we put it into action.

The pick-up from the prison went like clockwork and, as a dummy convoy made its way to the SSU HQ, the real, smaller one, driven by Keith and myself, slipped away and headed towards the hotel. Miller was whipped into the boss's suite and Keith and I, dressed as tourists with our Glocks concealed in bum bags, took up positions on the coastal approach road.

Miller's nephew, 'Massive', had featured heavily in our enquiries and had been dragged in for questioning several times. He drove one of the small tour buses that collected tourists from the cruise ships. Most were battered old bangers that wouldn't have passed a UK MOT but his, a mark of his criminal connections, was a brand new Toyota with blacked out windows, a custom paint job and wide alloys.

The Toyota rounded the sharp bend and crawled along the narrow road, the sun glinting on its windscreen. I glimpsed him behind the wheel but the tinted windows obscured any passengers. The hairs on my neck stood up. I drew my pistol discreetly, concealing it behind the engine compartment of a parked car. Massive's electric window slowly opened revealing a toothy grin glinting below his tacky sunglasses and, sensing a slight movement in the rear of the vehicle, my grip tightened on my Glock.

'Wha'gwan?' he asked, cheerfully.

'You tell me?' I replied. He bullshitted about wanting some property returned that we'd seized as evidence. It was obvious that he knew his uncle was in the hotel and my sixth sense was in hyperdrive as I noticed him throw a discreet glance into the back of his van. It was enough for me and I whipped up my Glock, pointed it at his face and watched him recoil so quickly that his sunglasses fell off.

'Fuck off now!' I shouted.

'Wha …? You can't …!'

'Fuck off or I'll shoot you right now!'

I watched him fumbling frantically with the gears before the engine screamed and his wide wheels span on the hot tarmac, the van shooting off like a scalded cat. I looked across at Keith, his pistol also drawn and we laughed simultaneously.

'Better tell the boss we're compromised here,' I sniggered.

The SIO wasn't happy. He'd completed his 30 years having deliberately avoided any dealings with guns and thought I should have reasoned with the suspect rather than resort to threats of violence. I took my bollocking but the next day was called to see the island's commissioner for a second pasting. Apparently, Massive had driven straight to police headquarters and filed a complaint.

The commissioner's view of Scotland Yard seemed based on reruns of *Dixon of Dock Green* rather than *The Sweeney* and he seemed saddened that one of its officers would draw a pistol on one of his citizens. I explained that someone had been hiding behind the tinted glass who, given the circumstances, may have been armed. Nevertheless, he said, I should have waited until coming under fire before drawing my weapon. I realised I was wasting my breath.

'If this is an official complaint, sir, am I going to be served with a complaints form?'

'We have no complaints form,' he said, confused by my request. *What a shame,* I thought – *a framed one would have made an interesting talking point in my new flat.*

Christmas was looming and the enquiry wound down to allow us to return home for the holidays. It would start afresh in the New Year but my time was up and, suffering from a mild case of island fever, I was happy to get back to the UK and the normality of SFO operations. My stint away had helped me save up enough for a deposit on a flat though and after 18 years in married quarters I was now a proud property owner. Things were starting to look brighter but a storm cloud that had been hanging over the whole of the Met was getting ready to burst.

EIGHTEEN
DO NOT PASS GO

Following a stint as chief constable of Kent, Paul Condon became the Met's new commissioner in 1993. Our county neighbours hadn't been sad to see him go; their gain was our loss. He'd stamped his 'mark' on their force by introducing a highly unpopular tenure policy before flitting off to the next rung of his career, leaving a trail of disgruntled officers in his wake. The policy meant that officers could only stay on a geographical division or in a specialisation for a set period before being moved to pastures new, but while Kent immediately reversed the damaging policy, Condon introduced it to the Met.

Thousands of perfectly content and diligent officers were being moved against their will, resulting in plummeting morale. Detectives on squads were sent back to divisional CID offices; uniform patrol officers were dispatched to different divisions, wasting all of their hard-earned local knowledge; and officers in specialist units were forced to abandon their skills to return to what was now known as core policing or, in other words, square one.

In 210 BC Petronius Arbiter had written: 'We trained hard but it seemed that every time we were beginning to form up into teams, we would be reorganised. I was to learn later in life that we tend to meet any new situation by reorganising; and a wonderful method it can be for creating the illusion of progress while producing confusion, inefficiency and demoralisation.'

It seemed we'd learnt nothing in the subsequent 2,000 years but I'd always prided myself on being a good copper at heart and the prospect of returning to street duty didn't concern me. What held me back was the thought that if I left for the compulsory 12 months, I wouldn't get back into my chosen profession. Privately, with my divorce recently completed, I was keen to catch up on lost time and, while I still held the responsibilities of parenthood, I longed for the single life. Perhaps it was time to leave my predominantly male enclave and go back to the real world. The quicker I left, I figured, the quicker I'd get back. Most of my severest critics had either retired or moved on and the Wing's new breed of senior officers knew me as a knowledgeable, committed officer who was an asset rather than a liability. I was fairly confident that if I left and did my time I'd get back in but nagging doubts remained.

I noticed Royalty Protection advertising for volunteers. On paper I was thoroughly qualified and I attended a recruitment day at Buckingham Palace where, in the opulence of a huge reception room lined with oil paintings and statues, I sat among the other hopefuls. Most of the women sported Princess Diana hairdos, pearl necklaces and twinsets, while the men wore brown brogues, moleskins and Barbour jackets. The murmur of conversation slowly died as an experienced Royalty Protection sergeant took to the rostrum to speak with enthusiasm about life in Her Majesty's protection team.

'When you find yourself in the finest hotel in Monaco with your Austrian-made Glock concealed under your specially tailored Savile Row suit, it's as near to being James Bond as you can possibly get,' he said.

I rolled my eyes to the huge chandelier. I'd heard enough and headed for the exit.

With the IRA carrying out increasingly spectacular attacks on the mainland, the Met had upped its game and we'd joined forces with the Territorial Support Group (TSG) to conduct high-profile patrols code-named 'Legions'. As the SPG's successor, they attracted like-minded characters. I quickly slotted back into the cut-throat banter of carrier life and arranged a week's attachment to my nearest TSG unit based at Lee Road nick. Walking through the gates of the old red-brick station was like a flashback to 1979 and my time on the P District Support Unit, and only served to remind me of what a retro-grade journey I was embarking upon. I only needed to get away from SO19 for a year, but if I joined the TSG I would have to guarantee them several years' service, and while the crews that I worked with were all sound, I just wasn't feeling the vibe and crossed it off my list.

Back at Old Street, Tom, Green team's new sergeant, sat me down for my annual appraisal. He wasn't his usual gruff self. It was all very positive, in fact, it was positively glowing, but I sensed him building up to some bad news.

Two weeks earlier, Green had been despatched to a domestic siege in Lewisham, where I'd bumped into the division's chief superinten-dent. He'd been a sergeant when I'd left to join the SPG and his rise through the ranks had been swift. We'd always got on and when I explained my predicament he was happy to help.

'I'm desperate for experienced officers, Tony; I'd take you here tomorrow. Give me 100 per cent for 12 months and I won't stand in your way when you want to get back to SO19.'

It would be a step backwards but at least I knew the ground. All the legislation that had come into force since I last performed regular police work would be hard enough to pick up without having to find my way around a strange new division and, after I'd served my stint, there would be nothing holding me back when SO19 called. I pondered my decision for the next fortnight.

Following the attempts to force me out of the unit, I'd been particularly concerned about my hearing. Recent results confirmed that the damage wasn't getting any worse but I still approached every test with trepidation. Unbelievably, a hearing test still wasn't part of our initial selection process and I figured that, if I left before my next one, after a year's grace on division, I could slip back in under the radar and it would be another year or two before the system caught up with me. I bit the bullet and contacted Lewisham's new boss. The ball was now rolling but I'd kept my plans close to my chest.

'Right, you're not going to like this last bit,' Tom said in his thick Belfast accent. 'You're right up at the top of the tenure list. I've discussed this with Andy and he is in agreement. In our opinion, you should show willing and jump before you're pushed.'

He looked up to gauge my response but I stayed poker-faced. I was enjoying this. He slid the report around, pointing at the final paragraph with a stubby finger. I took my time and read it slowly; it was a glowing testimony to my enthusiasm and ability, which finished with a guarantee that once I had completed my penance, both he and our team inspector Andy would highly recommend my return. I looked up from the paper and stared him in the eye.

'Don't let people think you're one of those wankers that's scared of division. You'll be missed but the sooner you go, the quicker you'll be back; you might as well be ahead of the game,' Tom added.

I picked up a pen and signed the bottom of the form. Turning the paper back towards him slowly, I paused for effect.

'You're pushing at an open door, mate. I'm already going back to Lewisham. I'm just waiting for a date.'

Tom gave me a rare smile and the stress disappeared from his face.

'I'll be back!' I said in my best Austrian accent.

NINETEEN
PAPA LIMA (SECOND TOUR)

Although much had changed in 11 years, I soon slid into the routine of police work. My colleagues were constantly telling me, 'We don't do it like that anymore, Tony,' but slowly, I started to get my head around the intricacies of the Police and Criminal Evidence Act (PACE) and other legislation that had changed the job significantly during my absence. Something's never change though and we were still dealing with the same social misfits and oxygen thieves that our moustachioed forbears had dealt with a hundred years before and they were still committing the same crimes against their fellow man.

One of the first things to hit me though was the proliferation of class A drugs. During the seventies, I'd had countless arrests for cannabis but despite my enthusiasm and my arrest rate I'd had one solitary arrest for heroin. Hard drugs may have been more prevalent in other parts of the capital but in semi-inner divisions and the suburbs, they were almost unheard of, but a seemingly insignificant arrest in 1980 would prove to be a tiny portent of things to come. Jock and I'd been punting around in the Area car when we'd seen two toe-rags sitting eating kebabs in a parked Granada. The passenger was a notorious car thief but neither of us recognised the driver and I jumped out, ran to his door and whipped the keys from the ignition.

They were immediately evasive. The car wasn't reported stolen but they were up to something and we searched them, the vehicle and even the greasy slivers of cold meat and warm salad in their discarded kebab rappers. Finally, under the car among the roadside litter I found a matchbox. Inside was a glass phial with the words diamorphine 500mg. The words meant nothing to me. I walked up to the handcuffed driver.

'What is it, mate?' I showed him the phial nestled in the tiny box; he denied all knowledge.

'Yeah? Well I thought you'd say that but I saw you toss it under the car as I approached so it's yours, mate. Get used to it!'

He didn't even bother to protest his innocence and back at the station I repeated my evidence to the charging sergeant who examined the phial carefully.

'What is it?'

'I don't know …'

'Well, lock him up and take it down to casualty.'

The sister loved us. She was married to a sergeant from Bow Street and half her nurses were dating coppers from Ladywell.

'It's heroin,' she replied, matter-of-factly. 'Medical heroin.'

I returned to the station and told the sergeant and his eyebrows raised in grudging respect. By the time we reached the canteen to complete our notes Jock and I were Popeye Doyle and Budd Russo and we'd just cracked the French Connection. So rare was a heroin bust that a round of spontaneous backslapping broke out.

The volume of drugs rapids I'd been on in recent years should have given me an inkling but parachuted back into the real world, the heroin epidemic was a shocking discovery. Skinny, zombie-like creatures with sunken eyes, their skin stretched across their prominent cheekbones, were everywhere. Every petty shoplifter was stealing items in bulk to pay for their daily habit. Every car or house that you searched had the charred remnants of silver foil and blackened spoons and every suspect potentially had syringes in their pockets. The criminals hadn't changed, just their motivation. Now they stole just to get high. Nothing else mattered any more. It was all about the habit.

If the criminals hadn't really changed, neither had the coppers, or had they? I soon began to discover that, older, wiser and more cynical than I'd been as an enthusiastic probationer, I now looked a lot closer at an individual before treating them with respect. The advent of the ARVs had resulted in SO19 being offered regular advanced driving courses and, despite my history, I'd successfully passed mine, earning a class one, the highest standard.

Back on division I was soon posted to the Area car and had been given a young enthusiastic probationer as my operator. After a couple of hours of aimless patrol we dropped into Brockley nick so that he could check his correspondence tray and grab a swift brew. Tea in hand, I stood at the noticeboard checking out the cars for sale, villas for rent and notices for retirement functions.

The fat sergeant sat his coffee down and prodded my stomach.

'Are you that SO19 bloke?' he said with a soft Scottish brogue. 'Bit fat for a ninja aren't you?'

I looked down at the slight bulge of my armour concealed under my uniform shirt and then towards the buttons of his own shirt straining to contain his huge beer gut.

'I'm wearing body armour, Sarge. What's your excuse?'

The rest of the room stifled their laughter. 'Body armour? Och, you don't want to be wearing that, it's dangerous. They proved that in Vietnam, you know.'

'Really?' I replied sarcastically.

'Yes, if a bullet gets trapped between the back of the armour and the front it'll rattle around and destroy all of your internal organs!'

I picked up a toilet roll used for wiping ink from the neighbouring white board and handed it to him and he looked confused.

'Wipe your mouth, Sarge. You're talking shit! You should be encouraging your officers to wear body armour, not telling them bollocks. Come on, Scott. Let's go.'

Subdued laughter swept the room. I put down my mug and walked to the back door.

'Anyway, when I joined the Job,' he blurted, 'my sergeant told me that all I needed was the Queen's uniform. He always said, "See this, Jock? Blue serge, bulletproof!"'

'Blue serge is bulletproof is it?' I snarled. 'Tell that to Pat Dunne's family.'

The nineties had not started well for the Met. PC Dunne had been just one of seven officers killed in knife and gun attacks in the first part of the decade, one less than the NYPD and two more than the LAPD had lost during the same period. The press asked a senior officer if now was the time to consider arming the police.

'A gun wouldn't have saved Pat Dunne,' he replied, which may have been true but as his colleagues searched desperately for his killers perhaps they may have felt less vulnerable had they been armed. The same senior officer was also asked if it was time to issue bulletproof vests.

'Body armour wouldn't have saved him, either,' he said, which wasn't true. As he reached across his chest for his radio mike, the 9mm had penetrated through the home beat officer's arm and into his chest. Had he been wearing a vest, he would undoubtedly have survived.

Fellow officers in the States had even set up a charity that sent their used armour across the pond to their unprotected cousins, but by way of thanks, the Home Office advised officers not to accept it as it hadn't been tested to their exacting standards and wouldn't protect them from knife attacks, something that wasn't totally true either. Presumably, they were happy for officers to remain protected only by blue serge until they eventually got around to issuing them with authorised protection. Cost probably had a lot to do with it but mainly they hated the change of image which would be an admission that Dixon of Dock Green was finally dead.

A few years previously, sufficient sets of body armour had been purchased to go with every revolver held on divisions and while Lewisham had only 12 sets I'd noticed several officers wearing them routinely. Others had bought their own, or had them bought for them by worried love ones. The armour wearers, particularly those that had bought it themselves, had to tolerate the usual piss-taking from their unprotected colleagues as my colleagues and I had done when we'd bought our own handcuffs back in the seventies. Long American-style batons had been issued, and knife and bulletproof armour and CS spray were on the way, but throwing equipment at the problem wouldn't make it disappear; what was needed was a substantial shift in mindset.

Back in the seventies Ted Stowe wouldn't allow women on the Area car, let alone a probationary WPC, but it was Marge's first posting to it and she was my operator for the month; it was going to be a long one. A late joiner and recent addition to the relief, she was in her mid-forties and had waited until her daughter had gone to university before undertaking what she described as her lifelong ambition to become a police officer.

She was a nice person, but the world's full of nice people and the last thing we needed was another one. I'd been unhappy about having her on the Area car with such little service but I'd been overruled and it was our first early turn together. It was only 0630 when she acknowledged a radio request for her to return to the nick to liaise with the CID in the canteen and I manoeuvred the Cavalier back into its parking bay, reclined my seat and closed my eyes while she left on her errand. The night before had been another late one; bachelor life was proving to be exhausting. Seconds later, she was knocking eagerly on my window.

'They want both of us.'

I reluctantly readjusted my seat before following her into the canteen. The counter shutter was still down and the only people present were a small gaggle of plain-clothes officers sat around a corner table, drinking tea. It was the 'proactive team', headed by their young DS.

'All right, Tone?' he said. 'Thanks for helping out. We're just going to spin a gaff and need a couple of uniform along in case it gets fractious.'

Their chairs scraping, his team got up and left for their vehicles, expecting us to follow blindly.

'Whoa, hold on!' I said. 'What's it all about?'

The DS reluctantly told me that they had an arrest warrant and their man was living in a ground-floor room within a bail hostel.

'We really just needed a plonk with us in case there are women or kids in there, but it can't hurt to have a couple of uniform along just in case.'

I would have liked a more thorough briefing but I reluctantly followed him out into the yard. A minute later Marge and I were tail-end Charlie on a four-vehicle convoy for the short hop to the target, a large Victorian red-brick semi. Marge and I tagged along at the rear of the search party, led off by the DS and a big lump lugging an 'Enforcer' battering ram.

At the back of the stick I expected to hear the impact of the Enforcer and the splintering of wood but instead there was a brief but heated discussion and seconds later a fist banging on the door and shouts of 'Police, open up, search warrant!'

Big lump scurried past us *en route* back to the cars, muttering about the glass front door. Moments later, the search party entered the house and as we reached the front door I could see the team in the first room dealing with a tired, bedraggled man in a frayed dressing gown. A few minutes later the DS spoke to us in the hall.

'Thanks for coming. He's as good as gold but it had the potential for being a bit fractious, so it was good to have you along. We're fine now, you might as well leave.'

It was the second time he'd used that word.

'Fractious? Why, what's the story?'

He lowered his voice to a stage whisper. 'Our man is good mates with the main suspect for the Essex Range Rover shootings, so there was always the chance he might have been staying here.'

I couldn't believe what I was hearing. Just a few weeks before, Essex gangsters Tony Tucker, Patrick Tate and Craig Rolfe had been lured to a farm track in Rettendon, Essex, where they had been ambushed and killed. I could barely contain my anger and prodded the DS in the chest before rapping my knuckles on the steel upgrade plate of the body armour hidden under my uniform.

'Just as well one of us is wearing body armour then!' I said, sarcastically.

He shrugged his shoulders and smiled weakly as I turned and stormed off, Marge struggling to keep up. I was angry with myself for not insisting on a more thorough briefing. No one else had been wearing armour and their research clearly hadn't even extended to a proper recce of the premises or they would have realised that an Enforcer wasn't going to work on a double-glazed, alloy-framed door.

'All right, Tone? You off?'

It was the big lump returning with a large, clear plastic property bag containing more bags and rubber gloves. His cheery tone snapped me out of my anger.

'Yeah, all done. Interesting, though; I didn't know that was a bail hostel. I'll keep an eye on it now that I know.'

'Yeah, it's a right little ants' nest. We've got some good info that a couple of Paddies on the top floor are renting out a nine mil pistol as well!'

Knowing an armed, underworld hit man and a 9mm pistol might be in the property, it was bad enough that they hadn't even asked for tactical advice, let alone a firearms team, but failing to brief us of the risks was downright criminal. I got in the car, slammed the door behind me, and as I fiddled with my seat belt, Marge climbed in. 'That was exciting, I enjoyed that!'

I glared at her and her enthusiastic grin morphed into a hurt frown. Kicking down out of anger, my wheels span as I headed away from their Mickey Mouse operation. Sadly, it was just one of many during my brief stay on division where the criminal use of firearms was treated with such a lack of professionalism.

Shortly after returning to ground zero, I bumped into a sergeant in a similar downward career spin. I'd first met him on my brief TSG attachment the year before and like me he had been forced to return to divisional work. Six months on and he'd been asked to take over the proactive team and given the opportunity to handpick his crew and he offered me the position of his APS. While I had enjoyed my stint in uniform, the opportunity to work in plain clothes against targeted criminals was a more attractive prospect.

I wasn't sad to hang up my uniform, never to wear it again. While I'd been busy and made plenty of arrests, I still hadn't got my head around the current custody and interview procedures and I'd allowed those who knew how to navigate the system to do a lot of the work for me. Now I was working with busy, proactive coppers I was concerned that I wouldn't be able to pull my weight but I needn't have worried. Unlike my time on the crime squad back in the seventies, I had nothing to really prove, and knowing that I had my sights set on returning to SO19, my new team seemed happy for me to simply tag along, go witness whenever required, and generally ride on their coattails. Time raced by and before I knew it I was eligible to reapply. I hadn't shown the commitment to police duty that I'd had in the past; I simply no longer had the enthusiasm for it. If I'm honest, I only ever really had one foot back in the real world.

Back at Old Street, tenure was tearing the teams apart and I found myself regularly attending leaving dos in the team bars in the area. Some would follow my path for a short stay back on division while others chose to go to units where they could still make use of their firearms skills. Some of the most talented would go to close protection in Royalty or Special Branch, and while all of them missed the camaraderie, they all went on to establish successful careers. It was no coincidence that the prime minister's team and those protecting dignitaries at the highest risk would become top-heavy with former SO19 operators, whose commitment and talent shone. Some of the more bitter and less dedicated just slid off to the uniform protection branches and waited for retirement. It was as if their morale had been sucked out of them and it was sad to watch.

My career plan had always been to return though, and while my old bosses seemed happy at the prospect of my return, I left nothing to chance, approaching the training team at Lippitts to obtain a study list and find out about the current selection process. Despite having left as an SFO, and one of the department's most experienced instructors, I would need to reapply as an entry-level ARV officer and while I wouldn't be required to go through basic ARV training, I would be expected to attend the one-day assessment for potential applicants. I left nothing to chance, spending hours revising the required legislation and use of force policies that we'd be tested on and upping my personal fitness programme. I wasn't prepared to just pass the assessment, I was determined to excel and when the day finally came, I paraded in the canteen at Lippitts with the rest of the hopefuls. It seemed strange to be back in the familiar surroundings of the old prisoner-of-war camp as a candidate rather than as an assessor, but everyone I knew greeted me warmly.

I found a seat at a table together with four other former members who, like me, had served their time and were aiming to return to the fold. Each one of us was prepared with fresh haircuts, neatly pressed uniforms and highly polished shoes. We were pushed through various stations throughout the day, testing our knowledge of the law, observation skills, statement writing, physical fitness and leadership. One phase was the formal interview by an inspector and two ARV sergeants. They had all joined in my absence, but my file was in front of them and they knew my history. I was politely asked about my time away before they got around to asking the test questions listed on a sheet in front of them.

'A lone gunman, who has already killed a hostage,' began one sergeant, 'comes out of a house armed with a shotgun in his hand but pointed at the floor. You challenge him but he threatens to kill another hostage and then turns to walk back into the building. What would you do?'

'Shoot him,' I answered calmly, almost before the question had left his lips.

All three looked shocked.

'What, you're going to shoot him in the back?' asked the inspector. 'Are there no other conventional methods that you could resort to before opening fire?'

'You've just told me that I've challenged him, sir, so I've told him to drop the gun, he hasn't, and if I don't act immediately he's going to go back inside where we have no control over him and potentially kill another hostage. Yes, I'd shoot him in the back, sir. This isn't cricket.'

They all looked at each other, raised their eyebrows and moved on to the next question. Over 200 candidates had attended over a four-day period and with just a wee bit of help from our assessors, the top four places went to my three colleagues and me. Previous experience in the department wasn't a guarantee of success though and one former instructor and SFO failed after turning up ill-prepared, not realising that no one else realised just how important he thought he was. I'd taken him on his first selection years before. He was a perfectly competent operator but had proved over time to be arrogant and lazy, earning himself the nickname of 'Blister' because he always appeared after all the hard work had finished.

Back at Lewisham, I was on wind down and finally, 14 months after I had left Old Street, I got my date to re-join SO19 and organised a hasty leaving do. The drink flowed, everyone wished me luck, and I slowly drifted into amiable drunkenness. Simon, the least experienced member of the team, slid up to me and asked for a quiet word. An easygoing late joiner, Si was straight out of his probationary period but had good local knowledge and a nose for wrongdoing that was impressive.

'Here, Tony, can I ask you a question?' he slurred, spilling beer from the three bottles he was nursing. 'You've killed people, right?'

I wasn't sure where this was going. I'd worked with him for just under half of my time at Lewisham and, despite sharing numerous pints, my past had never been discussed.

'How do you live with yourself?' he asked.

I looked him in the face while I tried to fathom a response. I couldn't think of one and, turning my back on him, went back to the rest of the group.

The following day as I nursed a hangover, I thought back to Si's question. It had taken six months and who knows how many pints to bring it up, but at least he'd had the courage to ask it. I wondered how many others had been thinking the same.

TWENTY
BACK IN THE FOLD

Back in the fold, retirement seemed a long way off and I was looking forward to another decade in the job that I loved. My first six months were spent on the ARVs, patrolling the streets and responding to armed calls. I was working with good people but my heart was still with SFO work. Nursing a damaged knee sustained during training and recuperating from surgery, I returned to training duties, overseeing SFO selection courses, which had grown from three to nine testing weeks and refresher training. We were still haemorrhaging experienced operators but at least the demanding selection process was providing us with some talented newcomers to fill the void.

I'd enjoyed my short stint back at Lippitts but it was soon time to go back on to ops and I found myself back on Blue. It was a great team and we worked, trained and played hard. The IRA was still very active and there was plenty of crime work to ensure that we were constantly busy but strangely, despite our hostage rescue remit, we'd never been deployed on kidnaps. Historically, detectives from the kidnap squad had conducted them but in 1997 we deployed on our first four. We soon became a key element in all kidnap operations and in only a few years we were executing between 50 and 80 rescues annually. They mainly involved low-level criminals, taken hostage because of a drug debt, but some involved genuine hostages. Either way, they were an opportunity to deploy our whole range of tactics and equipment.

I had written our Close Quarter Combat (CQC) instructors' course and, although I was back doing operations, I was sent to Malmö in Sweden to train their SWAT team in our hostage rescue drills. It was well received and resulted in continuing close ties with Sweden's tactical teams. Word spread and I was soon asked to run similar training for the Garda's Emergency Response Unit (ERU) in Dublin. With the IRA still active, some were concerned about exporting our skills to the Garda but the ERU operators that I came in contact with were sound and as keen to take on the IRA and organised crime as we were.

Back in London, operations carried on at a break-neck speed with one good job merging into another. Drugs were still a major issue, with us targeting crack houses at a local level and supporting Customs and Excise and the South East Regional Crime Squad (SERCS) on large importation operations that, together with counter-terrorist jobs, took us all over the country. Our covert vehicle fleet had grown so that we no longer had to rely on the Flying Squad to drive us and we were becoming more adept at providing support to surveillance teams, lending our backing to a far wider range of squads. Our work with the 'Cuzzies' and SERCS also identified the need to enhance our maritime capability and we worked with our colleagues from Thames division to develop it further.

Most operations could be dealt with by using one team but if short for a specific task, we could always draw on manpower from another team. One job in particular required every operator on the teams and, with the box empty, we even borrowed colleagues from our sister unit in the City of London Police. Operation Le Grande couldn't have been better named and soon became bigger than *Ben-Hur*. Located in the centre of the West End was a small triangle of Victorian buildings ripe for development and a team of Yardie enforcers were conscripted by developers to put the tenants under pressure to leave. When they did, the Yardies moved in, converting the vacant properties into one huge drug den. They'd converted the top floor into a strong room from where they dealt weed through a letter box in a steel-clad door and the ground-floor entrance was manned by armed guards who would vet punters before letting them in. Equipped with two-way radios, they also manned foot patrols, watching for police activity.

Blue had picked up the job and research told us that it was going to be a hard nut to crack. The Yardies always seemed ahead of the game and every time we found weak points in their defences they'd plug the gap. Corruption was suspected and the operation was taken over by a commander from one of the Met's outer districts.

Freddy, one of Blue team's more extrovert officers, went into the club with undercover officers making test purchases and befriending the guards and their pet Rottweiler. Heroin-chic thin and looking like a smackhead, he was perfect for the job and would return to the base to get his head down, eyes red raw and stinking of dope.

Finally we were given the green light and I was to be part of the roof party that would carry out a direct assault on the attic strong room. Throughout the day our 20-man roof team inserted under the noses of the Yardie patrols, settling in for the long wait. Nearer H hour, the time the assault would commence, Henry, another Blue team character, took up position in the alleyway, just feet from the club's entrance. Dressed in rags, his hands and unshaven face smudged with dirt and the flaps down on his winter hat to conceal his earpiece, he sat and begged. The Yardies avoided eye contact with the grubby vagrant and those good Samaritans who stopped to give him money, cigarettes and beer failed to notice the bulk of the Remington shotgun under his old parka. Later still, Capital radio advised drivers to avoid the area due to a broken-down lorry, while inside the back of the broken-down vehicle the main assault party stood waiting for the go.

Eventually the sniper team, inserted hours before, reported that everything was perfect and, on the 'Go', I pushed up the roof hatch, leading my team quietly out on to a metal stairwell and down to the drug den's flat roof. We'd mapped out a replica of the target on Old Street's roof and everyone knew their role. Two officers lay down on the roof while three pairs of abseilers attached their ropes to their human anchor points, and while three of us gathered around a roof hatch preparing to fast rope down into the strong room, the abseilers, lugging their breaching tools, clambered over the edge and down the sloping roof to attack the dormer windows.

As soon as we had radioed that we were in position, Freddy led his deception team to the front door where, together with our smelly, shotgun-bearing vagrant, they overpowered the bouncers and the rest of the main assault team poured out of the lorry, down the alley and into the target.

Back on the roof, we lifted the hatch to reveal a suspended ceiling. One kick and the flimsy tiles fell into the strong room in a cloud of dust and I dropped in a flash bang before following the lead man down the short length of fast rope and into the empty, smoke-filled room. I could hear my colleagues downstairs shouting commands and the screams of the punters over the smashing of glass and the dull thud of the abseilers' enforcers as they struck the concrete blocks that, unbeknownst to us, the Yardies had bricked up the windows with.

With the strong room breached there was no point in smashing through but the abseilers were determined to finish the job. The dealers had abandoned the room as soon as the flash bang exploded. Inside a pair of CCTV monitors showed images of the surrounding streets and rooftops and an abandoned two-way radio lay discarded on the desk next to bags of weed and a large pile of cash. We'd definitely spoilt their day.

Only a few years prior, we could never have mounted such a huge operation and we'd grown to a point where we could no longer operate without some form of logistical support. In my absence Mad Jack McMad, one of the team's more eccentric operators, had been given the new role of ops manager, doing a sterling job managing the vehicle fleet, ensuring that kit was maintained and attending important meetings.

Eventually my time on Blue was up and after another short stint on the training wing helping to run the first dedicated training for the Flying Squad, I was looking forward to my 'back-to-ops course' when I was asked if I would be interested in taking over Jack's job. There was a lot going on that I wanted to be involved with. Lippitts Hill had been slapped with a noise abatement notice and the Met had purchased the old sea-training college at Gravesend to create a purpose-built facility. We'd also outgrown Old Street, identifying another disused East-End nick as a replacement.

Mike, my old nemesis, had left on promotion and returned from division shortly after me. Now the unit's commander, we'd thrashed out our differences and buried the hatchet. He was a complicated individual who often struggled to communicate with his troops but was passionate about the unit. The main driver behind the new training site, he asked me to become involved in its design. Being office-based at Old Street would permit me to be involved with both projects and allow me to further develop our operational capability but still get involved as an operator when jobs like Le Grande came in. I wanted to remain kicking doors for as long as possible, so I thought carefully about the offer, discussing it with my new partner Katharine before finally accepting the job.

Working nine to five from a desk proved more difficult than I'd imagined, but I started to make some real progress. The teams were working flat out and supporting them while working on long-term projects was equally exhausting but when Operation Magician came in, all else was forgotten. The Flying Squad was looking at a team of robbers with a very distinctive MO. Their first job of note had been in February 2000 when they'd attempted to rob a security van in Vauxhall. They'd planned to ram the box with a stolen lorry on to which they had bolted a substantial battering ram, but bad luck came calling and they were forced to abandon their £10,000,000 goal, escaping across the Thames in a speedboat, leaving their signature for future jobs. In July they struck again, this time in Aylesford in Kent, firing shots at unarmed police before escaping, again empty-handed, in a speedboat.

The Squad's Tower Bridge office had a lead and contacted us for tactical advice. The robber's new target was the Millennium Star, a two-inch high, perfectly cut diamond, and 11 other rare blue diamonds on display in the Millennium Dome at Greenwich. The gems, totalling a staggering £350 million, belonged to De Beers, the world-renowned diamond dealers. What the Sweeney didn't know was how they would carry it out or whether they had an insider in De Beers. They believed the diamonds were due to be moved from the Dome, in which case the robbers were likely to hit them in transit, however they were unable to confirm this without the risk of spooking the robbers. It was also possible that they would attempt a direct attack within the Dome; we had a few days to come up with a plan that would cater for either contingency.

The Greenwich peninsular was perfect for a robbery. Easy to seal off, denying police the ability to respond, and perfect for their signature escape over water. Our first stop was the Marine Support Unit at Wapping and Blue team worked with them on a plan to thwart their getaway. If the roads were blocked, we would need 4x4s and trials bikes and I set about tracking down suitable transport, acquiring some unmarked Land Rovers and trials bikes. With no job-trained bikers, phone calls were made and Hendon driving school laid on some emergency training.

Black team took on the landside of the operation collecting the additional fleet but we were still concerned about reaching the robbery site. More calls were made and we secured the use of some military helicopters. I talked myself on to the air option; all big kids like a helicopter ride. Others wandered around the Dome dressed as tourists, taking the opportunity to take their families as cover for reconnaissance, and attendance figures for the ailing attraction doubled overnight.

The day before the robbery was due to take place, I went with Grey team to Woolwich Barracks to meet the helicopter crews and brief them. I was just going into detail when one of the pilots put his hand up. 'Excuse me,' he said in a rather posh voice, 'is this an exercise or is it for real?' He had a point – the whole thing did sound like the plot for a Guy Ritchie movie.

In the wee hours of the following morning, in full ops kit and ready to roll, we regrouped at the barracks and were taken to three Lynx helicopters parked on the parade square. Periodically the engines were turned over, the smell of aviation fuel and the vibration of the airframe combining with adrenalin to churn our stomachs, but the robbers weren't ready and the op was stood down.

By autumn, the intelligence picture was clearer. Surveillance teams followed the main players constantly. A CROP was dug in at the main players' farm in Kent and technical assets provided additional intelligence, helping the Squad to conclude that the target was the vault itself. The gang had stolen a JCB digger, they had their trademark speedboat and were keen to get the job done. In response, our plan balanced the needs for maximum evidence with public safety, and involved covertly inserting and concealing SFOs within the Dome prior to the robbery.

Key to the plan was an area in the basement underneath the central arena and I came up with the idea of building a large hide to conceal the team and its equipment. When the robbery was imminent, they would leave the hide, moving down a tunnel that gave direct access to the entrance of the diamond display. Others, disguised as cleaners, would make their way in advance to the flanks and act as cut-offs. The team needed to insert covertly, remain undetected for up to eight hours and, if necessary, leave without raising suspicion: no mean task. The Met's engineers rose to the occasion and with the cooperation of the Dome's management built the hide using the basement's concrete pillars for support.

We knew from intelligence and the tide state of the Thames when an attempt by the gang was most likely and, in early October, we received a warning order to prepare for insertion. With the helo option binned, I was still determined to be on the ground with a gun in my hand when the job came off and talked my boss into letting me join the cut-off team. In addition to their main role, they were responsible for driving the team to the site and smuggling them in with all their equipment. Their task fitted perfectly with my logistical responsibilities and I sorted out security passes and uniforms allowing us to move about freely inside the Dome. I was convinced that there was a good likelihood that that one or more of the robbers would run with a gun and it would be our responsibility to stop them, so in preparation I took my four-man team down the range to carry out rehearsals in our cleaner's kit. Several hours and hundreds of rounds later we could discard our brooms and the weighted bin bags concealing our MP5s and engage our targets in just seconds.

At midnight we all attended a detailed briefing. It was a multi-agency affair and took several hours but by the end everyone knew their roles, responsibilities and rules of engagement. It would be a daunting task and the sense of quiet excitement was palpable. Finally John Shatford, the SIO, addressed us. We would, in his opinion, get one shot at this. In the event of the robbers calling it off, he wanted the assault team, dressed as tourists, to leave in ones and twos over a protracted period to minimise any chance of compromise. He was happy for those who hadn't had a chance to visit the attraction to use the opportunity to give their eyes a treat and then leave the area using public transport but, and this came with heavy emphasis, without using their warrant cards. He didn't want the staff at North Green-wich tube station to notice any increase in plain-clothes activity.

At 0200 we were cleared to insert and the cut-offs, dressed as cleaners, drove the team across south-east London in the back of a hired lorry. On target, we opened up the roller shutters and one at a time, like a scene from *The Great Escape*, each assaulter, in civvies and carrying his kit in a packing container, jumped out and scurried down to the hide. With the whole team safely hidden we parked up the lorry and joined them. The hide was a hive of silent activity, every one quietly sorting out their kit and their bed space. There was no talking, just hand signals and the occasional whisper. No movement was expected until at least 0800 so the team got their heads down, leaving the cut-offs to stag on.

As day broke and the team stirred, sounds of activity, faint voices and distant music began to penetrate our subterranean lair. Some started to kit up while the older hands held back waiting for more intelligence. Periodically, Mark, the team leader, would take a whispered phone call finishing with a disappointed shake of the head. Three hours later, he put down his mobile for the final time and drew a finger across his throat. Stand down.

It was the signal we were all expecting. No one asked why; the team simply re-packed their kit into their boxes, got back into their civvies and prepared to leave. With quiet efficiency we reversed the insertion procedure and, one at a time, each assaulter left the hide carrying his box, made his way up the stairs to the fire exit door where, after an all clear, he'd handed it to the waiting cut-off and slid off into the Dome to make like a tourist. All Metropolitan Police officers received free transport on London buses and tubes so most had never had to buy a ticket like a regular punter. So in another scene reminiscent of *The Great Escape*, the lobby of North Greenwich tube station was full of escaped SFOs clustered around ticket machines, pretending not to know each other, whispering, 'What zone is Old Street in?'

The robbers' plans relied on the tides, and the demands of the rest of the job had to be met, so we returned to the usual cycle of ops but the subject of conversation always came back to the Dome. We were forced to go through the whole insertion and extraction process several more times without putting our arrest plan into effect, but on 6 November we received a warning order for the following day. On 7 November a main command post, high in Canary Wharf, oversaw 200 officers primed and ready for action. While we remained concealed in our hide and our boat team bobbed on the river, the Met's helicopter sat at Lippitts, its engines turning. Inside the Dome's control room, detectives monitored the CCTV while surveillance units covered the suspects' homes, the stolen JCB and the surrounding area,

At 0930 we were kitted up and ready when the first signs of movement reached us in the basement. The digger was on the move from the yard in Woolwich; everyone's heart rate stepped up a pulse. We had confirmation of the getaway boat making its way to the Dome's pier, and each assaulter's face sported a huge grin. When the JCB breached the attraction's perimeter fence and then the skin of the Dome itself, the team moved quietly towards their start line while myself and the other cleaners made our way to our cut-off positions. On the ground floor of the attraction, the surveillance team put into action a complex plan to ensure that no staff or visitors were in the area but, as we put on our plot caps and drew our MP5s, there were startled gasps from several passers-by and we ushered them away with urgent whispers of 'Armed police! Leave the area!'

My earpiece hissed into life. 'Standby, standby, attack, attack, attack!'

Immediately shouts of 'Armed police!' echoed around the huge Dome and I moved out into the concourse to see the JCB stationary outside the vault, its engine running. I covered as Black team dealt with the driver and another suspect on the ground. Purple smoke from the robbers' smoke grenades drifted to the ceiling in the Dome's still air. Suddenly the distinctive cadence of a nine-bang Nico stun grenade boomed around the attraction as we entered the diamond vault with more shouts of 'Armed police!' It was all over in minutes. The forlorn-looking robbers all wore gas masks and body armour and were equipped with two-way radios and earpieces. Inside the vault they had used an industrial nail gun and a sledgehammer to breach the exhibits' supposedly impenetrable bulletproof glass. Not knowing that the priceless gems had already been replaced by paste replicas, they thought they'd been just seconds from reaching their goal.

Out on the Thames, Blue had swooped on the getaway coxswain in his speedboat and, north of the Thames, the Flying Squad rounded up a sixth member in the gang's stolen getaway van.

It had been a faultless clean sweep and the next day it dominated the headlines. Praise was poured on the Sweeney by the press and the Yard, and rightly so, but together with SO11 surveillance, Thames division and the air support unit, we received barely a mention. None of us really cared, we weren't in it for the praise and despite huge advances in experience and capability, none of us were under any illusion that, in the eyes of the Yard, we were still regarded as anything other than the unacceptable face of policing and we quietly cracked on.

Back behind my desk, I found myself overseeing the move to our new operational base and attending regular site meetings down at Gravesend. With a completely new command staff in place I seemed to have put my past completely behind me and become a highly trusted, senior PC. With retirement just a few years away and with my tenure in the ops office over, I returned to Grey team under the command of Ian, an eccentric Jock with a shock of white hair. Graham, another old hand and one of the original Level 2 team members, was already his number two and I was quite happy to take a back seat and simply be one of the team.

The Good Friday Agreement had come into place in 1998 and we had turned our attention from terrorism towards supporting the newly created Operation Trident, set up to deal with the upsurge of black on black gun crime, and although we had done several jobs connected to Islamic fundamentalism, none had dealt with direct threats to the UK. We had all now been trained to respond to potential biological threats, now referred to as CBRN, or Chemical, Biological, Radio Active and Nuclear, but the reality of the threat hadn't really hit home until 9/11. Katharine and I had been in a bar in Cyprus when we saw it unfolding on TV and, like the rest of the world, realised that life, as we knew it, had changed forever.

Within the unit it was obvious that our tactics would have to adapt to deal with an enemy that wasn't interested in giving 20-minute warnings or spending days in negotiation, and a small team were sent to the States to participate in the Federal Air Marshal course, bringing back tactics and ideas used to create our own Aircraft Protection Officers' course. APOs were a contingency in case the US decided to refuse access to international flights without them and, while we threw ourselves into the training, few of us thought we would ever be deployed. Months later, six of us found ourselves sitting in an Irish bar in Times Square.

'Who here ever thought that one day they'd find themselves being paid overtime to sit in a bar in New York?' said Ali, one of only three women ever to have successfully passed SFO selection. We all raised our glasses to the war on terror.

Back in the UK, under the code name of Operation Kratos, we set about developing our tactics for dealing with suicide bombers on foot and in vehicles. Teams were sent on fact-finding trips to Israel and our sister units in Europe; the snipers upped their game and the offroad bike tactic, dabbled with during the Dome operation, was revisited as a means of getting a team rapidly through the capitals gridlocked streets and our covert vehicle fleet had become the largest in the Met. Our explosive entry capability (EMOE) was being progressed and there was more cross training with our colleagues from both Special Branch and the SO11 surveillance teams; liaison and exercises with our colleagues in Special Forces were stepped up; all of which had to be balanced with our daily war on armed crime. A war where enemy lines were drawing closer every day.

TWENTY-ONE
ECHO SEVEN

Operation Tayport was a random name selected by a Scotland Yard computer programmed to supply random names for all its operations. A system designed to avoid inappropriate names like 'Operation Money-Spinner' being picked by its bored officers.

The operation had commenced the day before with a 0600 parade. I was 100 days from my 30 years and, I hoped, a seamless transition to civilian life. After a short tactical briefing by Phil, our new team leader and Ian's replacement, we drew our weapons from the armoury, kitted our cars and made our way to Albany Street nick for a fuller brief from the Silver commander for the operation, a DI from the 'projects' team, a secretive squad dealing with, among other things, contract killings.

It was just like any other job; nothing more, nothing less. We were shown two A4 sheets with 12 photos, all mugshots of predominantly young black males with a couple of white Europeans and at least one Hispanic thrown in. They were all part of a gang of drug dealers, some of whom planned to rob some rival Colombians of several kilos of cocaine. Their victims lived in a flat somewhere close to Edgware General Hospital, the exact location unknown. They'd done business with the Colombians before, felt they'd be easy to rob and had arranged a meet later for a further buy but were still attempting to get firearms for the robbery. It was obvious that the Colombians were marked for death. In the world's league of violent drug dealers, they're right up in the premier division, and if they know who you are, you don't go and rob them without leaving them dead, not unless you want to end up wearing your tongue as a necktie.

We kitted up and deployed in support of the surveillance operation designed to identify the participants and locate the guns. Our role was to intervene prior to the robbery if at all possible. With a typical British sense of fair play we had a duty of care to both robbers and drug dealers alike and it would be a balancing act between their safety, that of the public and the acquisition of sufficient evidence to prosecute. As usual, we'd come a poor fourth.

Lars, a senior officer from the Sweden's counter terrorist team, was with us. With a crime level much lower than ours and terrorism an even rarer event, his two-week attachment was part of an on-going arrangement where their senior commanders would come out with us to gain valuable operational experience. Even with his liberal Scandinavian head on, he struggled with our interpretation of the European human rights legislation that governed us both. It was his last day with us and he was picking up his wife from Heathrow later for a romantic long weekend before returning home.

I was driving Bravo for the day with Smudge, a gobby ex-Para as my front-seat radio operator. After a long frustrating day we were eventually stood down. The bad guys couldn't get their act together. Unable to source firearms in time and after several phone calls, their victims, uncomfortable about meeting at night and growing impatient, postponed the deal until the following day. Lars hung around until the eleventh hour hoping for some action but, with a bit of help from the team, arrived at Heathrow on blues and twos in time to collect his wife. The day wasn't wasted though and with improved intelligence we now knew that the bad guys had access to fully automatic weapons. With the intelligence shaping up we reviewed our tactics for the following day.

The next morning we paraded early again. Phil had sourced another three lads to man a fourth gunship, call sign Delta. They were all from Black and included Stevie, an old teammate from the nineties. Smudge and I were back on Bravo with another Steve, an ex-marine and newcomer from Green. I hadn't worked with him before but we'd socialised together and I knew his reputation for being a 'hoofing' Elvis impersonator and solid operator. As the visitor, he took up the rear-seat position and was additionally armed with a shortened, breaching shotgun loaded with 'Hatton' breaching rounds for deflating tyres. Smudge was now driving with me as his operator.

Vehicle tactics were laid down and well-practised. They relied on flexibility as they depended totally on the actions of the suspects but if things went right, Bravo would end up as the side-blocking vehicle and the front-seat passenger would often end up extremely close to the suspects and vulnerable to hostile fire. My team knew that I was particularly hot on having static cover, but with so many visitors, I raised the subject again as a reminder.

The principle of having at least one team member static, covering while the remaining elements move, is a fundamental tactical principle and one that we always tried to observe. We all agreed that, if it came to a vehicle intervention, I would remain in the front passenger seat covering until the rest of the team were on foot and had eyes on the suspects, and my thoughts drifted back to July 1987 and my role on Operation Kincraig. Phil decided that with the suspects' potential firepower, each vehicle would have a H&K G36, a compact 5.56mm assault rifle, on board. I'd be carrying the one in Bravo.

In the team's underground car park we experimented with placing a small ballistic shield between my seat and the door but it proved impractical. Instead, I placed my ballistic helmet in the footwell and I'd try to don it immediately the hit was called. It was the sort of sound tactical thinking that had become our trademark. Every armed operation holds a potential risk and its own unique problems and we took pride in planning for them and resolving them beforehand, which is why we rarely came under fire and why we rarely had to fire our own weapons.

The previous day's activity had identified a SW6 address and so, following Silver's briefing at Albany Street, we moved to Fulham nick, immediately falling into the sit-and-wait routine we were all so used to. Some gathered in groups exchanging the latest news, interlaced with the usual stories of funnies and fuck-ups, while others sat in the cars and read or caught up on well-deserved sleep, but the surveillance net was always monitored. Our initial briefing would have been enough to keep less experienced teams fully equipped and on the edge of their seats but we'd all been here before. The potential victims were miles away; if the intelligence started to come together, then would be the time to kit up. Any fool can be uncomfortable.

The only vehicle not relaxed was the control ship. Silver, his DS, Phil and Mad Jack, his driver, remained alert listening to the surveillance chatter and taking and making calls to obtain the best intelligence picture they could muster. Periodically Phil would gather us round and update us, ensuring we were always at a suitable state of readiness.

Hours later and with a lull in surveillance, a couple of us sought permission to walk to the nearby supermarket for some food. We kitted up just in case the situation changed and I was in the queue to pay when my peanut crackled with the muffled information that three of our suspects were on the move. I made my way quickly back to a scene of calm activity. Those that had been monitoring the comms were updating the other lads, pointing at the suspects' location on the pages of police geographias while those listening buttoned their shirts over covert armour, radios and weapons. Soon each gunship was complete, their crews switched on to the task and waiting for the order to move. The radio hissed and Phil told Graham, Alpha's commander, to lead off.

The gates slid open and we forced our way out into the afternoon traffic, cutting up other vehicles to stay in convoy. The surveillance team were wrapped around the silver, five-door, VW Golf and its three black, male occupants, heading north through Shepherd's Bush, and we pushed aggressively through the city streets without the benefit of blues and twos, trying to remain as covert as possible while staying within striking distance of our surveillance colleagues. If the suspects were spooked, the lightly armed watchers would be heavily out-gunned.

The Golf stopped in a busy street in Harlesden and all three of our suspects were out on foot in the vicinity. The location was a known hub of criminal activity connected specifically to our gang. Alpha led us into a private car park. No permission was sought, we just split up, wheels crunching over the uneven gravel surface, and found ourselves spaces among the other vehicles where we could sit and listen. Harlesden was a hard place for predominately white surveillance teams to operate in and, unbeknown to us, one of the Met's best-kept secrets, a covert airborne surveillance platform, had been called in to silently watch the three young men as they made their final preparations for the robbery.

Phil tapped on Smudge's window. He was visiting each of the four gunships in turn. I leant across to listen. The intelligence was compelling, he informed us. The suspects had two weapons, probably

MAC 10s, and were awaiting the delivery of a third. We would soon be putting in an intervention on heavily armed suspects who were prepared to commit robbery and probably murder. We needed to be on our game and deal with them robustly.

The MAC 10 was the criminal's current weapon of choice. A back-street armourer had acquired a load of deactivated ones, reactivating them and then flooding the criminal market. Many had been used, particularly in Trident shootings, and taking them out of circulation was a priority. It's a crude but deadly weapon and with a cyclic rate of 1,100 rounds a minute, will empty its 32-round box magazine in under two seconds. A half-second burst will release nine 9mm rounds down range. In the hands of an amateur, it's a lead 'super soaker'.

Soon after, a meet was witnessed in a side street and a bag changed hands. They had their third gun. 'We've got two big Macs and a little one,' they were overheard boasting. They were ready to go and while we studied our maps trying to second-guess their most likely route to Edgware, they made their way back to their vehicle and the bag was placed into the back while they stopped, socialising with associates on the pavement.

The rear-seat passenger was now described as wearing a three-quarter length coat. It was a warm spring afternoon, why would he be wearing that? We asked each other: was it to conceal something bigger than a handgun? I made a note to pay him particular attention. He was the one with immediate access to the bag and the one most likely to have a weapon in his hand or under his coat when we put in the stop.

Suddenly they were off, followed closely by the surveillance team. We were still at state green. Silver needed to authorise the move to amber before we could start progressing through the surveillance caravan, positioning ourselves for the strike. Only then would we be given red and, before that, Silver would have to be satisfied that all the evidence was in place for a successful prosecution. All of that was beyond our worry factor. They've got the guns; we needed to hit them as soon as possible: give us Amber and let's start making some ground! Second in the train, Smudge steered our ageing Omega expertly through the late-afternoon traffic, keeping pace with Paul, Alpha's driver. Behind us were two more gunships and the control; 14 SFOs, all sharing the same thoughts.

After 30 years in the Met, I considered myself a Londoner, but I was north of the river and well off my patch. I scanned the pages of the well-thumbed geographia while Smudge called out street names and key features for me to pinpoint with my finger. Self-adhesive stickies helped me keep track of our position and that of the suspects. I looked up briefly scanning the horizon for a reference point. I saw the three tower blocks of Hendon Police College away to my left and finally figured where I was.

'State amber, state amber!'

At last Phil's voice came over the net and the team was unleashed. The pace picked up and one at a time the surveillance team pulled in to let us pass, gradually leaving us with just the eyeball and members of the public to overtake as we surged towards our goal. We were on the A1: a fast dual carriageway heading towards Edgware. It was great for making progress through the afternoon traffic but too dangerous for a stop. Time was running out!

'Lane one of three, brake lights, nearside indication and into the RA, the first, the first, Mill Hill Broadway, Mill Hill Broadway.' The surveillance eyeball indicated a sudden change of direction. Moments later, Alpha turned left at the same roundabout. We were on top of them!

'Eyeball permission, Trojan Alpha,' came Graham's calm voice.

'Go!' replied the eyeball.

'We have vision, two for cover, over.'

Immediately, Phil's voice came over the set. I imagined the tense atmosphere in the control vehicle. 'All units, state red, state red!'

Silver had given the go! The eyeball indicated left, pulling into the kerb and leaving one private vehicle between Alpha and our target. In giving red, Phil had passed temporary control over to Graham, his 2IC. At the back Phil would now have the least situational awareness of all of us and he'd have to trust Graham's judgement to call the strike at the optimum location. Graham was a seasoned professional with nearly 20 years' experience on the teams, so we were in safe hands.

'Trojan has it, entering the RA not one … the second, the second, Hale Lane, Hale Lane.'

Graham's voice was calm and controlled. The die was cast. The only other civilian vehicle ahead of us had taken the first exit at the round-about and now Alpha was right behind the target vehicle. I caught glimpses of it and its occupants as it negotiated the gentle bends and undulations in the winding residential street. It was an A road but comparatively quiet and the traffic flowed freely. I caught sight of the driver's eyes looking back in the mirror and the rear-seat passenger glancing over his shoulder. Surely we were burnt? Four high-performance saloons with three heavyset white guys in each. Why were they looking round if they weren't unhappy about us? The element of surprise is crucial to hard stops; without it the bad guys have time to create a hasty plan, arm themselves and take the advantage.

Time and distance were running out, Hale Lane led directly to Edgware. We needed to do it now before it was too late.

'If suitable we're looking to do it at the roundabout if he stops,' Graham's voice came over the radio, then almost immediately … 'Attack, attack!'

The G36 was already on my lap. My fingers tightened on the pistol grip and my thumb felt the resistance of the safety catch. I watched as Alpha commenced its overtake. My driver, Smudge, throttled it to close the gap on the accelerating lead vehicle and our target, the Golf, and its three edgy occupants. My eyes locked on to the rear passenger; he was in the nearside seat and unusually animated. I now had no doubt we were burnt. I sensed the atmosphere in the VW and imagined a heated discussion between the three men. I could taste the iron tang of blood. Adrenalin surged through my body.

Our car closed in rapidly. I wound down my window and felt the fresh breeze hit my face as I flipped on my Kevlar helmet. No time to worry with straps. I shouldered my weapon, instinctively brushing the safety to fire, my finger hovering beside the trigger guard. I was oblivious to anything other than that rear-seat passenger.

We were close now, just yards away. His hands were on the front seats and he was leaning forward as if he was bracing himself. Suddenly he pushed himself backwards and twisted to look over his left shoulder, then spun to look over his right. He seemed to look straight through me, oblivious to my presence.

Abruptly he threw himself down across the back seat. I was really close now, so close that if his window wasn't up I felt I could have reached out and touched the top of his head. Was he trying to hide or was he reaching for a gun? Just as quickly, he was up again, his shoulders hunched, his hands out of sight below the window of the rear passenger door.

He was armed, I was certain of it! He'd picked up the heavy, box-like, MAC 10 and was readying himself to fire. I held my breath as I aligned my iron sights on his centre mass, my finger curled around the trigger. No more time. I was going to have to shoot him and I was going to have to do it now. At any second my colleagues would be on foot and vulnerable, not only to the murderous rate of fire of the MAC 10 but also to my shots. Our car was alongside . No time to shout a warning! The rear half of the back passenger window shattered as the 65-grain soft points exploded from the stubby barrel of my Heckler & Koch.

I felt the slight recoil of each shot but despite its vicious muzzle blast I heard nothing. I fired again and again and again. Just like a recurring nightmare that I have, my weapon was as quiet as an airgun, and while I was sure I must have been hitting, I saw nothing to confirm it. I watched my iron sights bounce over the dark figure framed by the crystallised halo of glass until suddenly he was gone, obscured behind the remains of the rear window. I thought my vehicle had moved forward and I pushed myself back in the seat. He was still there, still a threat! I fired twice more and he pitched towards me across the back seat. Target down! I was in condition red, autopilot, back on the range and instinctively following drills. I needed to get out of my static position, NOW! I flipped off my lid and applied my weapon's safety. Smudge had already deployed, so I scrambled across his seat, debussing away from the threat.

My spare hand felt the warm, rough tarmac: stay low! Delta was abandoned alongside us and I moved between our two vehicles, emerging at a crouch with my weapon shouldered. Looking through my sights and safety back on fire, I closed on the rear of the Golf. Everyone was on task. Steve was by the rear wheel, breaching shotgun in hand. Others were dealing with the other occupants, aggressive commands filled the air. Was he still a threat? I tried to scan the rear of the vehicle through the hatchback window but all I could see was the sky and the face of a worried stranger. I drove my flash suppressor through the glass, watching my face disintegrate as I raked out the remains. Still nothing. The rear parcel shelf obscured the back seat and the interior was dark. I rolled around the rear nearside corner of the Golf and my eyes met Graham's. He was covering the shattered window of the rear passenger door; I thought he must have fired, too. He nodded at the door and I covered as he reached for the handle and pulled it open. I could barely make out the figure slumped across the back seat.

Graham reached in, grabbed his clothing and pulled him upright and I saw the vicious gunshot wounds to his scalp, the white of his skull and the grey matter beneath. His head lolled and blood and brain matter sprayed on to Graham's trousers. Graham's eyes asked me if this was my work. He knew the answer. Just like at Northolt and Plumstead, I felt the need to keep busy and returned to the Omega. Its front wing was in contact with the driver's door of the small hatchback and Smudge and Paul were on the bonnet, struggling to secure the driver.

'TL, move the motor!' Smudge ordered.

Clambering into the driver's seat I double-checked my safety and threw the G36 on to the front passenger seat. Reaching down I altered the seat, adjusted for Smudge's stubby legs and as I did so I saw several spent cases on the dash, a stark reminder of what I'd just had to do. I backed the car up a few yards, whacked it into park, clambered out and called Smudge.

'My G36 is on my seat.'

Smudge looked at me as if to say, 'Why are you telling me? Can't you see I'm busy?'

I was on my own again. Everyone seemed to have something to do. *I've done enough*, I thought. I looked for Phil. His back was to me and he was shouting orders. I looked to the rear of the scene and for the first time saw that there was a pub within yards of us. A detective wearing a yellow recognition cap was standing by the door trying to keep the curious drinkers inside. I suddenly realised that, since ditching my lid, I wasn't identified as police. I was wearing a torn and baggy T-shirt over my covert armour and my plot cap was folded into the cargo pocket of my paint-splattered combats. I considered putting it on but the moment had passed. No one needed to know who I was now, better to stay anonymous. I walked over to near the door of the pub and winked at the detective, his face discreetly acknowledging recognition.

'What's happening, mate?'

I looked past the detective to the source of the question. A tattooed skinhead in an England shirt looked at me in anticipation. His mates crowded behind him, equally curious.

'I dunno, mate. I think the Old Bill have just shot someone.' Dressed like a builder, I figured I should speak like one.

'The Old Bill have shot someone!' The skinhead shouted back into the pub.

A huge cheer went up from within and I turned and walked away. Looking back at the scene I caught Phil's eye. He walked towards me, his mouth beginning to form the question. I beat him to it.

'The rear-seat passenger was going for a gun. I saw him reach down for it and come back up. I had to shoot.'

He looked worried as if that wasn't the answer he'd wanted to hear. 'Okay, did you see the gun?'

'No, his hands were below the level of the door but he had a gun, trust me,' I replied, confidently.

It had been a shot in the dark, literally. Everything about his body language had told me that that was what had happened but, like all those years before at the abattoir, I was on my own. I'd tried to look on the back seat as Graham had reached in but the body was in the way. I hadn't seen a gun and I was starting to doubt myself. Déjà vu.

'All right, mate, well done. Go and sit in the control ship. What weapon did you use?'

'My G36. It's on the passenger seat of Bravo. Smudge is aware of it.'

'How many rounds? Do you know?'

I was pretty sure it was seven or eight but I couldn't be certain. 'No … enough to do the job.'

Phil returned to the chaos, leaving me to take the short, lonely walk back to the Ford people carrier parked about 20 yards behind the Charlie car. I clambered in and slumped down with my head back and stared up at the roof. A feeling of overwhelming tiredness swept over me. I looked ahead at the mass of activity. The three suspects were all lying down on the pavement in a row and the team were kneeling around them carrying out first aid and searching and securing them.

Because of the angle, for one awful moment, I thought that I might have hit the other two suspects as well, or perhaps they'd caught some frag from my rounds or secondary projectiles like flying glass or metal but almost immediately they were unceremoniously scooped up and led away, their faces etched with shock, and I sighed with relief. Four or five of the lads were still working furiously to try and keep the wounded suspect alive and the contents of one of the teams' large med packs were spread out around them on the pavement.

A surveillance officer in a bright yellow plot cap stood overseeing the scene. We'd both been on the SPG together. It seemed a lifetime ago. I'd only spoken to him on a job a week or so previously and knew that, like me, he was due for retirement. He was capturing everything on his video camera. We had nothing to hide and it was important that whatever we did at the scene was seen to be transparent. From prior experience we all knew that, in the months and years to come, clever, overpaid lawyers would argue over what had just happened, twist our words, allege malpractice and corruption and tell us how we should have done it. Hindsight is the only precise science.

Silver came up to the open door of the control vehicle. I'd watched him talking to Phil moments earlier. 'You all right, Tony? What happened?'

'I didn't have a choice, Boss. I saw him duck down and come up suddenly. I'm sure he'd picked up a gun and was preparing to fire it.'

'You all right, though?' I nodded, unsurely. 'Don't worry. You did the right thing.'

Phil returned with Paul, tasking him to keep me company. I was happier on my own. I'd taken Paul on his SFO course five years earlier. He was a sound operator and a good friend, but a shit counsellor. I closed my eyes.

'TL, there's a pistol on the back seat, mate. Right where he was sitting!'

I opened my eyes to see JC and Stevie, grinning.

'What is it?' I asked.

'Not sure … a black SLP,' JC replied. 'Well done mate!'

It was like the effect of Taff's words on that hot summer day in 1987: I was overcome with relief. There was a gun; I knew it! I knew it! It was a self-loading pistol, a semi-auto not a full-auto MAC10, but it'd do.

'Any others?' I asked eagerly.

'Don't know yet. The bag's in the back as well so hopefully the info was right and there's a couple more.'

Despite the seriousness of the situation, I could feel my facial muscles forcing me to grin in relief. I knew I'd been right. It had been the most difficult decision of my career. When you're confronted with a psychopath stabbing a four-year-old girl, or three heavily armed robbers in balaclavas threatening a security guard, its gold standard, it doesn't get any better. But when all you've got to go on is intelligence and body language, that's a massive leap of faith.

I threw my head back against the headrest, punched the seat and felt the stress drain away. The lads went back to work, leaving Paul and me in silence. Local uniform, an ambulance and Uncle Tom Cobley and all had arrived at the scene. Incident tape was up and traffic was getting diverted around the location. If we stayed much longer 'T-Pot one', the Met's mobile canteen, and the press would be arriving. Phil and Silver returned to the car.

'Tony, he's dead mate,' said Phil. It was no surprise, I'd seen the head wounds. I felt numb. 'You know about the pistol on the back seat, don't you?'

'Well done, mate, well done!' added Silver. 'I reckon the other shooters are in the bag in the back, but it's not our scene any more. We'll have to leave it to the DPS.'

The DPS, or Directorate of Professional Standards, was the Yard's internal affairs department. I was now under investigation.

Time slowed down. I felt helpless. I just wanted to leave, to get away, back to the base, anywhere but here, but there was nothing I could do but sit, wait and try to catch some shallow sleep. After the arrival of the ambulance, any attempts to resuscitate the suspect had ceased and now his lifeless, broken body lay underneath a bright red ambulance blanket next to discarded field-dressing wrappers, tuff-cut scissors and an abandoned oxygen bottle. A life wasted through reckless, selfish, greed; I was starting to feel angry. Angry at a nameless corpse going cold in a suburban London street. The body of a young, stupid gangster who had forced me into killing, again. I knew that my life was about to go on hold yet again but I had no idea for just how long!

The four gunships, the used med kit and anything else relevant to the incident would have to remain at the scene for evidential reasons. Replacement transport was being brought to our location to get the team back to base and Phil was briefing the late-turn ARV duty officer who had now arrived. It was important that she had all the relevant information to brief the SIO and other senior officers before we were able to leave the scene. A thorough handover was critical. Too many successful operations became flawed, not by the actions of the team but by lazy or incompetent senior officers and civil staff that arrive afterwards. Misinformation and speculation were always the consequence and the team would be the inevitable victims.

I would be travelling back in the control ship and I knew that we would be the last to leave. Eventually, Phil returned to the car and we slipped away from the scene like thieves in the night. Jack pointed the bonnet of the control ship east and by the time we'd reached the A1, I was sound asleep, waking up with a jolt as the back gates of the base slid open. We had several hours of post-incident procedure ahead of us before we'd be allowed home and I was grateful for the sleep. I scooped up my kit and made my way through the security doors to the stairwell. Ryan, a relatively new ARV lad, was fixing the chain on his bike in the lift lobby.

'I can't wait to read the last chapter of your book, Tony,' he said with a smile.

I barely knew him. Phil had been careful to use our anonymity codes set aside for incidents such as this. The base should have only known me by a single letter and a number. So much for anonymity! The lift doors closed.

'How the ...?' My colleagues shook their heads in disbelief.

Stepping out of the lift on the third floor my phone rang. The screen read Lyn. I hadn't spoken to her for several years, since she'd retired from the job and moved up north. What could she want at this time of night?

'Hi, stranger,' I said. 'How are you doing?'

'More to the point,' she replied, 'how are you? A little bird tells me that that you've been involved in something. Everything okay?'

'Yeah, good, thanks. Listen, I'm going to have to go … statements to write and all that. Thanks for calling. Keep in touch, yeah?'

'You know where I am if you want to talk. Take care.' And she was gone.

'Unbefuckinlievable!' I sighed. I was incredibly grateful for her concern but how the …? So much for operational security. If an ARV officer and an ex already knew I was the shooter, it was guaranteed the press did as well. I was too knackered to be angry. *Let's get this over with and get home*, I thought as I headed for the crew room. Waiting with his arms outstretched stood Phil Manns, our ops superintendent and the lead on post-incident procedure or PIP as it had become known. He gave me a big man-hug.

'Well done, Tony. Are you all right?' he asked, with a slight slur.

I caught a whiff of booze. He was off duty and had been attending a social function when the reserve officer had mistakenly called him in. There was always an on-call PIM or post-incident manager available out of hours but he wasn't it. The actual PIM, an ineffectual chief inspector who rode a nine-to-five desk, stood watching our exchange with an uncomfortable look on his face. I was glad to see Phil Manns. He wasn't really pissed and he was one of the good guys. It was a mark of his concern that he'd left his function to come in and give his support, but I hoped that he would thin out before the DPS arrived or at least have a strong coffee and suck a mint.

Phil, my team leader, took me into the boss's office and shut the door; he looked serious. 'Mate, Stevie captured the whole thing on video from the Delta car,' he said gravely. 'I didn't know that he was filming but it's done. I've decided that we'll hand it to the DPS unseen. We've done nothing wrong and I'm sure the footage will support that, but you need to know that it may have captured your actions.'

As an experienced instructor I knew that in a life-threatening situation an individual's recollection might not match that of a video recording. Unlike a camera's memory card, the human brain will automatically wipe footage that it considers irrelevant and will later fill in the gaps to make sense of a situation. On the other hand, a camera's lens sees only what is in its limited field of vision, whereas the human eye can move rapidly and pick up on things that the camera can miss, but the biggest problem is 'hindsight bias'. With video to play with, a critic can replay it, freeze-frame it, and advance it frame by frame in comfort and safety forgetting that the shooter didn't have that luxury and had to make a split-second decision in real time acting on perception and instinct.

'Why was he filming?' I asked.

'Fuck knows. Apparently we've got no current footage of hard stops to show during MAST training. He had all the best intentions but it doesn't alter the fact that it exists and we'll just have to live with it.'

He was right, of course, and I was confident I'd done the right thing.

Detectives and surveillance officers were also arriving and there was the satisfied buzz that came from a job well done. We'd mounted a successful operation resulting in the disruption of a crime, recovery of firearms and the arrest of two men. No one gloated over the death of the third but no one seemed to care either. Summoned to the main office, most of the team sat around the large coffee table while the detectives grabbed seats or stood, like me, at the back of the room. Silver spoke, thanking us for our hard work.

'Our task was to prevent a robbery, and that's exactly what we have done. Unfortunately one of them decided not to play ball and he's paid the ultimate price but that was his decision, not ours. We have done nothing wrong.

'Ninety-nine per cent of the time we achieve our aim without having to resort to shooting but today was one of those one-percenters and it is exactly why we need the SO19 lads with us. It's been a long day and we are all tired but we still have our notes to do and we need to make sure we get them absolutely right.

'We all know that it is minor, genuine mistakes that counsel will pick up on and use to discredit us. The most important person in this room is Tony. We owe it to him to ensure that we make no silly mistakes at this late stage of the day. Likewise, we must make sure that his name doesn't leave this room.'

A few faces turned towards me, and one or two gave me a subtle wink or a guarded smile. The surveillance officer standing to my right tilted her head towards me and whispered from the corner of her mouth, 'Which one is he?'

I smiled as a colleague whispered in her ear. She immediately blushed.

'I'm really sorry,' she murmured, burying her face in her hands.

Graham stood next to a white board, felt pen in his hand and as the loggist ran through the time line, street names, vehicle index numbers and the other basic details, he logged them on the board and we found a spare writing surface and, in our own words, put pen to paper.

It was a duty statement, a brief summary of the facts to satisfy the SIO before we could be released home. The policy, based on expert medical and legal advice, allowed 48-hours to relax and adjust to normality before completing a full evidential statement. After a traumatic incident, the brain needs time to comprehend the jumble of memories and attempting one earlier could result in mistakes and omissions. I wrote:

0630 3rd floor HD tac brief by PS / E1. Posted to B together with E6 (driver) and E8 (rear seat) 0800 attended main brief by silver at Albany St Pol Stn. 0810 Reminders, then to Fulham Police Station. As a result of radio transmissions at about 1943 we intercepted a silver VW Golf HV 52 VWX with 3 x IC3 occupants in Hale Lane, NW7. As a result of intelligence and the behaviour of the rear-seat passenger I believed that he was about to open fire with a fully automatic weapon. I opened fire on the suspect. At 2040 I left the scene and returned to HD.

I signed it 'Echo Seven'.

Later that morning after a tired drive home and a short, heavy and uninterrupted sleep, I woke up straining to remember the content of a dream. There was something tantalisingly close to my consciousness. Was it something I needed to tell Katharine? My brain kicked in with gruesome images from Hale Lane. I'd killed someone; it wasn't a dream after all. I'd fallen asleep as soon as my head had hit the pillow and somehow managed to shove it all into the dark recesses of my mind but now I remembered it only too clearly.

I shook her gently. 'Wake up,' I whispered. 'We need to talk.'

We'd been together a long time. We both still loved each other but we both knew things hadn't been right for a while. Half awake, her immediate conclusion was that I was about to finish it.

'I don't want you to worry, everything is all right. I'm not in trouble but I had to kill someone last night.'

She instantly bombarded me with questions while we held each other tight. It was Sunday morning but no ordinary weekend. We both did our best to carry on as normal but it hung over us both like a storm cloud.

On the Monday Phil rang. The dead man had been named as Azelle Rodney. Wanted for a double stabbing, he had been the subject of one of the photos on our briefing sheet but hadn't been identified until later. Two more loaded guns had been recovered in the car although neither were MAC 10s.

The following day I slid out of the house easing the door shut behind me. It was a relief to start my car engine, hear the radio kick in, and pull away into the early rush-hour traffic. We were all in early and several other teams were chilling in the crew room, hungry for information about the weekend's events. Press reports had got it wrong, saying that Rodney was brandishing a gun before I had opened fire. Eventually the corrective statement would make it look as if we'd lied. Azelle Rodney would forever be described as the unarmed black man shot dead by police and neither the Independent Police Complaints Commission (IPCC) nor the Job would ever bother to correct the mistake.

Scott Ingram, the Federation lawyer, arrived, and together with our Fed rep Mark, we regrouped in a spare office. Urns of tea and coffee had been laid on and piles of blank statement forms covered the large desk. I'd been involved in several PIPs in the last two decades but this time, as the shooter, I realised just how much we had progressed since Kincraig when we'd had no Federation or legal representation. There had been dark times in between where good friends had been treated like common criminals for simply doing what they had been trained to do. Now, we were told, we were looked upon as witnesses rather than suspects.

Scott addressed us. We would break the 30th of April down into manageable chunks, starting with a brief description of our background and experience and a caveat that we were aware that the incident had been filmed but that we hadn't seen the footage and that our statements were based on our own recollection of the events. There would be a general discussion before each phase to establish details such as timings and street names, then we would sit down around the table and, in our own words, record our private recollection of the events. It would prove to be a long, stressful day. The devil was in the detail and years later, when the case arrived at court, barristers would scrutinise your every word and, if you weren't careful, use them against you. When we were finally finished, we retired to our local hostelry, where we chilled out over a few pints. For my colleagues, the next day would be business as usual; back on the treadmill of dig-outs, rapids and squad jobs, but for me the future was less certain.

It was just over three months to go before I was entitled to retire on a full pension but I would need to carry on working. Several months earlier, I had been at a friend's retirement function in the sergeant's mess at Royal Marines Poole. Dave's top table, a celebration of his 22 years' service, reminded me that I too needed to make plans. Another friend, a former sergeant major and mildly eccentric Scouser, had pulled me at the bar and asked me about my plans. Mick worked with a government agency and was setting up a team to provide armed protection for their personnel in some of the world's more hazardous destinations.

He was keen to have a mix of experience and I was the first copper that he'd approached. There would be interviews, a medical, a fitness test and a challenging selection course run in the USA by an American sister agency. Then there would be vetting, after which he'd be looking to employ me straight away. It seemed like the perfect exit strategy and I said I'd give it serious thought. I discussed it with Katharine and she wasn't happy but I knew that it was going to be a one-off opportunity. I rang Mick and said yes.

Back at the base, I threw myself into various projects. I could have gone to the SFO training team at Gravesend but I didn't know how long it would be before a course in the States became available and attached to the operational support cell it would be easier for me to cut away at short notice. Besides, petty restrictions and paperwork were sucking the fun out of training and even if I couldn't get back on ops, I wanted my last months to be spent with the teams. A retirement do in Gravesend's austere and depressing bar was often a sad, lonely affair, where a once-respected operator could just slip away without his former teammates even knowing he'd gone.

Based with the teams I would still see my own team every day and go training with them every six weeks to remain current and share a laugh and a few pints, and I thought that there was still a good chance that I might be cleared to return to full operational duties fairly quickly. Shooters in several recent incidents had been reinstated within weeks and Tayport was being viewed as a relatively straightforward case. Many saw no reason why I shouldn't be cleared and reinstated quickly as well.

The IPCC, keen to build better relationships with the police than its predecessor, had signed an undertaking that they would report back within 28 days of a shooting and if they'd found no indication of wrong doing, the police could, if they saw fit, reinstate the officer. Unfortunately, by disregarding the 28-day rule and refusing to give the Met the necessary report, Tayport's SIO wasn't playing ball.

TWENTY-TWO
TERROR ALERT

The 31st G8 summit was due to be held in Gleneagles and the Scots had sensibly asked for support from forces all over the UK. I thought back to 1983 and the SAS exercise in Beith, where their chief constable had made us box our weapons. Now they wanted as many English guns as we could provide and the Met would be providing the lion's share. Responsibility for organising much of the Met's armed contribution fell on SO19 and, in particular, the SFO bosses, and as the spare prick in the office next door, I found myself attending meetings and writing reports. Phil Manns was to be our senior man on the ground and, keen to keep me involved beyond the planning phase, asked me to be his driver and bag carrier. Grey and Blue picked up the task and together with officers from all over the country, we headed north.

It was 7 July 2005, Britain had just won its bid to host the 2012 Olympics and with everything at the conference going well, the sun was shining and there was almost a holiday spirit among the team. It was Phil Manns who received the first call that put an end to that … There'd been a number of explosions in London's Underground system and everyone's phones were soon ringing. I went to the control marquee to watch Sky news on one of the giant flat screens and as news of a fourth explosion on a bus flashed onto the screen we knew London was under attack. The capital was in turmoil and with a chunk of our resources at the opposite end of the country, at least some of us would have to get back down to London ASAP.

Suspended from carrying, I was of limited use at the base and was dispatched to the Yard to man our desk in Central 1600, the control room of Special Branch (SB). It appeared possible that a fifth suspect might still be alive and on the loose and while detectives ran the murder enquiry, the control room's efforts were geared to catching the missing suspect and any of the bombers' support network. Special Forces were desperate to get in on the act but, like the Libyan siege 21 years earlier, there was nothing for them to do. Nonetheless, a small mixed contingent of SAS and SBS had arrived in the capital and had set themselves up in barracks close to the Yard.

Paul Robinson, SO19's new commander, tasked me with being their liaison officer (LO). Some of them had recently completed short attachments to our teams and I knew several of their older guys and barriers were soon broken down, but it soon became apparent that all of the bombers had perished and the attack's mastermind had fled the country before their rucksack bombs had even detonated. The military returned to their bases, leaving the Met to continue with their multiple murder enquiry alone.

Exactly two weeks later, bombs carried by three more jihadists failed to detonate on board London Underground trains and a bus; a fourth terrorist, deciding against martyrdom, abandoned his device in a park. CCTV had captured the attempts, giving good footage of the fleeing suspects, whose abandoned rucksacks left a treasure trove of evidence; the hunt was on!

Once again I was dispatched to 1600. A potential address for one of the bombers had been identified in Scotia Road, Tulse Hill, and one of our teams was covering it but by the end of the day the SAS were back in town and once again I found myself as their LO. The capital was in the grip of what could prove to be a concerted terrorist attack and Operation Theseus Two, the most high-profile manhunt in recent history, was in full swing. There may come a time when we might need to call upon the SAS's expertise, my boss said, but now wasn't it.

I would need to keep them abreast of developments, manage their expectations and, most importantly, keep them out of the Yard's hair. I joined them in their holding area and settled in. Urns of tea and coffee sat on a trestle table and their intelligence cell had set up situation boards on easels but, with nothing to do, the assaulters prepped their kit and hung around in small groups chatting. Every hour, I'd stretch my legs and take a walk over to 1600 for an update and pick up on any gossip. The following morning I sat with some of the squadron over breakfast in a nearby café and at 0933, as we sipped our cappuccinos, Theseus Two kicked up a notch.

As Black team prepared to take over the Tulse Hill plot, a suspect bearing a striking likeness to wanted bomber Hussein Osman, code-named Nettle Tip, left the Scotia Road address. A special reconnaissance regiment soldier attached to SB, more sensibly code-named Frank, spotted him from the back of his cramped OP van but midway through pissing into a plastic bottle, he'd been unable to take a photograph, describing him on the radio as a possible.

The SB surveillance team quickly wrapped themselves around the potential bomber in an attempt to get a positive ID. Working from grainy CCTV images of him fleeing the tube station, his watchers stopped short of positive identification, continuing to shadow him as he boarded a Brixton-bound bus. Describing him as being very jumpy, his behaviour at Brixton station convinced some that he was practising anti-surveillance. By the time he'd re-boarded the same bus and reached Stockwell tube station, the majority of the surveillance team were convinced he was Nettle Tip.

Stockwell was significant. Analysis of CCTV had identified it as the entry point for two of the bombers the previous day and at 1002, as he stepped from the bus and headed towards the station's entrance, tension on the ground and in the control room was palpable. A minute later, the SFO team's control vehicle received the radio call from 1600.

'He must not get on the tube. Stop him getting on the tube!'

Previously briefed that they would only be deployed in the event of a positive ID and warned that they should be prepared to carry out unusual tactics, the message meant only one thing to the team: Kratos!

Cleared to deploy and convinced that they were just moments away from confronting a suicide bomber, nine operators sprinted to their possible deaths. Knowing that the suspect might already be on a crowded platform, or worse still, a packed train, they vaulted the ticket barriers and rushed down the escalator, rapidly losing any chance of a radio signal from the surface: there was no going back. At the bottom, one of the watchers pointed them to the northbound platform and a packed, waiting train.

As they boarded the suspect's carriage, he inexplicably stood up and, thinking that he was about to detonate a suicide vest, one of the surveillance officers, code-named Ivor, grabbed him in a bear hug and both men fell back into the seats. Two of my best mates were closest and, expecting the struggling suspect to detonate at any second, fell back on their Kratos training, firing into his head at point-blank range until they were satisfied he was no longer a threat. It was a brutal, horrific death but the team and their surveillance colleagues didn't have time to dwell on it and started evacuating the carriages and platforms before taking cover themselves. Safe at last and experiencing a mixture of shock and euphoria, they hugged each other, thankful to be alive. EXPLO quickly established that the body wasn't wearing a suicide vest but they left the scene convinced they had at least taken out one of the terrorist cell. Proud that, in circumstances where normal mortals would have fled, they had run headlong into danger to protect the public and had come out alive.

Leaving the squadron glued to Sky News, I rushed over to 1600. Information was still coming in but there was a general air of victory: collectively we had struck back at the bombers. Stockwell was now a secure scene and back at the base Black were starting their PIP but the hunt for the remaining bombers was still on. For the time being at least, we were down to five teams and the two shooters, now to be forever known as Charlie 2 and Charlie 12, would be joining me in the Sin Bin. Throughout the day I visited 1600 several times but if there were any negative issues surrounding Stockwell, they weren't discussed openly and as far as my colleagues on the SO19 desk were concerned everything so far was going well.

The following morning, back at the Yard for my pre-breakfast update, I saw two of my bosses deep in conversation outside the control room and gave them a cheery good morning but their glum faces didn't crack.

'Yesterday's bomber,' one of them said shaking his head sadly. 'Innocent. He just looked like Nettle Tip and lived in the same building.'

'Fuck!' was all I could say.

It was obvious from the conversation that the team didn't yet know and, as I walked out of the building, I paused by Scotland Yard's revolving sign and rang their team leader. I knew from his cheerful answer that he didn't know and, using guarded speech, I updated him. After a brief silence, he put the phone down. I didn't envy him the task of breaking the news. The victim, of course, was Jean Charles de Menezes and his death remains highly controversial but the Met had to pick itself up and carry on. Tragedy or not, they had terrorists to catch before they could strike again and the next few days were a blur of activity.

The teams were now almost living at the base and bouncing from job to job. Red had already entered the cell's booby-trapped bomb factory in a grubby north London council flat. They'd felt the highly unstable triacetone triperoxide (TATP) explosive popping underfoot and witnessed the discarded hydrogen peroxide bottles and the hole where the toxic chemicals had burnt through the draining board, but the suspects had fled. On Friday morning, less than a week after the failed attacks, they had been busy on another task all night when they were redeployed to enter what was likely to be another empty flat in Dalgarno Gardens, a rundown estate in North Kensington, and they drew up a hasty plan.

In Madrid the previous April, Islamic terrorists had detonated explosives killing themselves and a police officer as Spain's national counter-terrorist team attempted to assault their hideout. Red team weren't about to make the same mistake and the suspects were contained and the neighbours covertly evacuated before contact was made. CS gas was quickly authorised but the team needed explosive entry for the front door. With our own EMOE still not cleared for operational use, a request went up to 1600 for military assistance and finally the SAS squadron escaped the confines of their barracks to provide some actual support. TK, Red team's inspector, had been anticipating two or three guys max, but when twelve troopers jumped out of the van with all their kit, he held out his arms and uttered the immortal words, 'Whoa! I only want you to blow the bloody door off!'

His Michael Caine impersonation was wasted on the regiment though – they didn't come in small packages – but after some negotiation a smaller, four-man team went forward, positioned their charge and withdrew. Shortly after, an explosion rocked the estate. Numerous calls were put in for the suspects to surrender but with no response and after several hefty doses of CS, Mark, one of our snipers on Black, finally saw a bedroom curtain twitch.

After a final dose through the back window, two suspects appeared at the front door stripped to their underpants, their hands raised and their eyes closed by the powerful irritant; both were totally compliant. Thorny, an old mate from our time together on Blue, led the group's leader down the stairwell, shoving him against the wall. I recognised him from the CCTV footage of his failed attempt to blow up the bus in Shoreditch. Code-named Royal Song, Muktar Said's fat belly wobbled as he sobbed like a baby and I couldn't resist whispering in his ear, 'Call yourself a suicide bomber? You couldn't even do that right, you fucking loser!'

Job done, we were redirected to a holding area near the Old Kent Road to be briefed about another location needing the squadron's delicate touch. This time the shockwave from their door charge set off every car alarm in the estate and as Blue team's CS drifted in the air, UK's Special Forces experienced the indignity of being jeered at by a gang of hoodies circling on their BMX bikes. I grinned through my gas mask at their respirator-less sergeant major, tears streaming down his face.

'Welcome to my world.'

With the remainder of the cell detained, the manhunt was finally over, normal operational life was resumed and I was joined by Black team's naughty boys in the support office, but it wasn't long before I found myself in the States for my selection course.

Run at various training facilities in Virginia and Arkansas by former Navy SEALs, there was a heavy emphasis on shooting, building clearance and evasive driving and I loved every minute of it. I was partnered with Gonzo, a former Royal Marine and the only other Brit on the course among 18 Americans. Gonz and I became close friends and, having smashed the testing seven weeks, we returned to the UK to complete an advanced medical course and the vetting procedure but my future employers weren't prepared to start the expensive process until I had the all clear from the IPCC.

First of all, I would have to sit through an hour-long interview at the IPCC's Holborn headquarters with Scott Ingram by my side. It was an uncomfortable affair where, having been read the official caution, I read out a pre-written declaration stating that I had already made a full statement and wasn't prepared to answer their questions. I would, however, listen to them and give written answers later if I felt I could answer anything not covered in my original statement. I understood my lawyer's reasoning but answering every question with the words 'no comment' made me feel like a criminal and with nothing to hide I would rather have answered them.

Finally, nearly 200 days after the incident, I was given the IPCC's concluding report. It read:

> The account given by E7 … is consistent and is supported by the evidence of other witnesses and the available forensic and video evidence. I believe that given the level of perceived threat E7 acted properly and in accordance with his training. E7 fired the number of rounds he did as he believed that the threat was still present and he continued to fire until he was satisfied his colleagues were no longer at risk. His action was within the powers accorded him by Section 3 of the Criminal Law Act 1967, Section 117 of the Police and Criminal Law Act 1984 and common law.

Following standard practice, they had forwarded their findings to the Crown Prosecution Service for them to review. Finally in December 2005, even though my case was now with the CPS, I was allowed to return to my team and the Foreign Office started my vetting process on the understanding that my clearance would be dependent on the CPS decision.

TWENTY-THREE
SERIAL KILLER

'Ah, Echo Seven. The Met's very own serial killer!'

I couldn't believe what she had just said, but the look of shock on my colleagues' faces confirmed it for me. One of the most powerful senior officers in the Met, Commander Sue Akers was in charge of the DPS, the very unit responsible for investigating allegations of police wrongdoing, including the use of inappropriate words and behaviour. She was at our base investigating the discharge of a firearm.

I'd seen guys checking their CBRN kit the day before and knew that they were being paraded later that evening but nothing about their secretive counter-terrorist operation and had arrived at work expecting the crew room to be empty; instead it was packed with tired assaulters. They'd carried out a rapid looking for a dirty bomb and in the course of the entry, encumbered by his bulky CBRN kit, one assaulter ended up in a struggle with one of the occupants. As they wrestled for his MP5 it had discharged, hitting the suspect in the shoulder, and the teams, who had been completing PIP for most of the night, were waiting permission to go home.

It was nearly a year since Tayport and, together with Akers, the IPCC's SIO was in the building and I was keen to speak to both about my situation. The IPCC man was friendly enough but pessimistic about whether they would be able to hold an inquest. Among other things, the Regulation of Investigatory Powers Act 2000, or RIPA, prevents intelligence obtained by certain technical means (such as phone taps) from being admissible as evidence, making half of my justification for shooting Rodney worthless. It also restricts those who are entitled to examine it and coroners, the SIO informed me, weren't included.

I'd found Akers deep in conversation on her mobile, just feet from our tea-making room. It was packed and I'd grabbed myself a coffee and hovered by the door waiting for her to finish her call. A couple of lads, twigging what I was up to, waited to earwig my conversation and when she'd finished her call, I'd stepped up and offered my hand.

'Morning, ma'am. I know you're busy but I wonder if I could have a moment of your time? Only you are dealing with my case.'

She'd held on to my hand but looked puzzled. 'Sorry, you are?' she'd asked.

'I'm Tony Long – ' but before I could finish my sentence she had uttered the words. Shocked as I was, I decided to ignore them and we had a brief discussion about my situation. She was aware of my predicament and was quite helpful and I offered my hand again.

'That's all I wanted to say. I just thought it might help if you could put a face to the name.'

'Oh no, that's fine,' she replied. 'I can't wait to get back to the office and tell everyone that I've met the Met's very own serial killer.'

I couldn't believe she'd said it again!

'I'm not sure it's a good idea to call me that, ma'am, do you?'

'Oh, don't worry about that. It's just the nickname we have for you in the office.'

Our conversation spread like wildfire and when I got home and told Katharine, she was outraged. Working in HR she couldn't believe that I wasn't interested in pursuing it, but all I wanted was to retire and transition quietly to my new job.

The next day, the personnel superintendent stopped me in the corridor. 'Please tell me, what I'm hearing isn't true,' she said before asking me to tell her exactly what the commander had said. She asked whether I wanted to take it further and I said no. I thought that would be the end of it but it had grown legs and the following day I was called in to see the unit commander. He was concerned that Akers' comments were a reflection of the way the DPS viewed us as a unit. He and Akers had been inspectors together; he was sure he could get an apology. Would that satisfy me?

The situation was getting out of hand and thinking that would put a line under it, I agreed, but a week later he called me up to his office. Mark the Federation rep was also present.

'She's not answering my calls and she's ignoring my emails!' he said angrily.

He wasn't in the mood for diplomacy. It was decided that I would write a statement describing the incident and, together with another from a witness, it would be sent to the Yard by the Federation's solicitors along with a letter demanding an apology. It did the trick and a reply quickly arrived, but it was a poor excuse for an apology, disputing our recollection of the event and finishing with an insistence that she would never condone the inappropriate use of such a nickname among members of her unit. Essentially she was calling my witness and me liars, and now I was seriously pissed off. The matter dragged on for weeks with letters bouncing back and forth between the Federation's solicitors and those of the Met as they tried to word an apology acceptable to both parties. Finally, worn down by whole process, I reluctantly accepted her final offering and a settlement of £5,000 on the understanding that I would be granted a personal, face-to-face and we met in her office at the Yard. It didn't start well.

'I have to say, I'm very disappointed in you, I expected more …' she began.

'You're disappointed in me?' I hadn't gone to get a lecture from her. She was supposed to be apologising to me!

For several minutes she sat with a slight look of shock on her face while I reminded her that she was the head of the Directorate of Professional Standards, and it was her not me that had made the inappropriate comment. There followed a frank ten-minute exchange before, having said our piece, we shook hands and I left feeling better for having got to dress down a commander.

It had been a stupid, wholly avoidable situation and I still couldn't fathom what she'd been thinking when she'd said it. It still amazes me that at her rank and position she thought it acceptable to call me a murderer, even out of jest; particularly when she was in the building in her official capacity, had never met me before and was overseeing my future. Frustratingly the incident would be repeatedly referred to in the press as having taken place over a drink at a social event.

Shortly after the altercation, I finally received the all clear from the CPS. I would not be charged with any offence; I was free to retire and take up my new career and my boss sent a confirmation letter to the Foreign and Commonwealth Office. Naively, I thought I'd be able to stand up at my leaving do and ask everyone to raise their glass to Sue Akers for paying for the bash but, of course, she wasn't, the taxpayer was, and in any respect there was to be no retirement for the foreseeable future.

After receiving no word from the FCO, I contacted my vetting officer to find that my job offer had been withdrawn. If I was to proceed with my application, I was advised, I would not be given my security clearance and this might affect future job applications. Mick, my recruiter, hadn't been consulted and was furious about the decision. We appealed but it was pointless and having written a formal letter, withdrawing myself from the process, I resigned myself to staying within the Met until something else came along. I never really did discover why I lost the job, although I had my suspicions.

A reshuffle at the Yard had us moving from specialist to central operations and being rebranded as CO19, Specialist Firearms Command (SFC), a name picked by a soon-to-retire Phil Manns, a passionate Southampton Football Club supporter, which of course had nothing to do with his choice of acronym. Partly as a result of lessons learnt following the previous summer's terrorist attacks and partly in preparation for the 2012 Olympics, a review of SFO operations made us look at how our sniper capability could be improved.

Phil and I were both due a training posting when the bosses tasked him with starting up a dedicated SFO sniper team and he offered me the role as his number two. I jumped at the opportunity and White team was born. We were soon set up and running and very much learning as we went along but it felt good being at the centre of something ground-breaking. The team was small and, along with our training commitments, could only put out a single sniper pair with each shift with another covering night-duty call-outs. Many were sceptical wondering what we could bring to the party but we soon started to prove our worth.

On top of helping to run White team the bosses asked me to travel to Jamaica on a training task. Their government had approached the Met asking for assistance in making their Constabulary Force's firearms training UN human rights compliant and I was to carry out an analysis. I'd been involved in a similar team task in Guyana several years before, receiving a commendation for my efforts. I suspected that it was another ploy to keep me out of any further trouble but Katharine and I had recently split and it was a timely opportunity to get away and reflect on the future so, never looking a gift horse in the mouth, I accepted gratefully and spent a month travelling around the island looking at how the officers were trained and deployed.

Later in the year I returned with a small team and spent several months training their instructors. It was an interesting environment to work in with murders and police shootings almost daily occurrences, but I also met some of the friendliest people you could imagine and the two extremes gave me an insight into Jamaican culture that I wish I'd been given at the beginning of my service. The novelty soon wore off though and while most of their instructors were enthusiastic, one or two made it hard work and I was happy to get back to the real world and rifle ops.

The ditch under the gorse bush was full of split rubbish bags, soiled nappies and other household debris and Badders and I shared the space with an abandoned bike frame and an abundance of fox shit; it had been home for the last two hours. We were covering a drugs rip-off in a pub car park ten miles outside the Met. Radio comms were bad, the heavy rain had eventually percolated through our gorse ceiling and we'd taken it in turns to slip out of our camouflage leaf suits and into our Gore-Tex before replacing the camouflage top layer. I'd passed 50, needed reading glasses and was getting too old for this shit. My phone vibrated in the pocket of my jeans, and I wriggled, trying to reach it without moving the bush. Finally, having released it through layers of fabric, I checked the screen only to discover that in the gloom of our hide, I couldn't read the text and was forced to repeat the whole process to reach my reading glasses. Finally I put them awkwardly on over the facemask of my leaf suit and read the text.

There had been a change of circumstances: the gangs had cancelled their meeting and we were to stand down. I turned to whisper the news to Badders and my oppo started to shake; his leaf suit rustling as he tried to supress the giggles. I was a spectacle-wearing, whispering bush and realising the absurdity of the situation I too started to snigger uncontrollably.

'It's time to retire, isn't it?' I whispered and my fellow bush replied with a nod.

In addition to working on White team I'd continued to run several equipment projects and one earned me another trip across the pond. Edgar Brothers, one of the companies we procured kit through, suggested that it was quicker and more cost-effective to send a small evaluation team to the States rather than try and import the kit for trial. One day was spent with a Virginia Beach company who were helping us to develop the equipment and I spent much of the day standing at a white board in their conference room, sketching out my ideas and answering their designer's questions.

That evening, over a beer, Mike and Paul, the two young guys that ran Edgar Brothers's Police and Military Division, impressed with my presentation, offered me a job. I hadn't seen myself working in the commercial world but I thought about it for a few days and accepted their offer. It was late September 2008.

TWENTY-FOUR
THE INQUIRY

Back at work, I handed my papers in, only to find I was owed 50 days' leave, and so, having booked a date and a venue for my retirement do, I went home to find an official-looking envelope containing a kind invitation to complete jury service and, with nothing better to do, I dutifully attended Croydon Crown Court to do my civic duty. After 33 years as a copper, watching how the diverse group of jurors eventually came to their verdict was fascinating and disturbing in equal measure and I came away secretly hoping that our heavily redacted statements would preclude a jury inquest in the Rodney case. It turned out that it would.

My leaving do was held in the Sergeants' Mess of the Honourable Artillery Company. The beer flowed, and the speeches, especially mine, were too long. My daughter Josey had travelled down to proudly see me off and my only regret was that Mark, deployed to Afghanistan, was unable to be there.

I'd been recruited into Edgar Brothers, not as a salesman but as a subject matter expert, a door opener and a point of contact for countries' Tactical Firearms Units. I was on a good wage with a commission, company car and benefits and there were trips to the States and Europe to visit companies and trade shows. I was kept busy but, hovering in the background, there was always Azelle Rodney.

In August 2007, as expected, the coroner had ruled that he couldn't hold an inquest because of our heavily redacted statements. Because of the source of the intelligence, any mention of the planned robbery, the fact that the potential victims were Colombian or that they lived in Edgware, and any reference to the type of weapons we believed them to have, had been laboriously scrubbed through with thick black ink and we were forbidden from ever mentioning what lay underneath for fear of prosecution under RIPA.

The Justice Ministry were looking at ways around the stalemate but Susan Alexander, Rodney's mother, was a frail voice in the wilderness. Her son's accomplices had pleaded guilty to firearms and drugs offences back in 2006 and been given custodial sentences. They'd soon be released, but her son was dead and no one could tell her why. As I am a father, she had my sympathy. Rodney had died in a white, middle-class suburb and not an ethnically diverse, inner-city borough like Hackney or Lambeth where his death may have caused uproar; no one had heard of him and those that had simply didn't care.

In 2009, I heard that she had gone to the European Court claiming fairly that her human rights had been breached by the delay in due process. I was equally keen to get the incident resolved and when, in March 2010, I got a call from Scott telling me that the Justice Minister had announced a judge-led, public inquiry, I thought I could finally see light at the end of the tunnel and could dismiss my concerns about facing an unpredictable jury.

In the autumn the Rodney Inquiry, chaired by 73-year-old, retired High Court judge, Sir Christopher Holland, went live and it asked me to complete several supplementary statements answering questions like 'what height was your seat set at?' I did my best to answer them but it was now five years on. I was finally allowed to view Steve's video and, together with access to my colleagues' statements, I had a better idea of what happened in Hale Lane that evening than when I wrote my original statement; making response to the Inquiry's questions problematic. What actually happened bore little resemblance to my own recollection, which had it as a textbook interception with us pulling alongside the Golf in one smooth movement. In fact, it hadn't been perfect at all.

I now knew that on the 'attack', Smudge had swerved to avoid an oncoming vehicle and, in doing so, had clipped the Golf but, focused on Rodney, I had no recollection of the near-miss or the collision. Because of Smudge's manoeuvre the Golf had stopped short, causing Alpha to overshoot, leaving a gap through which it could escape. Our vehicle also stopped for several seconds, to the offside and slightly to the rear of the Golf, until Charlie rammed the VW forward into the rear of Alpha, but again, focused on Rodney, I hadn't realised that we'd stopped or that the Golf had been shunted. It all served to demonstrate the effects of perceptual distortion in a high-threat situation but the video did however prove that I'd had 10 seconds of clear, unobstructed view of Rodney before opening fire; a lifetime in an adrenalin-fuelled situation.

Thirty-three years of paying my Federation subscriptions had my legal fees covered and periodically I attended meetings with Scott and Sam Leek, my diminutive barrister. She had represented several officers following shootings and my morale was boosted by her confidence in me. I was kept abreast of developments by regular emails but it was a slow process with most activity directed at administration and issues surrounding our anonymity and the redacted intelligence.

The Inquiry had recruited 'experts' and run a 'partial' reconstruction at a disused airfield. Photographs and video had been taken with a view to creating a computer reconstruction. The word 'partial' worried me and knowing that, in addition to Steve's video, they also had data from the black boxes, or IDRs, in each of our cars, I would have preferred them to have conducted a full one. I'd also received feedback about some worrying preconceptions held by members of the Inquiry who seemed to be overly influenced by hindsight. I knew that I'd acted correctly but was starting to worry that, if they continued to play Miss Marple, I'd be hung out to dry before I even got a chance to give my evidence in person.

The Inquiry's experts were two former Northern Ireland officers called Gary Gracey and Andy Mawhinney. I knew little of Gracey, a retired senior officer, but knew Mawhinney reasonably well. Prior to retiring, he'd had been a member of the HMSU (Headquarters Mobile Support Unit), which performed a similar role to our SFO teams in London. He had slightly less service as an operator and instructor than me, had attended our SFO course and participated in the APO programme. SO19/CO19's SFO teams and the HMSU had strong links and I hoped his experience would help give the Inquiry's lawyers some perspective on the realities of our work.

Steadily, we were served with all of the evidence secured by the Inquiry and I was disappointed to find that the computer reconstruction wasn't among the material. Scott made enquiries to be told that they wouldn't be using it because it wasn't accurate enough but, reluctantly, they eventually served us a copy. When Mawhinney and Gracey's statements were finally served, there was uproar in the Met's camp and I shared their outrage.

They were highly critical of our tactics and procedures, citing their own as the model we should aspire to, but tactics that work in provincial Northern Ireland don't necessarily work in a city the size of London. Their hindsight-based recommendations suggested, among other things, that we should have got ahead of the Golf and put out a 'stinger' or set up a roadblock to stop it safely but this wasn't some country lane in County Antrim. The Golf could have taken any number of routes between Harlesden and Edgware and we didn't have a crystal ball. I had massive respect for the HMSU and many good friends within its ranks who all knew that Mawhinney was talking shite.

Holland finally gave an undertaking that we would all be allowed to give our evidence anonymously and in October of 2012, nearly two years since the Inquiry had started and following a written assurance from the attorney general that evidence provided by witnesses would not be used in any criminal proceedings, the Inquiry began to hear evidence from all of the many witnesses. While technically a public Inquiry, the actual public, with the exception of Susan Alexander, were denied access, having to watch the proceedings from another room equipped with monitors.

The Met had a similar setup so that we could enter through a back entrance of the High Holborn courtroom, watching the evidence on screens in our own rooms adjacent to the court. As with coroner's and other civil courts, witnesses were free to listen to others give evidence before giving their own. Having grown a full beard as a makeshift disguise, I attended several times to get a feel for the setup, but I had a day job and, as the hearing was scheduled to last for weeks, I kept abreast of proceedings through daily phone conversations with Scott.

The Inquiry began with Ashley Underwood QC, their lead barrister, giving a summary of the incident starting with all of the redacted evidence that had been inked through in our statements and which we had been told couldn't be given in open court for fear of breaching RIPA. If it was possible to release it all for public consumption now, we asked, why couldn't it have been put before a jury at a coroner's inquest seven years ago? I was livid and made more so by the revelation that Rodney's mother had just received a substantial sum for the delay in due process. She now knew exactly what her son had been up to and why he'd been shot. It was his selfish, criminal behaviour that had forced me to take his life. I didn't want compensation but what consideration had been given to the stress caused to my family by the seven-year delay?

Underwood also introduced Steve's video during his opening address and it featured heavily in the media. Steve had used the words 'Sweet as ... Sweet as!' as Delta came to a halt but you could clearly hear him start to utter the words before my first shot. Despite that, elements of the press made out that they were a callous reference to Rodney's death when they'd simply been instructions to Tom, Delta's cockney driver, to stop, an explanation accepted by the Inquiry.

The witnesses were dealt with chronologically, starting with the Customs and Excise intelligence officers first alerted to the robbery. Restricted by the RIPA laws, they weren't allowed to divulge in open court the source of their intelligence but it was extremely valuable evidence underlining the gang's involvement in serious criminal activity but, following their feeding frenzy the previous day, it went almost unreported by the press.

Exactly a month after the hearings started, I was finally called to give evidence. Booted, suited and with my beard camouflage freshly trimmed, I was sworn in as E7. First up was Underwood. I'd decided months before that I didn't like the man but I responded to his questions politely. They started about my background and experience, including, in guarded terms, my previous shootings. Holland had directed that they could not be mentioned in a way that would identify me and both Northolt and Plumstead were lumped crudely into one. It fooled no one, particularly the press.

He dragged out an incident in 2004 where a report had criticised me for leaving my vehicle to get my crew some coffees prior to a shooting. Phil had also been criticised for his lack of supervision. Our bosses had decided that Phil and I had done nothing wrong, but somehow the criticisms had remained on our files. The second, more serious blip on my otherwise clean record had taken place in 2000 when, following a stupid altercation with some bouncers in a West End nightclub, I'd been ejected but had stupidly attempted to get back in to retrieve my coat and phone, ending up in a one-sided fight with five knuckle-draggers. Drink was obviously involved and when the local Old Bill were called I'd been rightly arrested for failing the attitude test and suspended from ops for several months before being given a written warning.

'You were arrested and taken away in handcuffs by the Metropolitan Police?' Underwood probed.

'Yes, sir,' I replied. 'Not one of my proudest moments.'

On the positive side, he asked about my commendations and I told Holland of those that I'd received, including one in the nineties when a colleague and I had confronted a suspect armed with what appeared to be a Browning Hi Power. We had managed to arrest him unscathed and the pistol had turned out to be a realistic replica. His attempted 'suicide by cop' was put down to his partner having just died of AIDS.

I was hit by the naivety of Underwood's questions and his seeming inability to understand that when confronting dangerous armed suspects, no two situations are ever the same. We had laid down tactics that we tried to adhere to but flexibility is the name of the game. He seemed to struggle with the concept, wanting a textbook solution to every problem he put to me. In particular, he saw our experimentation with the shield in the car as proof that Tayport was too dangerous an operation to have undertaken.

'Did you say to anybody, "Look, this is a very dangerous operation. Should we really carry it out?"'

Who the fuck else was going to deal with it? I thought to myself while politely explaining that our job was to confront armed criminals and we did so on a daily basis but I could tell that neither he nor Holland could grasp the concept. Eventually we got on to the events on the day: the briefings, the period of waiting in Fulham's yard and the intelligence build up, the activity at Harlesden, leading to the move from state green, through amber to red and, eventually, the events in Hale Lane. I described in detail what I had seen and my thought process before opening fire.

In my career I had shot five men, killing three of them, and over the years, alone with my thoughts, I had contemplated many times how it was that I'd coped with that responsibility without feeling guilt or remorse. Sometimes I'd even wonder if there was something wrong with me but I would always come to the same conclusion: they had all been criminals prepared to use knives and guns to intimidate, wound or even kill people weaker or more vulnerable than themselves and I had simply acted to stop them.

I'd not lost a moment's sleep over Rodney's death and yet, as I described Graham pulling him up from the rear seat and I pictured his gunshot wounds, I felt a lump developing in my throat and tears welling up and had to pause, shocked by the sudden, unexpected outbreak of emotion. As I struggled to compose myself, I heard Rodney's mother shouting something about me lying and hurried footsteps as she left the courtroom.

Eventually we got to Steve's video and I explained how little it resembled my own recollection of the incident. I had shot Rodney through the rear passenger window but knowing what I knew now, I was certain that I must have seen at least some of Rodney's final movements, not through that window, as I'd described in my statement but through the rear hatchback window. I knew what I'd seen but not exactly where I'd seen it from, and in trying to piece together those final critical moments, my brain had filled in the gaps.

Underwood took me through their partial reconstruction at the airfield. They'd used only two cars, a Golf and an Omega, and had taken a series of photographs and some video to try and demonstrate my view of Rodney as the Alpha car made its final approach. Their attempts looked like a school project put together by a bunch of kids in the playground on a wet Wednesday afternoon. I couldn't believe that after two years of preparation, this was the best that they could come up with.

Just three days before giving my evidence, we'd received a letter from the Inquiry's solicitor. In it she admitted that the partial reconstruction had, unbelievably, 'Failed to take into account the movement of the Golf relative to the Omega during the interception,' and stated that 'it was not possible to accurately determine the distance between the Golf and the Bravo at any time, except when they were in contact.'

As a consequence, two weeks before, they had had another bash at recreating it in the tiny courtyard at the rear of the Holborn court. In such close proximity to the surrounding buildings, it was barely possible to see into the Golf because of the reflection and the photographs bore no resemblance to the environment or the light conditions I'd experienced in Hale Lane. It was another example of highly intelligent, legal minds playing amateur sleuths and failing miserably.

Despite evidence of the unit conducting hundreds of similar stops each year without having to resort to lethal force, the Inquiry seemed convinced that Rodney's death was inevitable; Underwood suggesting that he could not have avoided being shot.

'He makes some movements and tragically, you take those movements to be the movements of a man reaching for a weapon. Do you accept they may not have been?'

'No, sir!' I countered. 'My belief is absolutely that he picked up a weapon, almost certainly from the floor, and I believe that he had a gun in his hand when I shot him. That is my belief. I still believe that to this day, sir!'

Holland chipped in, pushing the point and suggesting that it would have been dangerous for Rodney to have either put his hands up in surrender, sat absolutely still or to have dived down to avoid being shot.

'He could have done all three of those options, sir. He could have raised his hands, in which case I almost certainly wouldn't have fired. He could have sat still, in which case I almost certainly wouldn't have fired. If he'd ducked down and stayed down, I would not have fired, for several reasons, not least of which is that I would have nothing to shoot at.'

I could still see no reason why he should have ducked down and sprung back up again and was still certain that he had picked up a weapon. I described the MAC 10's rate of fire, explaining that, factoring in my reaction time, he could have fired a half-second burst before I could have squeezed my own trigger, and that assuming I'd the luxury of seeing the weapon, which could have been fired from below the level of the window. In explanation, I drew parallels with stopping for traffic lights and the distance you will have travelled by the time the brain has processed the change from green to red and applied the brakes.

Finally, Underwood directed his questions at the number and sequence of my shots. I'd been confident that the Inquiry would understand my reason for opening fire but was concerned that a layperson would struggle to understand why I'd fired eight shots so rapidly and had expected to be questioned in depth. It was accepted that one of my shots, quite possibly the first, had struck several inches below the level of the sill and come to rest within the bodywork. The first round to strike Rodney had hit him in his upper arm at 90 degrees, shattering his humerus. The next struck him by his right shoulder blade, travelling at a slightly downward angle. These, the experts told us, were unlikely to have been fatal.

The next two, they felt, had hit him in and around his right ear, again at a slight downward angle, and these were likely to have rendered him unconscious and killed him eventually. Another round from this first tranche of six had missed Rodney, passing through the opposite window, making Graham, now referred to as E3, believe that he had come under fire from the rear-seat passenger. This was the point at which I had lost sight of Rodney behind the shattered remains of the rear window and, having pushed myself back, I'd described him in my statement as still upright.

I fired my last two rounds before watching him fall below the level of the window. These two shots, we were told, were the two near the top of his head. Knowing this now, I realised that Rodney must have been slumping towards me but, intent on neutralising the threat as quickly as possible, I hadn't been aware of it. Had he been standing, I would have seen him falling and probably ceased fire much sooner but strapped in by his seatbelt and sitting, the effects of my rounds had been less obvious.

We are trained to fire at the centre mass and that is exactly what I had attempted to achieve. Obscured by the car door, the hit to his arm was the centre mass of what I could see and was the first round to penetrate the window, shattering it. The subsequent shots enlarged the hole in the now frosted glass but it was still like shooting into a pond through a hole in the ice. Focused on my front sight rather than Rodney, I fired all of my shots in just over two seconds, maintaining my centre mass hold throughout.

I hadn't deliberately aimed any of my shots at his head but failing to register him slumping towards me, that's was where some had struck. In the same way as it takes time to identify a threat and open fire, I tried to explain, it takes time to register that the threat is over and stop firing. We are taught to fire while assessing the threat and to continue to fire until we are satisfied that the threat is neutralised. I'd done exactly what I'd been trained to do.

It was getting close to lunchtime. I had an afternoon with Leslie Thomas, the family's belligerent lawyer, to look forward to but Holland was confused and wanted to revisit old ground: I'd fired one shot, why didn't I stop there? Why fire again?

We'd gone through all this already but clearly Holland hadn't got it. Adrenalin flowing, Rodney was probably unaware he'd even been shot at and even when the first shot hit him, would he have instantly registered pain? Who could say? I repeated that I'd seen no indication that my rounds were having any effect but he argued on. Surely, as he'd been shot at once, he must have known he was going to die if he didn't give up? I started to despair; he and Underwood had immersed themselves in the minutiae of the case for two years, picking apart statements and studying the video, freeze-framing and reviewing it in slow motion so many times that they could no longer grasp the speed with which these things happen.

Thomas was like one of our nine-bang distraction grenades. He went on a bit, was noisy, distracting and very annoying, but didn't actually cause any real damage. Except for giving him a look of disdain when he asked a particularly dumb question, I never bothered to look at him and could tell it was annoying him. He went over all the ground that had been covered by Underwood but naturally dwelt on anything that made me look bad. My 'no comment' interview and my nightclub scrap were well hammered, both having to be brought to a finish by Holland when he repeatedly overstepped the mark. He brought up my previous shootings again, predictably accusing me of being trigger-happy. When he eventually got round to the actual incident he tried to break down the moments prior to my first shot by numbering each key point.

'Number one. "I remember seeing him with his hands on the seat in front of him. He appeared to be looking forward …" Correct?' he asked, condescendingly, while reading from my statement.

'That's correct, sir. Yes.'

'Okay. Then you said this, number two. "He seemed to push himself back in his seat …" Yes?'

Holland was writing furiously and asking him to slow down, but between the struggling judge and my numeracy issues, Thomas's simple numbering technique was doomed to fail. Soon he was getting confused himself and my refusal to look at him and answer only to Holland left him an outsider in his own cross-examination. He became increasingly annoyed, with Holland frequently asking him to calm him down and telling him to 'lower the volume'. I did my best to calmly answer his increasingly irrelevant questions. Eventually he got to the amount of rounds that I had fired, pouring scorn on how I'd continued to assess the effect of my rounds as I fired and he played the video.

'Where I come from in south London, we say, "You're having a laugh aren't you?" Are you telling me that between "da-da-da-da-da" you were thinking?' he said, incredulously. He moved back to the forensics, analysing the trajectory of each shot and once again I explained the principles of action and reaction. Human beings aren't cardboard targets on a range and when they are hit they fall, twist and spin around so that a quick follow up shot fired deliberately at the chest may still strike the suspect in the back or even the head.

He chuntered on, covering old ground, and I glanced at my watch hoping it would all soon finish. Not one of his questions unsettled me. I was confident in the rightness of my actions and the laws and procedures that surrounded them and then he accused me of getting my colleagues to plant the pistol, always a sign of desperation.

'Sorry, sir! That's outrageous!' I responded.

'No, you say it's outrageous, but we say that – '

'I think it's insulting, sir!'

Thomas was practically shouting when Holland finally interjected.

'Mr Thomas, we've been through this before. First of all, you have to define planting, which as we all know in this case is rather different from a … you have to be fair to E7!'

I was grateful for Holland's intervention but what did he mean by 'different in this case'? Planting was planting, however you looked at it. Rodney had the gun in his hand when I shot him and that was an end to it. Finally he wrapped up his cross-examination with his killer punch. Tutting and shaking his head he said, 'No blood on the gun … there was no blood on the gun. You shot him six times and there was no blood on the gun!'

He stared at me with smug satisfaction, but I'd read all the forensic reports in detail. Traces of Rodney's DNA were found on the weapon but the expert had been unable to say whether they had come from blood or sweat. But the gun had been retrieved from under his body, which may have shielded the weapon from blood splatter and there was pooled blood in the magazine well of the pistol where he had lain on top of it.

'That's not my understanding, sir,' I said to Holland. 'I thought there was blood on the gun.'

'No,' Thomas replied. 'There was no blood on the gun … there was some blood inside the barrel.'

'So, there was blood on the gun, sir,' I said, staring him down.

Once again Holland stepped in to stop the bitch slapping and, after Thomas had finally finished, he asked his own final question about one of my rounds missing E3. Graham had left the front passenger seat of the Alpha car, his responsibility being to cover the front-seat occupants of the Golf. They had appeared scared and compliant but his attention was immediately drawn to Rodney ducking down across the back seat.

Considering him the bigger threat, he'd advanced along the side of the Golf to see what he was doing but couldn't see into the rear because he was now looking at the side windows at an angle and had obviously missed Rodney springing back up again. On the night he'd admitted encroaching on my arc, realising it only when the rear window shattered, showering him with glass. Holland looked perplexed, clearly struggling to get his head around a world so different from his sheltered nine-to-five courtroom.

After questions from my own barrister and five hours in the witness box, I finally stepped down. In our holding area, former colleagues queued to shake my hand and congratulate me. I'd smashed it, they said, but I was less sure. Sam and Scott arrived wearing wide smiles and we were left alone in a side room.

Sam jumped up and hugged me. 'Congratulations, Tony, that was the best evidence that I have ever heard from a principal officer. You were brilliant!'

'Well done, mate,' added Scott with a wink and a handshake. 'We had high expectations and you've exceeded them.'

'That's really kind of you both,' I replied, 'but Holland didn't get it.'

They tried to reassure me but my old copper's instinct was still strong. We'd see.

TWENTY-FIVE
CHARGED

'Anthony Long, you are charged that on the thirtieth of April, two thousand and five, you did murder Azelle Rodney, contrary to common law.'

I stood in the dock of Westminster Magistrates' Court like an exhibit in a zoo, the words echoing around the confines of my glass box. I'd spent my adult life helping to put criminals away but now I was the prisoner. The magistrate ordered that my name could not yet be released, his words drifting over me like fog. Behind my non-emotional mask I was distraught, wondering how it had come to this. It was September 2014, two years had passed since the Inquiry, and while I had tried to live my life normally, the future hadn't looked good. Holland had published his final report in June 2013 and I had been right; he hadn't got it. It was a mess of contradictions and legal terminology but the bottom line was, in his eyes, I'd acted unlawfully.

'It was the job of the police in the UK to protect its citizens and not to shoot them', a paragraph of his first draft report had stated and I knew then I was fucked. Another said that he'd seen no evidence that Rodney's gang would have harmed the Colombians in any way. Why would they? It wasn't as if the Colombians would have reported the theft of their drugs to the police! The naivety was breath-taking. The first drafts had been highly critical of the Met, the Silver commander and the planning of the operation but after submissions from all of the interested parties, his final effort levelled the most serious criticism directly at me. He explained that he'd looked at my actions inquisitorially and not with the same standard of proof required in a criminal court but that was of little comfort. He described me as a well-trained, very experienced and well-respected SFO but, referring to the nightclub saga, with a career that had suffered its ups and downs. He doubted my evidence, comparing it with that of E3 and a man called Leon Gittens who had witnessed the shooting. Both had seen Rodney duck down on the back seat but Graham had been moving and hadn't seen him spring back up again.

Gittens had seen him spring back up but, startled by the sudden, violent confrontation, had clearly confused the sequence of events. His statement broadly supported mine to start with, describing Rodney as being agitated, looking around and acting as if he had ants in his pants. Then Gittens described him ducking down across the back seat, just as I had, but interpreted him springing back up as being the result of my shots hitting him.

He went on to describe the simultaneous shattering of the nearside window, immediately followed by the hatchback window. Rodney, he said, had then slumped towards the nearside window and he had seen the gunshot wounds to his head. In reality, my evidence and the forensics proved conclusively that Rodney had fallen towards the offside of the vehicle, meaning Gittens would only have seen Rodney's injuries after Graham had opened the door, reached in and pulled him into an upright position.

Likewise, the rear, hatchback window of the Golf had been smashed, not by a bullet but by the muzzle of my G36 long after I had fired my last shot. Like me, Gittens honestly believed his recall but, like all humans confronted by such a situation, focused on the highlights, leaving his brain to fill in the gaps.

Holland had also cast doubt on my belief that Rodney had been holding a gun, stating that the only firearm available to Rodney, a deactivated Colt, was found in a position inconsistent with it ever having been in his hand, yet later wrote that the pistol, which a back-street armourer had tried to reactivate, was recovered under Rodney's body. The two other pistols, a 9mm and a .25, both of which, contrary to reporting, were loaded, were recovered from the bag in the back of the Golf together with handcuffs and three live .45 ACP rounds for the Colt, presumably indicating that the criminals had believed the Colt to be in working order even if it wasn't.

Holland rejected my account, saying that I couldn't be rationally believed, but went on to say that he didn't believe I'd deliberately lied, rather that I had unconsciously reconstructed the events to justify my actions. He went on to say that he believed that I had held an honest belief that Rodney had access to a sub-machine gun in the rear of the Golf and that he posed a threat to my colleagues and myself, but not that he had picked it up and was about to use it.

His conclusion was that, feeling vulnerable, I had overreacted with a pre-emptive strike, hoping to justify it later when a sub-machine gun was subsequently recovered from the vehicle. From day one I had always insisted that I had opened fire, not in fear for my own life but for those of my colleagues, and I'd been involved in enough operations to know that even grade A intelligence is rarely spot on. There was no way that I would ever have opened fire on Rodney based on intelligence alone!

I thought back to one occasion when we'd been briefed that Trident suspects had been overheard talking about having two dogs and loads of teeth. Criminals always talk in guarded speech and this had been decrypted to mean that they had two guns and loads of ammunition. When we dragged them out of their vehicle at gunpoint, the main man was screaming, 'Mind the puppies, man! Mind the puppies!' Sure enough, on the back seat, in a cardboard box, were two pit-bull puppies excitedly wagging their tails. He hadn't been doing a gun deal; he'd been selling off his bitch's new litter.

Holland went on to say that, even had I held an honest belief that warranted opening fire, the shot in the door should have been sufficient warning for Rodney to immediately desist. If it hadn't, he argued, then certainly the first round to strike Rodney in the arm, plainly neutralising the threat, made the following round, aimed at the back of a disabled man, unnecessary. What he didn't acknowledge was that at this point I'd been firing through a hole in the frosted glass and while my shots were aimed at centre mass, I had no idea where or if I'd struck him.

All of my subsequent rounds, in his opinion, were unlawful as they either caused death or were fired at a dead or dying man. He described the pair that struck his ear and the two that struck the top of his head as accurately aimed double taps, a term never once uttered during the Inquiry. Like the shot to the back, these rounds had been deliberately aimed not at their final point of impact but at the centre of mass of a man that, only now I was being told, had been falling towards me.

I felt a tug on the sleeve of my suit as the uniformed custodian pulled me towards a door in the corner of the glass dock. The magistrate had finished speaking but I hadn't been listening and I caught the eyes of my legal team smiling nervously as I followed the guard into an echoing, grey corridor where handcuffs were applied and I was led down into the bowels of the custody area. This wasn't meant to be happening, I told myself, I was supposed to be whisked away by my old SFO team to the Bailey to be granted bail.

Despite protestations from my solicitor, representatives from the Met and even the prosecution barrister, I was rudely deposited in a cell and the heavy door was slammed shut. SERCO, the civilian company responsible for prisoner security and transportation within London's courts, weren't interested in gentlemen's agreements or even the wishes of the magistrate: I was in their care now and they would be taking me to the Old Bailey in a prison van.

I took in my sordid surroundings, breathing in the familiar stench of stale sweat and urine. So this was what it was like on the other side of that metal door I had slammed on so many criminals in the past. Anger welling up inside me, I sat down on the wooden bench, stripped off my tie, lent back against the graffiti-scratched wall and closed my eyes.

I must have looked at my watch five times before I realised that only three minutes had elapsed and I made a conscious effort to ignore it, turning my concentration back to Holland's report and his advice to the Met to seek the expertise of Andy Mawhinney to improve its tactics. I smiled as I recalled a conversation shortly after the Inquiry with Brian, a long-retired SFO sergeant.

'Is that right, Mawhinney was an expert witness? Some expert! I had to take him off the range on his SFO course when he had an ND and nearly shot his oppo in the head!'

'It's no point telling me now!' I'd answered despondently.

With Holland's report published, the case was referred back to the CPS. My legal team had tried for a Judicial Review, arguing that his conclusions were irrational, but it was a long shot. Sam, my barrister, had been dubious about trying but to me it was a no brainer. If against the odds the Judicial Review found in our favour, it was possible that the CPS would stick to their 2006 decision and not prosecute. If we lost, I couldn't see that we were any worse off.

I heard the keys scrape in the lock, the cell door opened and a guard beckoned me out, applied the handcuffs and led me past his unsmiling colleagues towards the underground car park.

'Don't think I'll be giving you a good write up,' I said with a grin. 'The service was shit!'

I was secured in a claustrophobic cubicle in the back of a prison van and we started our ascent towards the outside world. The interior of the van brightened as the shutter went up and as we pulled into the street I ducked to avoid the press photographers pointing their lenses through the tiny window. As we crawled through the midday traffic I watched the world go by through the scratched plastic, jealous of the pedestrians wandering carefree in the mid-September sun. I watched the landmarks crawl silently by: Baker Street tube station, Madame Tussauds, Euston station, and then I closed my eyes and continued with my thoughts.

Sam had been right. We had lost in our bid to overturn Holland's findings but the reviewing judges had passed several comments in my favour. Firstly they'd condemned Holland's reliance on Leon Gittens's evidence and secondly they criticised the weight that had been given to my continuing to fire at what he'd described as the 'diminishing threat'. Holland's judgement had been based on hindsight and they felt that it was unrealistic to expect me to have known the effect of each round.

With the Review concluded, the Crown Prosecution Service commenced their review of the case. It was likely to take at least six months. I'd heard through the grapevine that the Rodney case was being viewed by the CPS as a poison chalice that stood little chance of achieving a conviction but finally, in July of 2014, over a year after Holland's report had been made public, they announced their decision.

The day before, to avoid potential press intrusion at our homes, CO19 had put my family and I up in a hotel close to the base. I'd been invited in to meet the unit's commander and assured that, whatever the outcome, I had everyone's support and well wishes. The following day, back in the boss's office and surrounded by my family, senior

312

officers, members of the Tayport team and the unit's Federation reps, I waited for a call from Scott Ingram. Coffee, biscuits and tense humour filled the waiting but finally my phone rang, and silence fell over the room. I listened to what Scott had to say, thanked him and put my phone down. It was what I had expected but I could feel the lump developing in my throat as I went to speak.

'I'm being charged with murder,' I said flatly and a nervous silence fell over the room.

The sound of a passing emergency vehicle, its two-tones blaring, snapped me out of my reflections and I looked out of the window as we slowed and turned right across the traffic and through the Bailey's huge gates. I thought back to the last time I had passed through these same portals. It had been 1986 and I'd been incarcerated with the rest of my team in the back of an armoured Land Rover as we arrived to give evidence at the trial of Errol Walker. How things had changed!

The door to the cubicle opened and I offered my wrist to yet another guard; I could hear raised voices and was led out of the van on to the turntable at the bottom of the ramp. Black team had tail-gated the van and Atters, their team leader for the day and tasked with getting me in and out of court covertly, was arguing with a group of SERCO staff. Backed up by a monster of an SFO wearing a smart, three-piece suit and a huge black beard below his massive bald head, Atters was beyond diplomacy; he wasn't leaving me out of his sight again and there was an uncomfortable standoff until the SERCO supervisor reluctantly let him sit in the cell with me. After a long, banter-filled wait, he accompanied me upstairs to the court, staying outside in the corridor while I was un-cuffed and led into another large glass-fronted dock. I took in my surroundings, staring back at Rodney's hostile family members glaring down at me from the public gallery. There was a heavy press presence and Scott and Ian Stern, my new barrister, were in deep conversation while next to them the CPS barrister went through her papers.

'All rise!' called the usher and together with the rest of the court, I stood up as Mr Justice Sweeney entered the room. I remained standing with my shoulders back as he addressed me before sitting to listen to the to-and-fro of legal argument. The Crown's barrister stated that she had no objections to bail and, for the time being, no objections to my maintaining my anonymity. The case was outlined and I was granted bail with the standard provisos, that I make myself available for two independent psychiatric evaluations and that I gave a bail address to the court.

My anonymity, granted at the Inquiry by Holland, would have to be authorised by the Justice Minister and another date was set for it to be resolved. I left the court a free man but no one had told SERCO and I was immediately re-handcuffed, led back to the cells and locked up with Atters while they processed my paperwork. An hour later, safely back in a covert gunship, I was whisked back to the base for a hasty de-brief. The late-turn team were sitting in the crew room on standby and as a cold beer was pushed into one hand, lads came up to me to shake the other.

Back home, I walked to the bottom of the garden and rang Mick, one of the unit's Federation reps. There was no way, I told him, that I'd tolerate my home address being made public in open court. Julie, my partner, and I hadn't even been together when the incident happened and her and her daughter Katie's right to a safe and private life was my absolute priority. He listened patiently while I ranted on. I would rather be remanded in custody than give up our home, I insisted. The Job would have to sort something out and quickly!

TWENTY-SIX
THE TRIAL

My first experience of court from the wrong side had been emotional but listening to the prosecution outline their case convinced me that I was being prosecuted simply because the CPS had been too weak to disagree with Holland's findings. There didn't appear to be any new evidence but they had taken heed of the Judicial Review, making the important decision of prosecuting me only on the grounds that I hadn't held an honest belief that Rodney posed a threat and not on the basis that I should have realised the diminishing threat and ceased fire prior to Rodney's death. They would, however, be using the sequence of my shots to prove that my account was a lie.

On bail for murder, I could no longer carry out my role within Edgar Brothers and reluctantly resigned. Good friends rallied around, finding me work doing private security. It was boring and unfulfilling and I had taken a substantial drop in wages, but being based in London, I was at least able to meet with my lawyers and prepare for the court case. The court still required me to specify a bail address and the Federation and the Police Firearms Officers Association (PFOA) stepped up and paid for accommodation at the Federation's headquarters. Elements of the press weren't happy, insisting that the public had a right to know where I lived, but other than those that wished me harm, I couldn't imagine that anyone else cared.

There was no stipulation that I had to reside there and no restrictions on travel so I was still able to get home regularly and even travel abroad. Despite my confidence, I had to prepare for the worst and Julie and I had to go through the process of rewriting our wills and having a power of attorney drawn up, so that she could manage affairs in my absence. Even then she wouldn't have been able to pay our mortgage on her own, so after much discussion, I decided to sell one of my two flats. I'd rented out my first flat when I'd moved in with Katharine years before and when we'd split up I'd had to buy another one to live in. I'd hoped to keep hold of them both as an investment but Rodney had put a stop to that.

Weeks from the trial I was required to attend a preliminary hearing at Southwark Crown Court. By now I had lost my anonymity, but the press still hadn't managed to get a picture of me. Expecting to keep it that way was a tall order but I was determined to give it a try and CO19 stepped in to get me in and out of court. Once again though, despite thorough planning, the court staff refused to cooperate and we had to enter on foot through the front entrance, so waiting until the press photographers outside were distracted and holding up my phone to mask my face, we quickly entered the court's lobby.

After the hearing, I left surrounded by a phalanx of SFOs who successfully screened me from the swarm of TV cameras and press but it was too late, they had caught me on the way in. That evening, as I watched myself on the news, I was shocked at how much I'd aged. The goatee I'd grown as a disguise hadn't helped but, nevertheless, it made me wonder if the events of the last ten years really had taken their toll on me.

The team's attempt to protect my anonymity had potentially compromised their own and I decided then that it would be unfair to expect serving operators to continue to be involved in my security.

Fortunately, TP, an old friend and colleague from the teams, stepped in. He had retired early, forging himself a successful career in the security industry, and offered his help. My name and face were now public property but I was still praying that my home address and the safety of my family could remain uncompromised. The Met's TSU had installed alarms and CCTV at our home but what I really needed was a plan to get my family to and from court without our home's location being discovered and without them being photographed or associated with me.

The case was set for Monday 8 June 2015 at the Central Criminal Court, ten years and just over a month from the day that I'd shot Rodney, and yet the prosecution remained seemingly unprepared. I'd had plenty of meetings with my legal team and was still confident but our preparation had been made difficult by the fact that we were still being served prosecution evidence just days before the trial.

The original computer reconstruction, deemed too inaccurate by the Inquiry, had been given to specialists to try and iron out the inaccuracies and we were served the new version. The original had merely shown a bird's-eye view of the VW and our gunships during the final ten seconds but the new version split the screen into three, showing their corrected bird's-eye view together with Steve's original footage from the rear of Delta and a new, computer-generated animation, showing my view from Bravo.

On the bird's-eye view, supposedly for clarity, they had kept the original version and shown what they suggested were the correct vehicle positions as ghost images superimposed over the old. The corrected version and in particular the new animation showing my view clearly proved that I'd had a full ten seconds of unobstructed vision before firing and seemed, if anything, to strengthen my case, but the ghost images and their jerky movements created a confusing presentation of the events, making me wonder just how accurate it actually was. The prosecution promised that the faults would be ironed out and that the jury would be shown a cleaner version without the confusing ghosting.

The Saturday before the trial Julie and I hosted a Before Bailey Barbeque and, surrounded by friends and trusted neighbours, we drank each other's health and did our best to forget about the coming Monday. TP took me down the garden and, over a beer, briefed me on his plans to get me to and from court. In typical SFO style it had been thoroughly planned and had even been given an op name. Operation Edge relied on over 50 former members of the unit volunteering to offer transportation, facilities and their time to provide my family and me with security to, from and within the court building.

Each day would start with one of the lads conducting a sweep of my street before picking us up and taking us to a rendezvous in the Old Kent Road. Here we would meet a black cab, driven by one of a small group of licensed cabbies, all ex-SFOs, who'd whisk us down bus lanes and back doubles to get us close to the Bailey where my family, including Lindsay, a close friend, would be dropped at a nearby coffee shop to be met by their minders. I'd be delivered to the front door of the Bailey where a small reception team would be waiting to whisk me past the press and into the court's lobby. At the end of the day the plan would simply be reversed. TP and I chinked bottles and I said my thanks. It was a massive weight off my mind.

I was up bright and early on the Monday for a quick three-mile run. I knew that the days were going to be long and sedentary and I'd promised myself a daily run where, alone with my thoughts, I could focus on the day ahead. TP's planning paid off and I was delivered bang on time to the front of the Bailey and ushered through the throng of press into the calm of the court's lobby and the inevitable security checks. As a defendant, I had to be escorted around the building so I waited patiently until I was picked up by my defence team and taken to the drab public canteen. Jacqui, my guardian angel from 19's Post-Incident Office, was there as she had been throughout, lending support and ironing out problems, and Steve and Mick, the unit's Fed reps and members of 19's management, were also there to offer support.

I would soon discover that the Old Bailey wasn't designed to cater for defendants on bail and I had to literally step over the feet of Rodney's family to enter the dock. I'd expected some overt hostility but, to their credit, they avoided eye contact and politely shifted their feet, allowing me to pass. The solitary SERCO guard opened the gate and after leading me through the dock to the adjoining cell passage to be searched, I returned to the now familiar glass box as the judge entered and the proceedings began.

Above me to my right was the public gallery and I looked up to the reassuring sight of Lindsay and old colleagues smiling down on me. The trial was scheduled to last between six and eight weeks. I hadn't imagined that it would take that long but as I sat, half-listening to the legal niceties and the trial's administration, I realised that it might and I closed my eyes and willed the trial to start in earnest.

That evening, the BBC was to air the first part of a documentary about Scotland Yard. The first episode covered the aftermath of the shooting of Mark Duggan by V53, an old colleague. The repercussions of the shooting had caused nationwide riots and much controversy and there was a long discussion as to how it might affect our jury's mindset. The barristers went off to view it with the judge, who decided to advise the jury that it was not evidence and shouldn't allow it to influence their verdict. Unbelievably, the Rodney Inquiry website, including Holland's findings and full transcripts of every witness's evidence, had still not been taken down and that too had to be resolved before we could proceed.

Worryingly, the judge also asked both parties to consider a charge of manslaughter, something that I for one was against. The last thing I needed was for the jury to be given an easy option. A mass of potential jurors were assembled at the back of the court and called forward one at a time where Justice Sweeney asked them if they had had any involvement with police firearms officers. One of the first was a smartly dressed man in a suit.

'I'm a detective on the Flying Squad. We work with CO19 on a regular basis,' he said flatly.

I reflected on how things had changed. A few years previously, your average Flying Squad detective would have just remained silent and taken his place on the jury. The process eventually resulted in a panel that seemed a fair representation of the inhabitants of a capital city where 300 languages are spoken. There were seven women of varying ages and ethnicities including one Muslim and five men of a similar mix, all with my future in the hands. For 33 years, London's public had entrusted me with their safety; now it was my turn to put my faith in the them.

Finally, on the Wednesday, the trial started for real. The prosecution's opening speech was long and the final version of the computer reconstruction featured heavily, being shown at different speeds a total of eight times. Contrary to their promise, they hadn't removed the confusing ghost imaging though and as Max Hill, their lead barrister, tried to explain what happened during the final seconds of Rodney's life, I could tell the jury was as confused as I was.

He made a huge play of the fact that I had opened fire 0.06 seconds after Bravo came to rest, suggesting that that was the time it had taken to make my decision. It was a ludicrous assertion that completely ignored the ten seconds of observation I'd had before coming to rest but he was holding me to having seen Rodney make all of the movements I'd described through the rear offside door even though I'd accepted at the Inquiry that I might have seen some of them through the rear hatchback.

The first prosecution witnesses were all former colleagues, some by now retired, others still serving, and the first to take the stand was the Gold commander. A highly experienced detective superintendent who had sanctioned the operation, laid down its strategy and authorised the deployment of surveillance assets and firearms. He was questioned at length on the intelligence build up, much of which I was hearing for the first time.

He painted a picture of a highly professional operation where every piece of intelligence was scrutinised and discussed before critical decisions were made and the Silver commander who followed him expanded on his evidence. Talking from behind a curtain that screened him from the press and the public, the career detective explained how, sitting with Phil in the control vehicle, he'd led the operation on the ground.

Phil, call sign E1, followed, describing in depth the events of 30 April 2005 and detailing his tactical decisions and his actions at the scene. During cross-examination, he described our long relationship, from our time together as PCs on Green in the early nineties to choosing me as his number two on White, speaking highly of my dedication, professionalism and my selection for responsible tasks and overseas deployments.

As the trial approached, I'd had dozens of offers from former commanding officers and outside professionals to appear as character witnesses but the two parties had agreed that the subject of my character would be dealt with later in the trial and, when the jury retired for a break, an agitated Hill objected to the defence having raised it with Phil. Stern argued that, as my team leader, it made sense to ask Phil about me while he was in the box and Sweeney, a prosecutor by trade, smiled wryly and smoothed the waters; Stern had managed to slip in my good character and, while Hill continued to sulk, it was done and time to move on.

The rest of my team followed in numerical order, referred to by their anonymity codes. Those still serving appeared in uniform, their medal ribbons on display, and I was proud at the way that they all gave their evidence in a quiet, professional manner. In cross-examination Stern questioned each one, carefully pinpointing errors in their recall of the events.

I was impressed by his attention to detail and while there was no questioning the honesty of their accounts, it became obvious, when you compared their evidence with the video and that of their colleagues, that every one of them, entirely focused on their own specific role, had made basic errors in their recall of those last critical moments.

Smudge (E6) had sworn that he had heard my shots only as he struggled with Golf's driver, when the video proved, beyond doubt, that he had still been exiting our vehicle as I fired. Likewise, Steve (E8) believed he'd debussed and was preparing to shoot the Golf's rear tyre when he'd felt the violent muzzle blast and seen the VW's rear window shatter believing, wrongly, that he was under fire from the Golf. In reality, he too hadn't left the Omega.

'That wasn't a lie was it?' asked Stern, 'Perception, under stress can produce mistakes, can't it?'

'Absolutely, sir,' Steve replied.

Relying totally on his colleagues to protect him, Alpha's Hatton gunner (E5) was so focused on disabling the Golf that he'd been completely unaware of the vehicle's occupants or of any shots being fired other than his own, and Paul, his driver (E4), was unaware of a gap between the Golf and the rear of his Audi or of the subsequent collision and, despite being the only one at the scene to actually see me fire, had still managed to get the sequence wrong.

Another operator from the Charlie car was convinced, like Gittens, that he had seen the rear hatchback window shatter at the moment he'd heard my shots. In all, not one of the team recalled the incident perfectly; proof, in my book, of their honesty and evidence that we hadn't colluded when writing our statements.

It had been a good day and as the judge left the court I looked up and smiled at my friends, cupping my hand to my lips and receiving a cheerful thumbs up. My silver-haired protection team, now affectionately known as the Expendables, swung into action, whisking my supporters away to a rapidly reconnoitred pub, while I was bundled into my waiting cab and taken to meet them. A cold beer never tasted so good and as we discussed the day's events, we realised that we were all part of the biggest reunion in the unit's chequered history.

I'd been looking forward to hearing the next witnesses give evidence. Despite the Judicial Review's criticism of his account, as the only useful independent witness at the scene, Leon Gittens still remained the prosecution's star turn. I hadn't listened to his evidence at the Inquiry but I'd read his statements and the transcript of his evidence and I knew he'd described the incident as an execution. I was fascinated to hear him speak, see what he looked like and watch Ian Stern tear him apart. He arrived the following morning with his own solicitor, insisting on time to study his statement before giving evidence. Sweeney, patient as always, granted him several hours but by lunchtime his lawyer stated that her client would require the whole day.

His Lordship wasn't happy and made his feelings known – it was a day wasted – but the application was reluctantly allowed and, the following morning, their star witness was ready to roll. Gittens, keen to sell himself as a victim, readily admitted to convictions for theft and a history of heroin addiction, blaming the shock of witnessing Rodney's death for a return to drugs and a diagnosis of PTSD. As he explained how he had been nursing a pint outside the pub, he came across as an affable rogue and when he described witnessing the violent incident, I couldn't help having some sympathy for him.

His first account, given at the scene was uncannily like my own but he had clearly been in shock and several days later was visited at his home by two members of the IPCC who had conducted a long and very thorough, tape-recorded interview. The content of the four tapes were turned into a transcript and distilled into a written statement, which also broadly supported my account but differed from a less supportive one made years later for Holland's Inquiry.

'It was like an execution! They didn't have time to surrender!' he told the jury. 'I can't emphasise how quickly this happened! It had a profound effect on me. I wouldn't place a lot of weight on what I said shortly afterwards.'

He claimed that his first two statements had been taken under duress and that only his final one, made years after the event, should be relied on. With the passage of time, the original transcript had been forgotten about; the prosecution hadn't even known there'd been one and it had been diligent research by my defence team that had revealed its existence. Copies of the original tapes and the transcript had arrived at Stern's chambers just weeks before the trial and their contents had revealed a very different story.

Under Stern's expert cross-examination, it was revealed that, far from being under duress, Gittens had been an enthusiastic participant in the tape-recorded interview and although he had claimed under oath to have just wanted to get it over and done with and for the IPCC to leave, he had actually been amicable and cooperative throughout, even offering to make them fresh cups of coffee. The honestly held but obvious errors in all of his accounts were highlighted to the jury but Stern had left the best for last. When he asked Gittens how his £50,000 lawsuit against the Met was going, the court cringed at his awkward response. *No wonder he had wanted a day to rehearse his evidence,* I thought.

Next up was the forensic evidence, but unlike the Inquiry, this time we took their experts to task over their conclusions. Ill health had prevented the original pathologist, a Dr Shorrocks, from giving evidence at the Inquiry and it had been left up to a Dr Crane, who had carried out a second post-mortem, and Mr Miller, a forensic firearms expert who had been present at the first PM, to give their conclusions.

Crane's PM was hampered by the removal of organs during the first, and he had needed to rely partly on Shorrocks's notes. While Miller had been present at the original PM, he was not a pathologist and his interpretation of Crane's findings were brought into question, in particular, his analysis of the angles of the wound tracks through Rodney's body. Under cross-examination, he was forced to admit that he had changed the description by Shorrocks of the angle of the wound to Rodney's back from slight to steep, and that on an anatomical drawing in his notebook he'd even drawn Rodney's scalp wounds on the wrong side of the head.

Miller had demonstrated the angles of each bullet by pushing steel rods into a foam dummy and the prosecution had placed photographs of the experiment in the jury bundle but their quality was so poor that the judge insisted they found the original. When the only photo was finally located and handed slowly around the courtroom, it only demonstrated that the rods had been inserted into the dummy at the wrong angles and had failed to take into account Rodney's movement.

In a world used to sophisticated computer graphics, it was a pathetic excuse for evidence.

A great deal was being placed on the sequence and angles of my bullets, with both Crane and Miller suggesting, as they had done before, that my final two shots were those to the top of Rodney's head, proving, said Hill, that my description of Rodney being vertical at that point was a lie. I had always argued that it all happened so quickly that I'd been unaware that he was falling towards me but more diligent research by my defence team had located an eminent surgeon who disagreed with the prosecution's experts.

Lieutenant Colonel Adam Brooks OBE had served as a surgeon in Iraq and Afghanistan and was one of the country's leading experts on gunshot wounds. His expertise was not in dealing with bodies on slabs but with the passage of rounds through living tissue and the dynamics that movement played in the resulting wound tracks. He hadn't, he admitted, been present at either of the post-mortems but he had studied Shorrocks's PM report and the evidence of Crane and Miller and felt that their conclusions were flawed.

'Can you say for definite that there were errors in the post-mortem report?' asked Hill.

'I can say that there are considerable differences between Crane's and Shorrocks's reports,' he replied.

The judge then read out a question passed to him from a juror. 'The jury would like to know if it is fair to say that the firer would have had no idea where his bullets would strike within the body?'

It was a simple question from the common man that, in ten years, intellectuals had failed to ask. Brooks explained that the wound tracks to Rodney's ear were at a steeper angle than those to the top of his head, making it more probable that my final shots were the two to the ear. This would mean that it was far more likely that my account was true and that Rodney had been in a near vertical position when I made my decision to fire my last shots.

'It's not my opinion that Rodney was toppling prior to the scalp wounds,' he insisted in response to Hill's cross-examination.

His evidence and two long weeks of trial finally over, I wished Suzzanne, my now permanent SERCO guard, a good weekend and stepped from the box looking forward to a cold one and a restful weekend.

'That is the case for the Crown,' said Hill finally.

It was lunchtime on the Monday of week three and the jury was sent home. Hill had spent the morning outlining the remainder of their evidence, explaining in detail the computer reconstruction and how it had been made, leaving his junior barrister to take the jury through a schedule of timings. Pens out, frame by frame they corrected errors made when compiling the data and which they would have to factor in when assessing the evidence. Yet another example, I thought, of piss-poor planning and preparation.

As the trial approached I'd been called to a meeting at Ian Stern's chambers. In his opinion, the prosecution appeared not to have considered key issues surrounding my honestly held belief that Rodney posed an immediate threat. We discussed applying for the case to be dismissed as there was no case to answer, but for tactical reasons decided against it.

Failing in our application before the trial had even started would have shown our hand and allowed the prosecution to rectify their error but Hill had failed to cover the point of law in his opening speech and, having now heard the whole of their case, Stern felt the time was right to make our move. His carefully drafted submission was handed to the prosecution and the judge who set the next day aside to discuss it.

By now it was clear that the prosecution's case rested solely on their assertion that I had lied about seeing all of Rodney's movements through the side window, meaning that, in their opinion this wasn't a case of honestly held belief.

Ian Stern detailed our submission, highlighting the accounts of Gittens and Echo 3. If I'd lied, he argued, how was it that Gittens and E3's accounts were so similar to mine? And why were the prosecution insisting that I was lying rather than simply being mistaken, when all of their witnesses had made similar honest mistakes in their accounts?

Hill had also suggested to the jury that I might have opened fire either through misjudgement or panic and Stern pointed out that either reason would negate a charge of murder. Why would I have panicked, he argued, if I weren't in fear? And why would I have been afraid unless I'd a genuine belief that my colleagues or I were in danger? I didn't like the suggestion that I'd misjudged the situation or panicked but it was a good point; misjudgement or otherwise, why would I have opened fire if I hadn't genuinely believed that Rodney posed a threat?

Personally, having gone this far, I wanted the jury to find me not guilty after hearing my evidence. Getting off on a technicality would always leave a nagging doubt about my innocence and the following morning I was almost thankful when Sweeney dismissed our application. The jury was called back and I found myself in the witness box, Bible in hand, reciting the oath. Just like my previous experiences giving evidence into the deaths of Payne and Flynn all those years before, and more recently at the Rodney Inquiry, my confidence grew with each question put to me.

Ian Stern led me through my evidence while behind him, the jury hung on my every word and, by the time he had sat down and Hill had started his cross-examination, I was deep in familiar territory. I had no letters after my name and all of my knowledge had been gained through practical experience. Hill may have prepared for the case but he couldn't compete with knowledge accrued over three decades. I knew there was nothing he could do to faze me and I stepped from the box confident that I had done everything that I could to convince the jury that I had simply done my job.

My team of supporters had been getting bigger by the day and had included two ex-partners, friends and former colleagues, some of whom had travelled from as far away as the States to show their support. Julie, who had been granted compassionate leave by her boss, and my son, Mark, fortuitously on leave, were now watching down on me every day. Both were stoic individuals but despite their outer calm, I was concerned about the emotional toll on them. The jury was equally difficult to fathom and I had no clue which way they were leaning.

Our minimalist defence was complete. We had discussed calling some of my character witnesses but however good they may have been, their introduction would have allowed the prosecution to introduce the irrelevant but potentially damaging nightclub incident and so, other than Brooks, I would be our only witness.

After more legal argument and discussion, the third week ended early on the Thursday. As I left the box, my guard Suzzanne told me that she was on leave the following week and wished me luck. The next Monday, refreshed after a relaxing long weekend, I climbed into the dock, knowing that I was on the final straight and was surprised to find her greeting me with a smile.

'I cancelled my leave,' she explained kindly. 'I couldn't let you sit here with a stranger.'

It was a kind gesture and I knew from TP's feedback that my family and supporters were receiving similar care from the Bailey's security staff with whom they'd built a rapport and, as I waited for the judge's arrival, I looked up to familiar faces and concerned smiles. The day was spent listening to Hill justify the prosecution case and Ian Stern tear it to pieces and, by end of play, the stage was set for the judge's summing up. His four-hour summary spanned two days and seemed to me a direction to a not guilty verdict, and at lunchtime on the Wednesday the jury were finally sent out to deliberate. As I left the dock I was quietly confident.

Less than an hour later, the public address crackled into life. 'All parties in the case of Long to court ten.'

We all looked at each other in amazement.

Christ that was quick! I thought to myself as we all stood up in unison. I made my way to the toilet, escorted as always by Scott and Mick. Nervous banter, an insurance pee and a quick check of my tie and we made our way up to the lobby. Somehow the news had already escaped the court.

'It's a question, just a question,' someone said in an urgent whisper and my heart sank. There were two irrelevant questions and Sweeney dealt with them both patiently. Someone on the jury was clearly thinking too deeply but he gently rebuked them all. They were, he reminded them, the judges of the facts and he sent them back to their jury room, directing them to focus on the facts and the facts alone. As they filed out I studied their body language and had no doubt who was the fly in the ointment.

An hour later, after the now customary warning not to discuss the case with others, they were released for the day and I looked forward to a pint with my supporters before a night in a central London hotel where Julie and I had been put up in anticipation of a verdict.

The next day morale was high and we were all anticipating a result later that day. Proceedings never started until Rodney's family were in court but no such consideration was given to my family in the public gallery. I was the defendant, but this was no ordinary murder trial and it galled me that Rodney's family should be treated with more respect than my own so I resolved to just take my time when we were called. I didn't want them to miss the verdict and, after all, the court couldn't start without me.

The public address system called us to court three more times that day. Once for another pointless question, once for the judge to inform us that a juror had developed a nasty rash and that he was sending her to see the court's matron, and finally at about three o'clock to tell us that she couldn't continue and he would be sending the jury home early. Each time we were summoned my heart rate soared and I suggested they put a defibrillator in the dock.

It was Friday 3 July, and I arrived refreshed and hopeful. Surely, I told myself, the jury wouldn't want to be back here next week? In the lobby outside the court, Rodney's mother was all smiles. She'd had a minor outburst during the judge's summing up, accusing him in a loud stage whisper of being biased. It had been a momentary lapse in an otherwise dignified performance.

The Canesten had obviously worked though and the complete jury was fit and raring to go and after the usual formalities, at 10:00, while my defence team and I filed downstairs to the now familiar canteen, they sat down to continue their deliberations. Two superintendents from CO19, together with senior Federation officials, Jacqui, CO19's own Fed reps and my defence team gathered round sharing stories and jokes to keep our minds from the main topic and waited. At 12:43 the call came.

'All parties in the case of Long to court ten.'

As we gathered in the lobby outside the court we were informed that it was not a question but a note and I knew straight away what it said. Sweeney informed us that the jury were unable to reach a unanimous verdict and I was pretty sure which juror was causing the problem.

Sweeney had reached a point where he was prepared to accept a majority verdict and the jury was called in. I looked up to the gallery to see Mark, Julie and George, my old mate from Blue team, looking down with concern etched on their faces. The jury filed in and took their seats and the foreman was asked to stand.

Sweeney leant towards him. 'Have you reached a verdict upon which you are all agreed?'

'Yes, my Lord,' he replied confidently and the whole court looked puzzled.

Sweeney looked over his glasses, a gentle smile on his face. 'I think you mean no, don't you?'

He said it kindly and everyone, including myself, smiled, the tension broken. The foreman blushed, apologised and replied that they hadn't and several of the female jurors looked towards me still smiling and I knew then the result. The judge sent them away for a final opportunity to deliberate and we returned to the canteen. No one else had noticed the jurors' smiles and no one could understand why I seemed so relaxed; everyone seemed more apprehensive than me.

'All parties in the case of Long to court ten!'

There was an air of anticipation in the lobby outside the court. Over the previous days the next trial had been setting up shop in preparation for ours coming to an end and I entered the court to see a man in a white shirt sitting in the dock with Suzzanne standing next to him. My first instinct was that he was the new defendant and that I had entered too early until I recognised him as another SERCO guard, there in case I was convicted and started to kick off.

I entered the box and was taken out to the cell passage for one final search before returning to take a seat, with Suzzanne and her colleague sitting on either side of me. The court was packed and I looked up to the gallery. Julie looked absolutely terrified. We all stood as Sweeney entered, sitting again as the jury entered to take their seats. A hush fell over the court as their foreman and I stood for the verdict. I gave Julie a wink and took a deep breath. Whatever the result, I was determined to show no emotion.

'Not guilty!' The foreman replied in answer to the clerk's question and, despite my confidence, a huge wave of relief rolled over me. Several members of the jury turned towards me and smiled and I mouthed 'thank you' to them, before looking up to the gallery. Mark had arrived, his face etched with relief, and Julie's head was in her hands; she was sobbing uncontrollably and several of my friends were comforting her. I thanked Suzzanne as she opened the gate for me; she too was crying. I stepped from the dock for the final time, proven innocent at last.

TWENTY-SEVEN
REFLECTIONS

It's February 2016 and I'm watching the powder settle on the Rockies as I finish my final chapter. Just like after Kincraig nearly 30 years ago, I'm back in the States to recuperate from a stressful experience. It's strange how history repeats itself. Shortly after the trial, Geoff, an old friend and colleague from my second tour of Lewisham and now a US citizen, invited Julie and I to come over to relax and go skiing and, as I type, I reflect on all of the support and other acts of kindness that have been shown to my family throughout my ten-year ordeal, and also the obstacles that have been put in my way.

Within minutes of my acquittal, as the Expendables whisked me into a pub to celebrate with my friends and supporters, my phone rang. It was Pat Gallan, the assistant commissioner for specialist crimes and operations, and she congratulated me. 'Tony, the commissioner and I are so pleased for you, you must be so relieved. I'm sure you just want to celebrate but if I could just take a moment of your time.'

She wanted to run her press release past me; giving me the opportunity to change anything that I wasn't happy with, and I listened carefully, only asking that she referred to me in the release as Tony rather than Anthony, a name last used by my mum.

'Okay, Tony, well thank you so much. Go and let your hair down and I'll call you next week to make a date for you to meet with the commissioner, if that's all right?'

The following evening, Saturday 4 July, Julie and I were guests of honour at the perfectly timed PFOA summer ball and, dressed up to the nines, we received a standing ovation and the champagne flowed. I'd made a small contribution to the creation of the organisation several years previously and its founder, my old Fed rep and friend Mark and his wife Debbie, had been a massive support throughout the ordeal. It was great to be able to thank them in person.

Early the following week, I received a call from Gallan but after a few moments the line went dead and 30 minutes later, when she still hadn't rung back, I left a message for her to call back at any time. She never did and three weeks later I left another message that finally prompted a call from her staff officer, and the following week I attended Scotland Yard expecting a meeting with the commissioner. Gallan met me, revealing accidentally that both she and the commissioner, Sir Bernard Hogan-Howe, had, weeks before, found time for a meeting with Susan Alexander. Sir Bernard wasn't, however, available to speak to me.

'It's just the way it turned out, Tony, and besides she's not a drug dealer,' she responded when I questioned why she was only meeting me now after I had prompted her and only after she'd already met Rodney's mother.

The meeting turned frosty and, attempting to ease the tension, she asked what I was doing with myself now that the trial was over; I looked her in the eye and told her I was going to write a book. She winced.

'We don't really like books, Tony.'

I assumed she meant the Yard didn't like its minions spilling the beans.

'Well, I'll make sure there's plenty of pictures for you then, ma'am,' I replied sarcastically.

The next day I was interviewed on LBC radio and despite speaking well of the Met's hierarchy, it prompted another meeting weeks later, this time with both Gallan and the commissioner, where it was made clear that, while a jury may have found me not guilty, Holland's ruling that I acted unlawfully still stood.

'Oh, I'm sorry!' I countered. 'I thought a judge at the Central Criminal Court and a properly directed jury would trump a senile halfwit's decision!'

By now I'd discovered that the Job were paying Rodney's mother off. What I couldn't fathom was why? As far as I was concerned, it felt like drawing a thick line in indelible ink through my not guilty verdict.

Rodney wasn't Stephen Lawrence, he was a violent gangster already wanted for a double stabbing and when he woke up on the morning of 30 April 2005, he knew that by the end of the day he would have participated in the robbery and murder of rival drug dealers.

By contrast, when I rolled out of bed that morning, I had no idea that I would be required to take another human life. It was a possibility, of course, I was a member of a specialist firearms team and our deployment wouldn't have been authorised unless there was a chance that we might have to resort to the use of firearms, but we rarely had to do so.

The US columnist Richard Grenier, prompted by George Orwell, once wrote: 'People sleep peacefully in their beds at night only because rough men stand ready to do violence on their behalf.' When I joined the job in the mid-seventies, it was full of rough men and women prepared to do violence on the public's behalf and do whatever had to be done to keep the streets safe for decent people.

Modern policing is far more complex, and over the last ten years, in my darker moments, I have sometimes thought back to those simple times and lain awake wondering whether it might have been a lot simpler to have said that I'd seen that gun in Rodney's hand. Thinking of what my family and I had been put through, I was sometimes forced to ask myself if honesty wasn't always the best policy.

In a police service proud to boast that it is predominantly unarmed, those that volunteer to carry firearms have always been looked upon as its bastard sons and daughters. When I joined, revolvers, referred to only as 'equipment', remained hidden under tunics, and while in the last 30 years armed policing may have come out of the shadows, with liveried ARVs patrolling our streets and overtly armed protection officers a regular sight, still the stigma remains.

There are a few exceptions. When ARV officers shot and wounded the murderers of Lee Rigby in 2013, they were unusually lauded as heroes. The prime minister sent them hampers and the mayor of London and the commissioner queued up to shake their hands and congratulate them. All three received Queen's Police Medals. On the day, they had turned up in their white charger to slay the dragon and their bravery and decisiveness had camouflaged the fact that the acceptable image of the Met, so cherished by the Yard, had stood by impotently.

There had been regular uniform coppers on scene for nearly 15 minutes before the ARV had arrived but, through no fault of their own, unarmed and hampered by health and safety legislation and protocols, they were forced to stand behind their incident tape and watch a public they were sworn to protect remonstrate with Rigby's murderers and protect his brutalised body. That day the ARVs had been the solution to the problem but when I killed Azelle Rodney or when C2 and C12 shot Jean Charles de Menezes and V53 shot Mark Duggan, neither our bosses, our government nor the press saw us as the solution: we were the problem. None of us would be receiving Queen's Police Medals.

The British people need to realise that when police have to fire their weapons, it doesn't mean that they've made a mistake or that they have done something wrong. Firearms officers spend hours on the range honing their skills so that when an armed suspect puts them in a position where they have to fire, they will be faster and more accurate than their adversary.

We are human and periodically there will be tragedies, but in 2005 the British police shot and killed two people, Jean Charles de Menezes and Azelle Rodney. Rodney was an armed criminal but Jean Charles was tragically an innocent victim of circumstances. In the same year, in his own his native country, police shot in excess of 1,000 Brazilians but that is of little consequence to the British public. His death was a tragic accident and it shouldn't have happened but neither, perhaps, should the deaths of the 44 people killed in the UK that same year in traffic collisions involving police vehicles.

One momentary lapse of concentration when driving a police vehicle at speed to an emergency call or in pursuit of a stolen car could wipe out an entire bus queue but no one is arguing that the emergency services should be issued bicycles. It is the word 'gun' that strikes an irrational fear in the national psyche and any discussion about police and firearms immediately draw parallels with what happens in America rather than what happens in Holland or Sweden.

The events in Paris, Brussels and elsewhere in the world have highlighted the need for highly trained armed police prepared to respond immediately to a terrorist attack, take the fight to the killers and neutralise the threat, protecting the innocent and minimising loss of life and serious injury. Those officers don't want recognition or immunity. They simply want to be treated fairly and judged with understanding when they are forced to do what they have been trained to do. If we don't there will be a distinct shortage of volunteers in the future.

Statistics bear witness to the truth that firearms officers and their commanders do everything in their power to safely arrest suspects in such a way that no one is injured. Perversely, police shootings in the UK are made more controversial because they are so rare, but criminals who go out with guns have to understand that by doing so, when fractions of a second count, they are severely limiting the officers' options to deal with them safely. If it comes to a choice between their life and that of a police officer or a member of the public, theirs will come a poor third.

I no longer have to carry a gun but if I did, despite everything I've been through, I would still rather stand again as a defendant at the Old Bailey and justify my actions to a judge and jury than stand in the witness box at a coroner's court and explain, in front of a family, why their loved one died because I hadn't done my job.

After the trial, I had a challenge coin minted for the Expendables who leant their support to Operation Edge. On one side is the blindfolded Lady of Justice dominating the Old Bailey's domed roof, the scales of Justice in one hand and her sword in the other. Underneath her is the classic London taxi that became synonymous with the operation. Above the two images, the words: 'It is not the critic that counts.' On the flipside is the SFO symbol of a Roman sword and shield with the number 19 in Roman numerals surrounded by the words: 'Never among the timid souls that know neither victory nor defeat.'

The words are taken from a speech by Theodore Roosevelt, the 26th President of the United States and a former commissioner of the NYPD. To those quick to criticise police whenever one of their brave men or women have to shoot a suspect, and to those who, from the safety of their sofas, think that they could do better, I leave them with his unabridged version:

It is not the critic who counts; not the man who points out how the strong man stumbles, or where the doer of deeds could have done them better. The credit belongs to the man who is actually in the arena, whose face is marred by dust and sweat and blood; who strives valiantly; who errs, who comes short again and again, because there is no effort without error and shortcoming; but who does actually strive to do the deeds; who knows great enthusiasms, the great devotions; who spends himself in a worthy cause; who at the best knows in the end the triumph of high achievement, and who at the worst, if he fails, at least fails while daring greatly, so that his place shall never be with those cold and timid souls who neither know victory nor defeat.

ACKNOWLEDGEMENTS

In 2008, after 33 years in the 'Job' – 25 years of which were spent in SO19 – I retired and took up a new career in civvy street. I cherished my anonymity and would never have stepped out of the shadows had I not been charged with the murder of drug dealer and armed robber Azelle Rodney. So I should start by thanking Sir Christopher Holland, the retired high court judge who oversaw the 2012 public inquiry into Rodney's death, and whose 'conclusions' led to my prosecution and ultimately to this book – a book that otherwise would never have been written.

Lethal Force started as a germ of an idea and a conversation with a journalist, Dave Matthews, who became my editor. He has been a constant source of support and advice and has become a close friend, to boot. He also introduced me to my agent Robert Smith and to Andrew Goodfellow at Penguin Random House who commissioned the work and who, together with Kelly Ellis, Liz Marvin and Jo Bennett, has worked tirelessly to get it on the shelves. To all of them my thanks.

This book would also not have been possible without the support I received throughout my ten-year ordeal between shooting Rodney, facing trial and beyond. Those who lent that support are too many to mention individually but extend from some very senior officers at Scotland Yard to the management at SO19 and, of course, my former colleagues and those currently serving.

When I joined the unit in 1983, there were 40 of us tasked with training 4,800 firearms officers and taking it in turns in our eight-man teams to cover our emergency call-out responsibility; we were enthusiastic part-timers. Now the unit is 600 strong and its team of instructors continue to train the Met's 2,000 shots and are struggling to cope with a projected increase. Its Armed Response Vehicles (ARV's) and its Specialist Firearms teams (now rebranded as CTSFO's to describe their enhanced counter terrorist capabilities) provide 24-hour cover to the capital, dealing with thousands of emergency calls and pre-planned operations a year. My own selection for the unit was very basic when compared with what current members have to go through, and in a country that is proud of its 'unarmed police service', none of us could sleep peacebly in our beds without them.

Some of those who deserve individual mention are: Jacqui Oliver from the unit's 'Post Incident' office; my Police Federation representatives Mick Burke and Steve Hartshorn; Mark Williams and all his staff at the Police Firearms Officers Association (PFOA); Scott Ingram, my solicitor, and his assistant Sally Tyers from Slater Gordon; my barrister at the Rodney public inquiry Sam Leek QC and my trial barristers Ian Stern QC and Dean George, who represented me so well at the Old Bailey.

An extra special thank you goes to TP and 'Scowler' who organised and ran 'Op Edge', and to all those who gave up their time to man it, including Kath W, Gonz (your nose isn't really that big mate!) and especially Walt and Gav L for travelling so far to lend their support. Closer to home I could not have kept my sanity without my stoic partner Julie, my son and daughter, Mark and Josey, and my step-daughter Katie. As helpless observers, in many ways I know their journey was more difficult than my own. I am proud of all of you and love you all very much.

So this is my story. It's all true…well most of it. Readers with a bit of inside knowledge may notice that I have taken some creative licence with a few events, names, places and dates, which have been changed to protect the innocent and the guilty alike…

Tony Long, 2016